LAND ART

LAND ART

Creating Artworks in and with the Landscape

JAMES BRUNT

SCHIFFER PUBLISHING
4880 Lower Valley Road • Atglen, PA 19310

Other Schiffer Books on Related Subjects:
Create Naturally : Go Outside and Rediscover Nature with 15 Makers, Marcia Young, ISBN 978-0-7643-6434-1
Nature Mandalas Wonders of the Garden, Tim Phelps, ISBN 978-0-7643-5044-3

Library of Congress Control Number: 2022947051

Produced by BlueRed Press Ltd., 2022
Designed by Matt Windsor
Type set in Anko and Bilo

ISBN: 978-0-7643-6605-5
Printed in India

Published by Schiffer Publishing, Ltd.
4880 Lower Valley Road
Atglen, PA 19310
Phone: (610) 593-1777; Fax: (610) 593-2002
Email: Info@schifferbooks.com
Web: www.schifferbooks.com

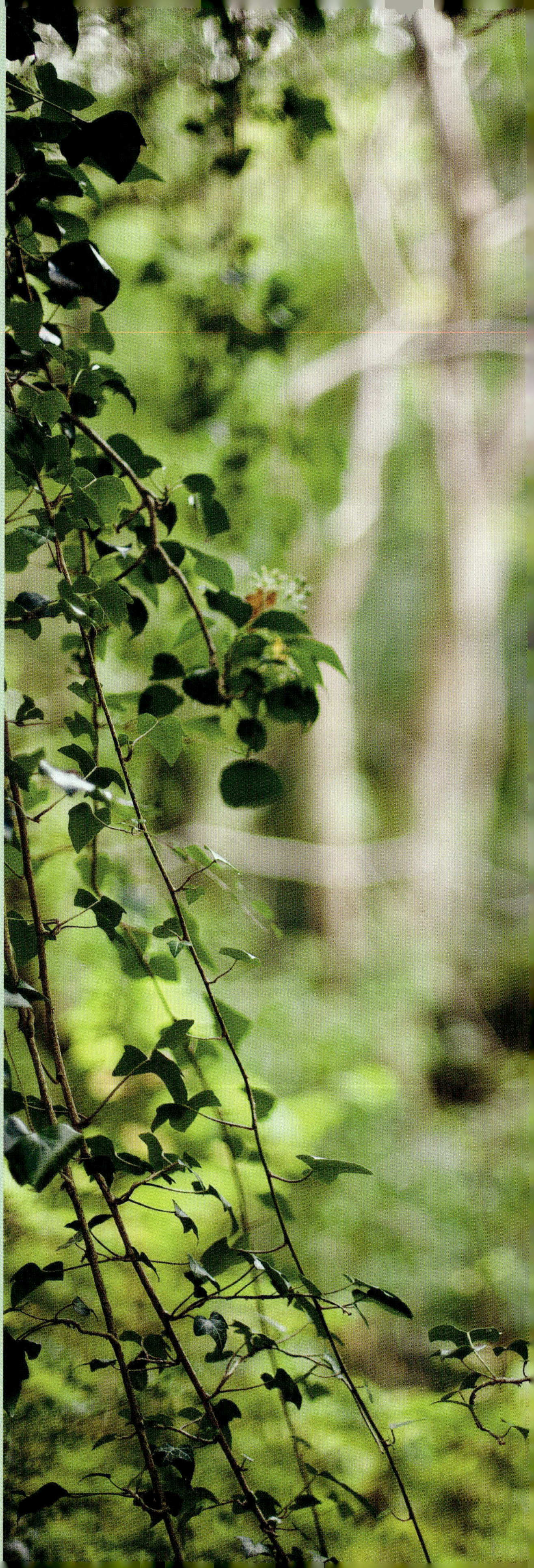

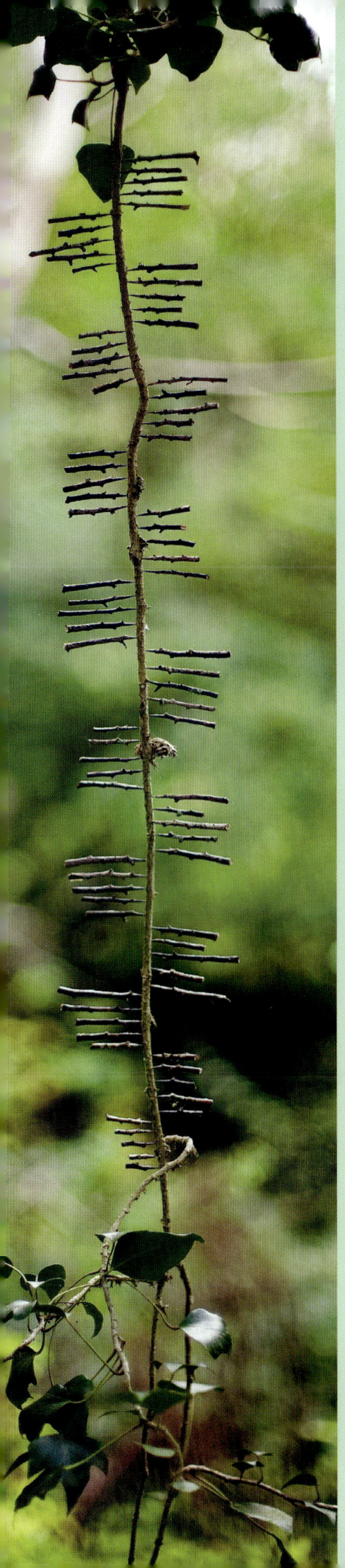

Contents

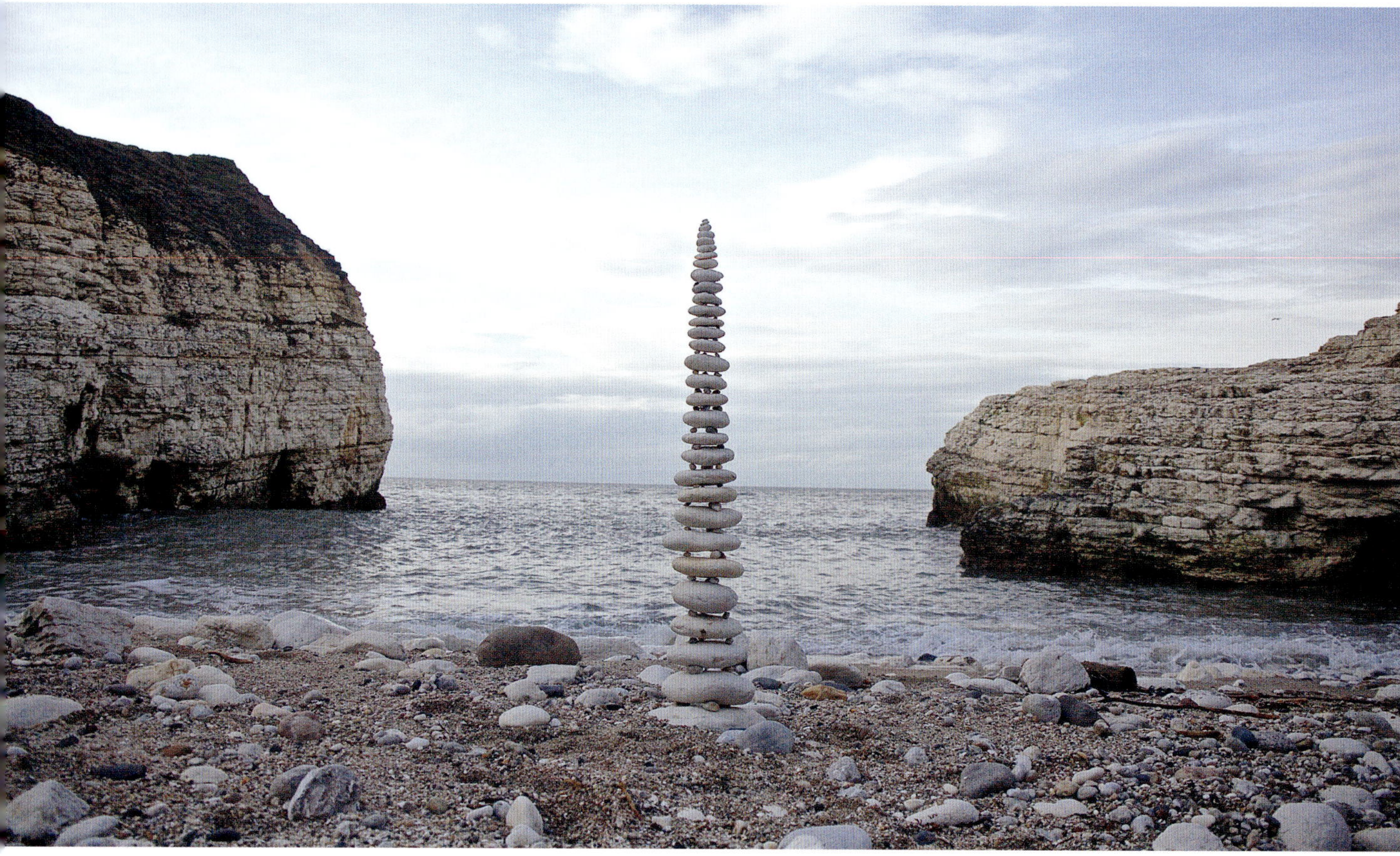

Introduction

The first thing to say is thank you so much for buying the book. Honestly, it means the world that it's in your hands or on your screen right now. From the outset, it was never intended to be a coffee-table art book (although please feel free to give it a nice spot on the coffee table—I'm sure it will look lovely). I wanted to produce an honest book about my relationship with the natural world—a book that wasn't just about showcasing an artist's work, but something more revealing about things that I believe to be crucially important: the outdoors, the flora and fauna we share the planet with, every person's right to have access to natural spaces. And the fact that no matter how old we are, we should never stop playing. Yes, there's plenty of pictures, most of which are of works previously unseen, a few that people may recognize, with the commonality being that every picture of work in this book was purely the result of me allowing myself to do what makes me well and content, in the places that make me the happiest. The result, the images you see, are the outcome of the real joy, the experience of creating, the relationship with the natural world around me, and that moment in time when everything is about the here and now.

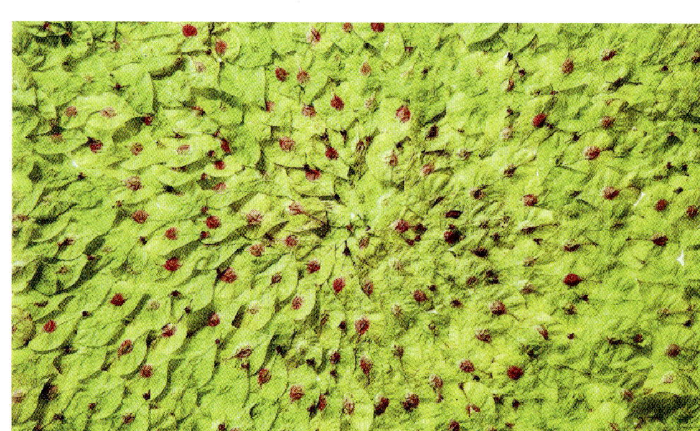

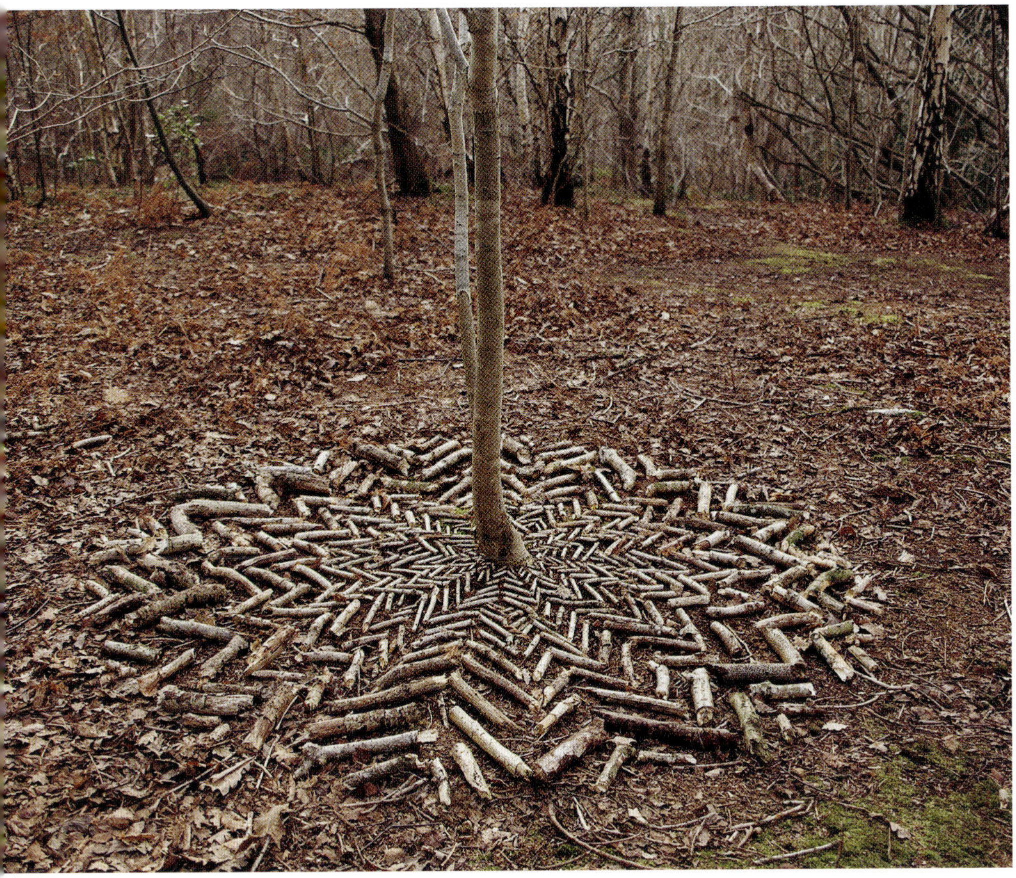

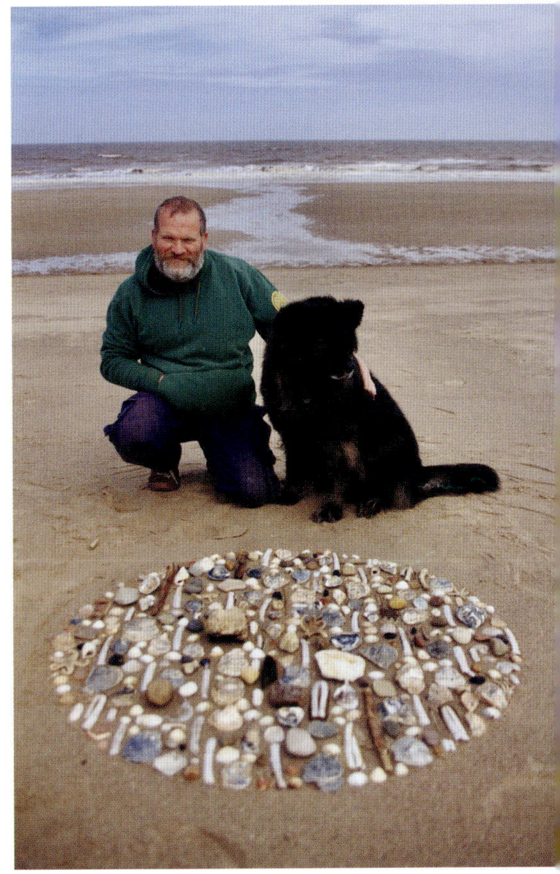

Trying to pinpoint when this current creative path began for me is difficult, but for the sake of not wanting immediately to get into questions about when an artist becomes an artist, I'm going to say 2012. In 2012, I was introduced to the work of a stone balancer by friends of mine, which planted the seed. A few weeks later, on a trip to the coast with friends Timm and Rob, I remember us all with two pebbles, trying to make one balance on top of the other in a seemingly impossible way. I wonder how different my journey would have been if I hadn't managed it! Then in 2014, inspired and supported by Timm, I left full-time employment to pursue my own artistic path. Since this very humble beginning, the rest is a work in progress.

I have tried to write a simple account of what makes me tick as an artist. I see my work as very simple, so I don't think overintellectualizing what I have to say would suit me. So I've attempted to share my thoughts and feelings as they appear to me. I hope that what comes out at the other end is an understanding of the connection I have with the natural world, how it ignites the creative spark in me, and how I hope my work temporarily sits harmlessly alongside the environments in which they are made.

More than anything, I hope the book is, like you, the reader, taking a walk with me, a walk through the forest as I seek that spark of inspiration—a walk through the journey that has led me to here.

I hope you enjoy our journey together and, importantly, that it encourages you to get out and immerse yourself in the natural world, develop your own relationship with the plants and animals with which you share the space, and, at the same time, have a go at making your own temporary natural artworks.

James

Art-Nature-Me

Let's get something straight from the start. I'm not a stereotypical "outdoors" type of person. What I mean by this is that I don't have all the gear, I'm not a walker, I don't climb mountains, I don't trek for days to seek solitude or to witness outstanding untouched natural beauty. My love of the outdoors is what I witness daily, in my garden or the local woods near where I live. The need to create far outweighs the need to explore.

From an early age, the natural world around me was always full of wonder, from the smallest insects to the seasonal changes that chart the years' progress. As a child, being outdoors was always the "happy place"; I spent countless hours looking under stones and such like, looking for bugs, making Lego "creature homes" for the things I found, and collecting caterpillars, sticklebacks, or whatever in jam jars. Looking back, I must forgive my younger self for the way in which I went about collecting and removing these unfortunate creatures from their natural habitat, trying to preserve them in totally unsuitable replacement homes; as a ten-year-old I honestly thought a Lego maze would be a wonderful adventure for the creatures I found. This was the foundation to my ongoing curiosity and love for all things natural.

Now, as an artist, supported, helped, encouraged, and loved by my partner, Caroline, and our two boys, Rudy and Sonny, what surprises me more than anything is the time it took me to combine this passion for nature, with my calling from a very early age—the arts.

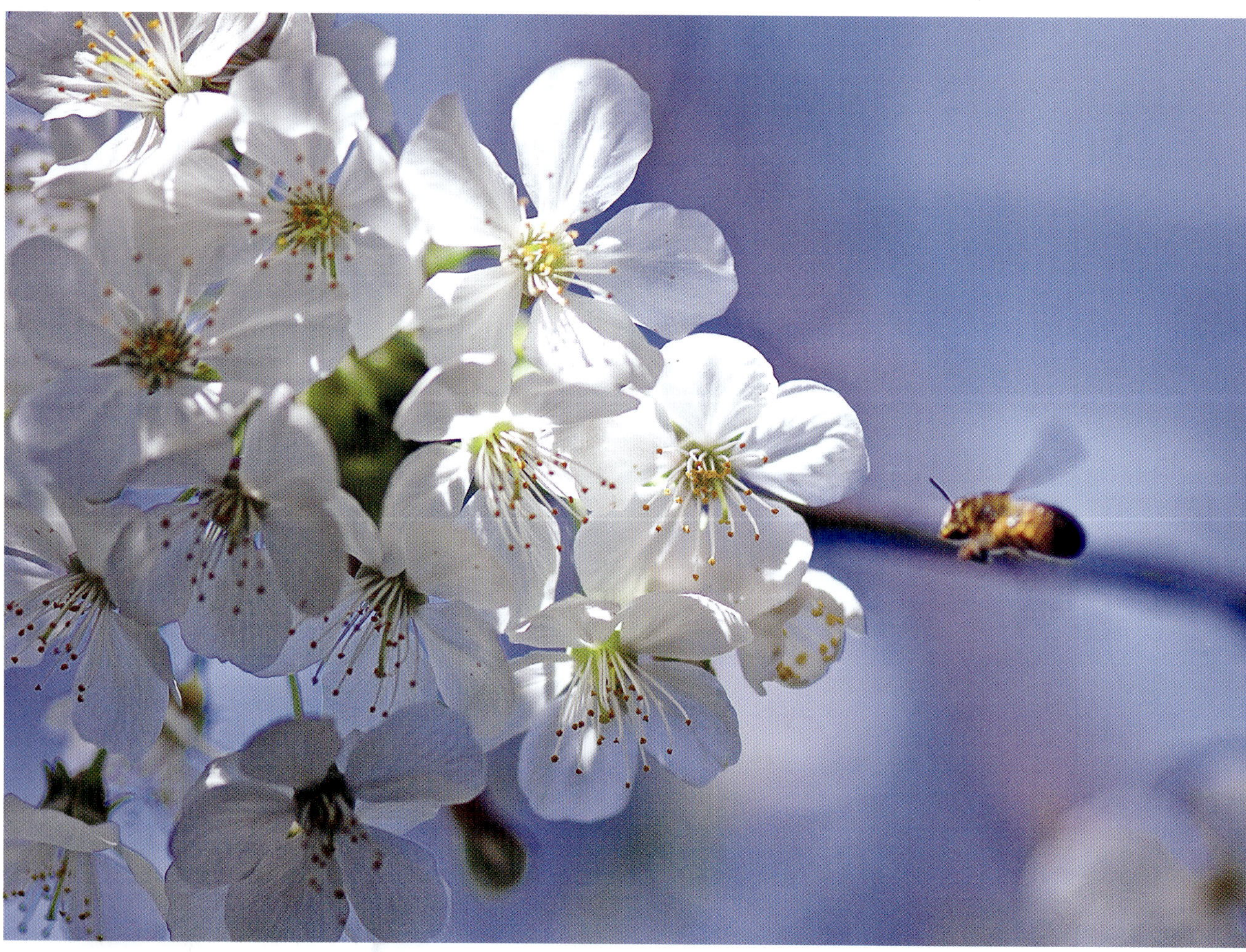

South Yorkshire, United Kingdom, in the 1980s was in no way a hotbed of creative opportunity, and for a child growing up in the small coal-mining villages, whose greatest gift was the ability to draw, the ambition of becoming an artist was one many will have lost en route to a more "acceptable" career.

But dreams of being either an artist or living a Gerald Durrell-type existence surrounded by animals never went away, and perseverance in the end paid off when I graduated from the Byam Shaw School of Art, London, in 1997. Fast-forward twenty-five years, time spent working in the arts industries, galleries, arts education, and arts administration—everything but my own art, basically—my two passions eventually came together, and for the first time my artistic calling fell into place.

The woodland near my house became my studio, the natural world around me my assistant, and the changing seasons an endless source of inspiration. But the discovery was bigger than finding a creative path; the relationship with the environment has become an intrinsic part of who I am, what makes me well and content. To be frank, my work, although definitely more like play, has an overwhelming connection to my well-being. It's no surprise that more and more doctors and health professionals are beginning to see the power of outdoors and natural settings as important tools in their job roles, and the prescribing of outdoor time, experience, and social and natural interaction is becoming a vital part of medical intervention. In addition to this, having this deep connection between art and nature has for the first time given my work a strong feeling of meaning and personal purpose.

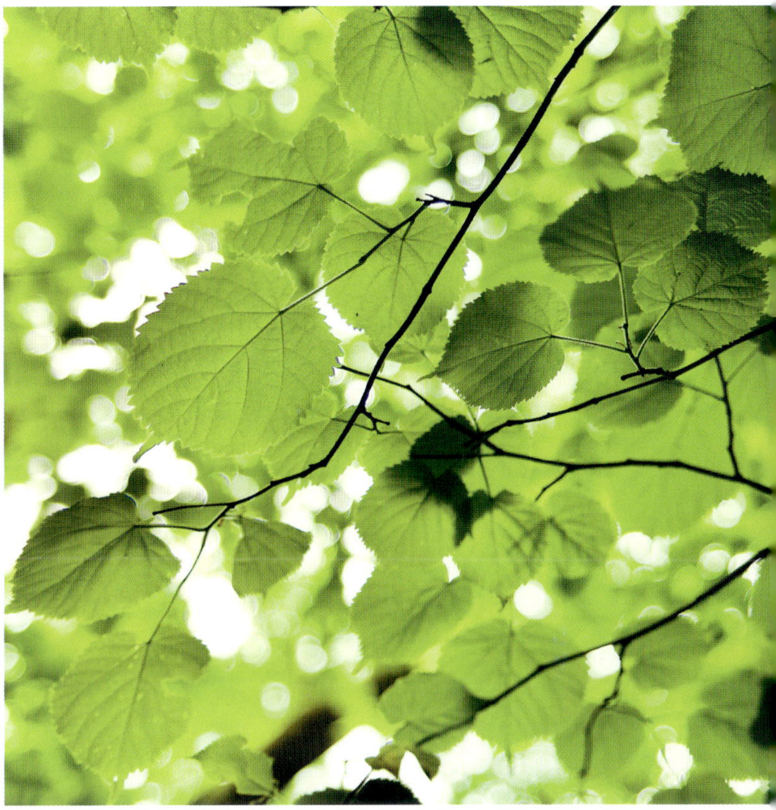

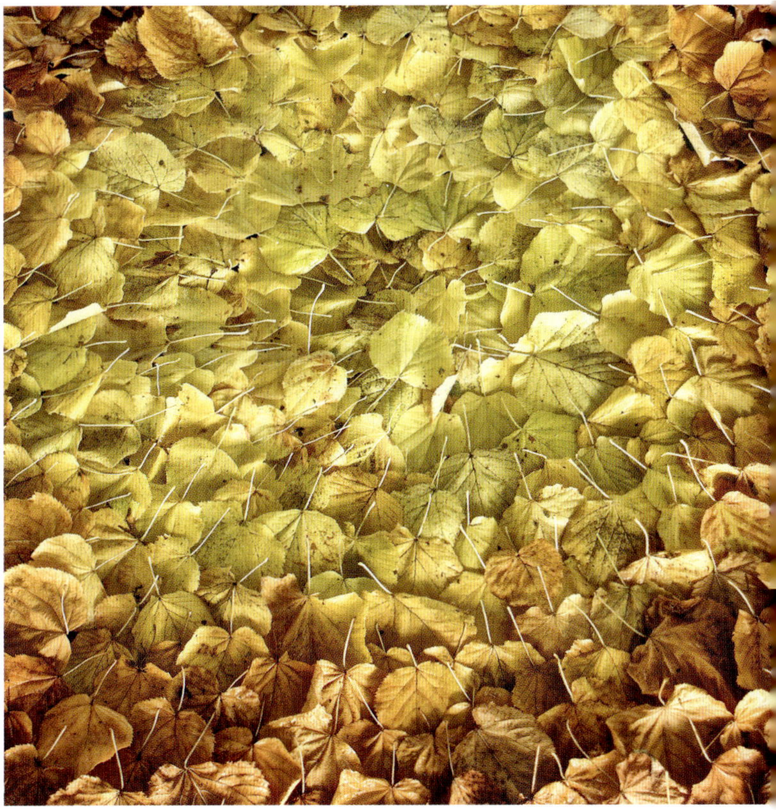

***Left:** A honeybee enjoying the blossom at Weleda, Derbyshire. It's moments like these that bring me so much joy when out in nature.*

***Above right:** Spring lime leaves. Looking up into the branches of spring trees hints at what fall will provide.*

***Right:** Lime leaves in early fall, Cusworth Hall, South Yorkshire. Lime leaves are delicate and turn quickly; the window of opportunity is short.*

I'm not unique. We all, if we allow ourselves, feel revived and uplifted when surrounded by nature; it goes back to those health benefits. What, where, and when that nature is will be specific to each of us—a park, a beach, a forest, a garden, a window box. The outdoors in our lives plays a huge role in our well-being. What is unique to me is the curiosity, love, and relationship I've forged with nature, since allowing myself to dedicate a huge part of my life to being within it, part of it. The more I create, the more I notice, and the more I crave knowledge and understanding, the more I then want to be able to share with others about the material I work and create with. Through repetitive experiences within the same locations, over and over again, you soon begin to witness on a deeply personal level the nuances of changes to that environment. I feel like part of the story of that space. As seasons change, I've lived it; when the wild garlic first pokes its green shoots out of the forest floor to the blanket of white flowers and the wonderful pungent aroma that fills the air, I've watched it all happen. Getting sidetracked by the journey of a beetle and trying to work out why the journey is being made in the first place. A kestrel patrolling a cliff edge, back and forth, back and forth, hardly an opportunity to strike, I get drawn in, willing it success, reward for the work put in. The oyster catchers, moving as one, walk, fly, walk, fly up and down the beach. This is the theater in which my works evolve, a sideshow to a much-bigger story—a story I urge you to connect with, to sit and watch, sit and be part of.

Each work has its own story to tell and a bigger story playing out around it, the location, the wildlife, elements, the defining factors of time and weather conditions all combining to become a partner in the process of rearrangement and a partner in that drama. The rearrangement of natural matter and for a brief moment a transformation of the environment in which each piece sits, and each story unfolds.

Right: *x10, a challenge in collecting ten of everything. I woke up with the idea to collect ten of many things and see how that would influence what I created.*

Below: *Fallen yew berries and twigs in Anston Stones. Happening upon materials by chance sparks new ways to develop and progress work.*

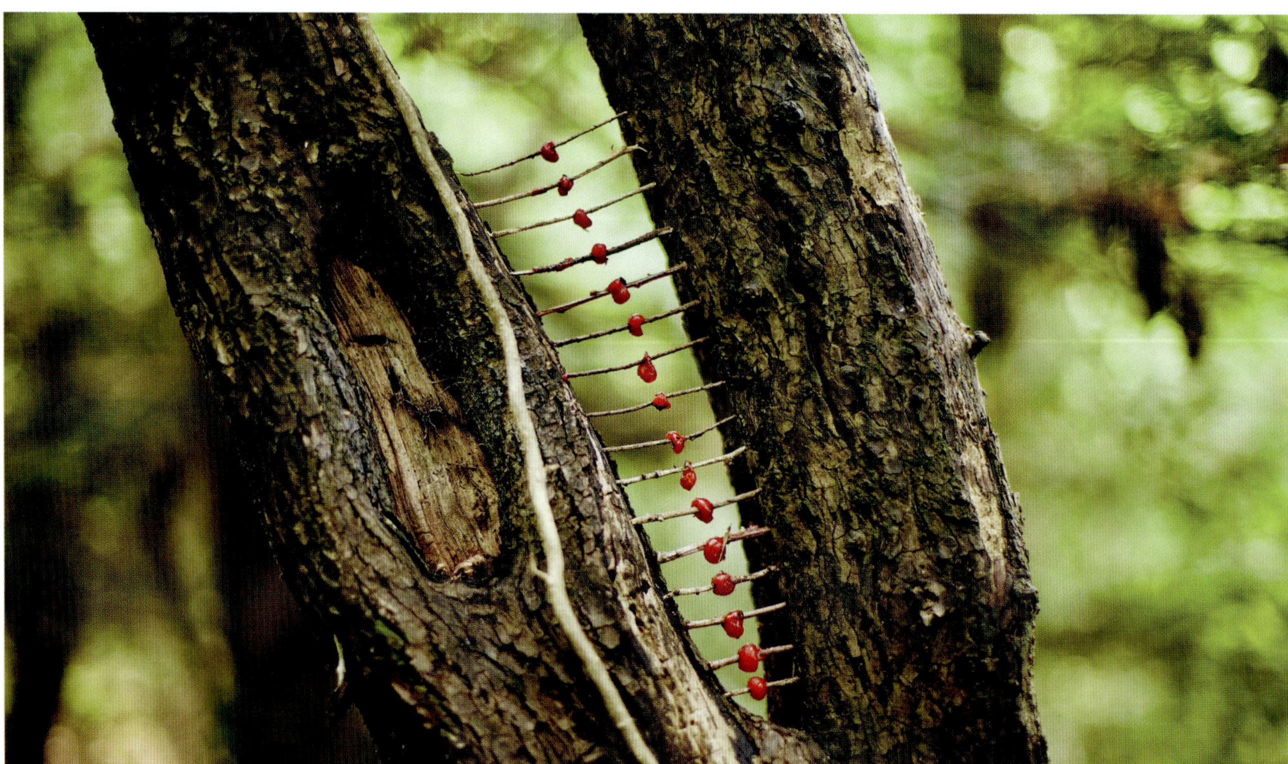

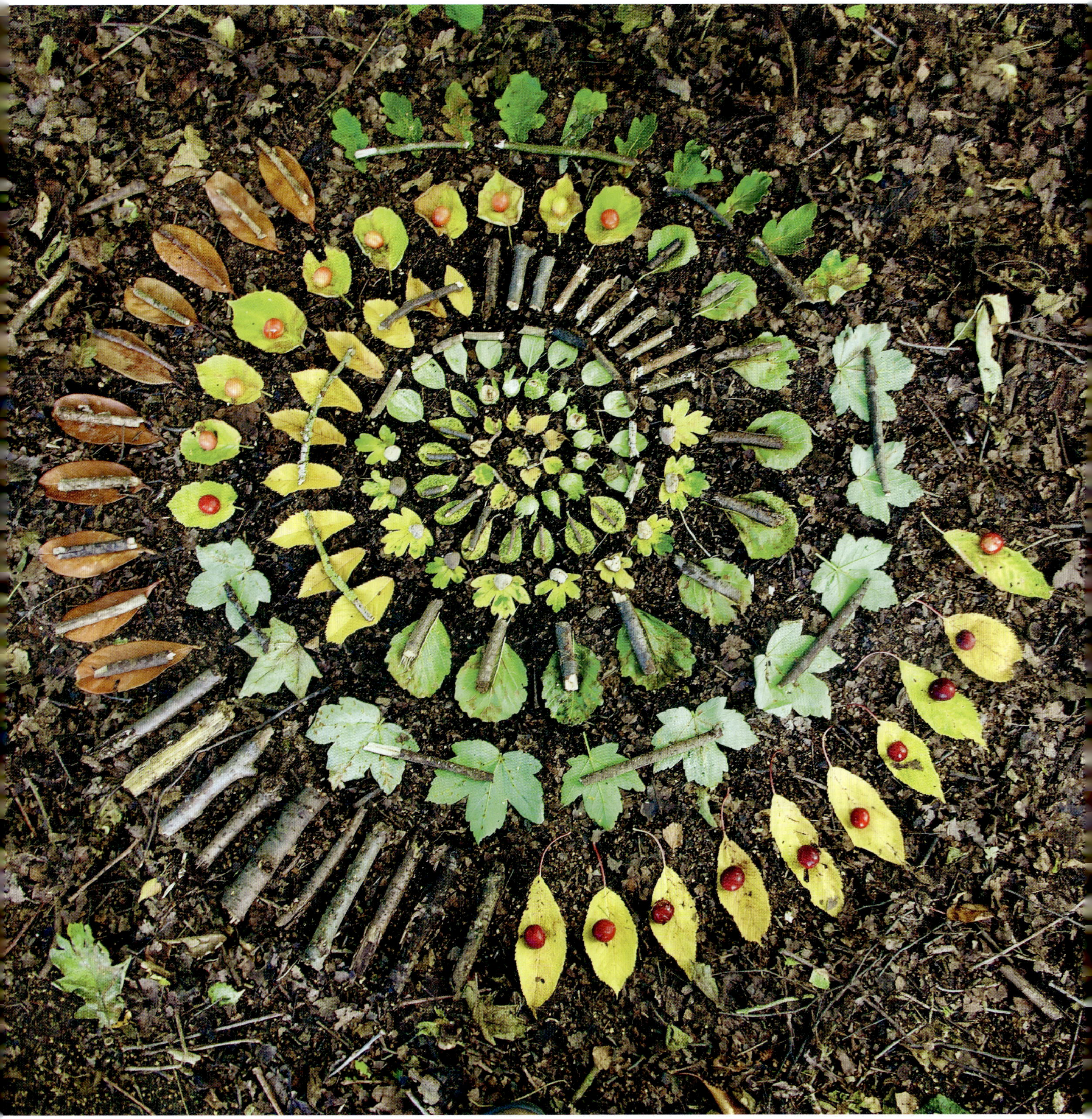

The Joy of Making

Recently a friend, Sterling Gregory, an artist himself and whose work I really admire, asked me how I "push through the feeling of repeating yourself," and it got me thinking. Was he asking about the repetition of constructing a piece over several hours, or was he questioning the lack of something "new" from my creative output? Either way, it was an interesting observation and prompted me to consider both options.

First, on the issue of making a piece of work. The key thing to understand is that I don't plan, draw, or sketch out ideas to create. My interest is in the discovery of a location, a situation in which the elements have come together to capture my attention, either with a composition or an abundance of resources, that somehow forces me to stop for a second and weigh up the options of how I could rearrange that setting. At this point, once an environment has me captured, my aim is to enjoy that moment, immerse myself in the landscape, and be aware and alert to the natural world around me. Thinking up and attempting to realize tricky, intricate designs at this point would go against this desire to be part of that environment for the time I have. Therefore, works I embark on are generally simple processes, processes that require minimal decision-making once started. Allowing me to arrange, collect, sort, and place in an almost instinctive manner, allowing the mind to empty and the nuances of the environment not to pass me by—the opportunistic robin just behind my shoulder, looking for a treat, the normally shy jay foraging nearby unthreatened by my presence, or the many insects wandering into my canvas to take shelter under a leaf, a twig, or shell.

***Below:** Holly leaves at Clumber Park. Evergreens such as holly, laurel, and rhododendron ensure color and texture all year round.*

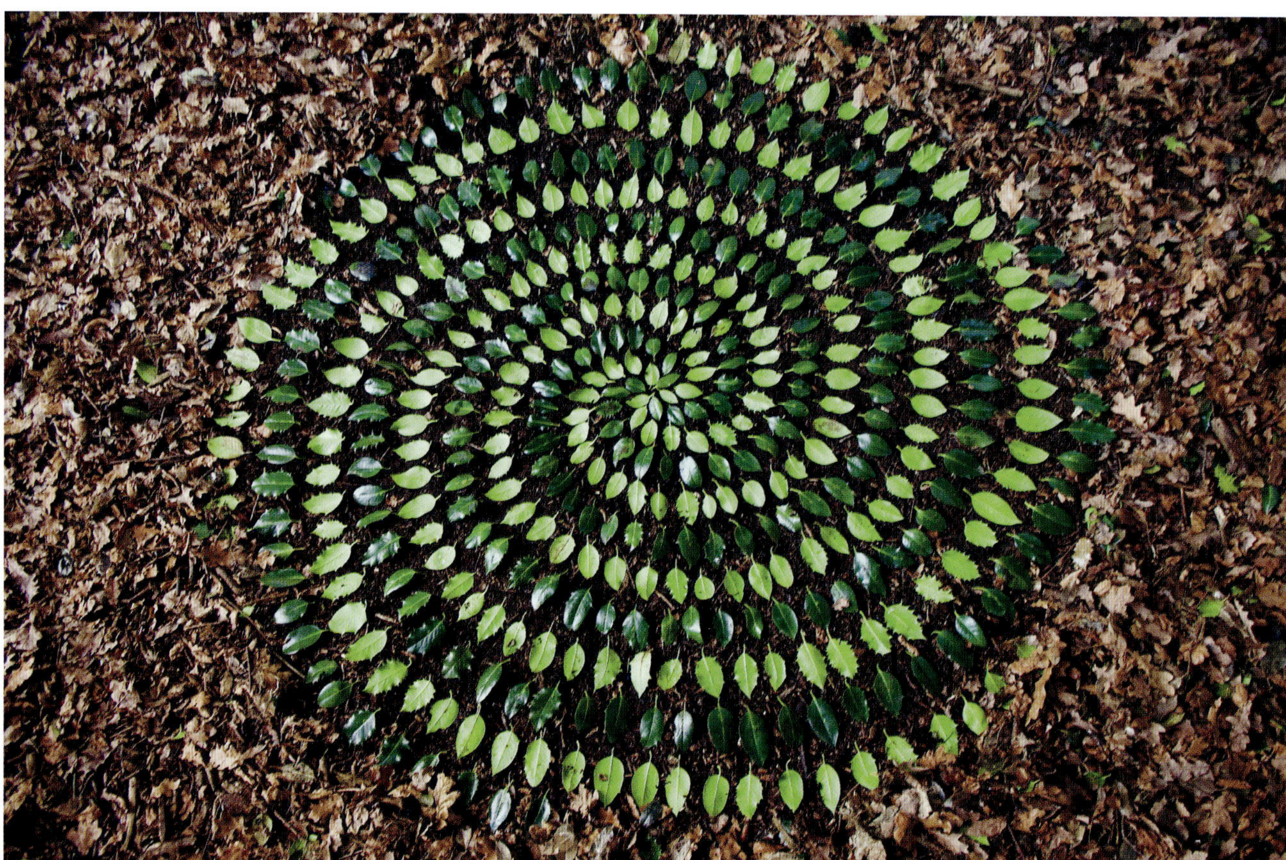

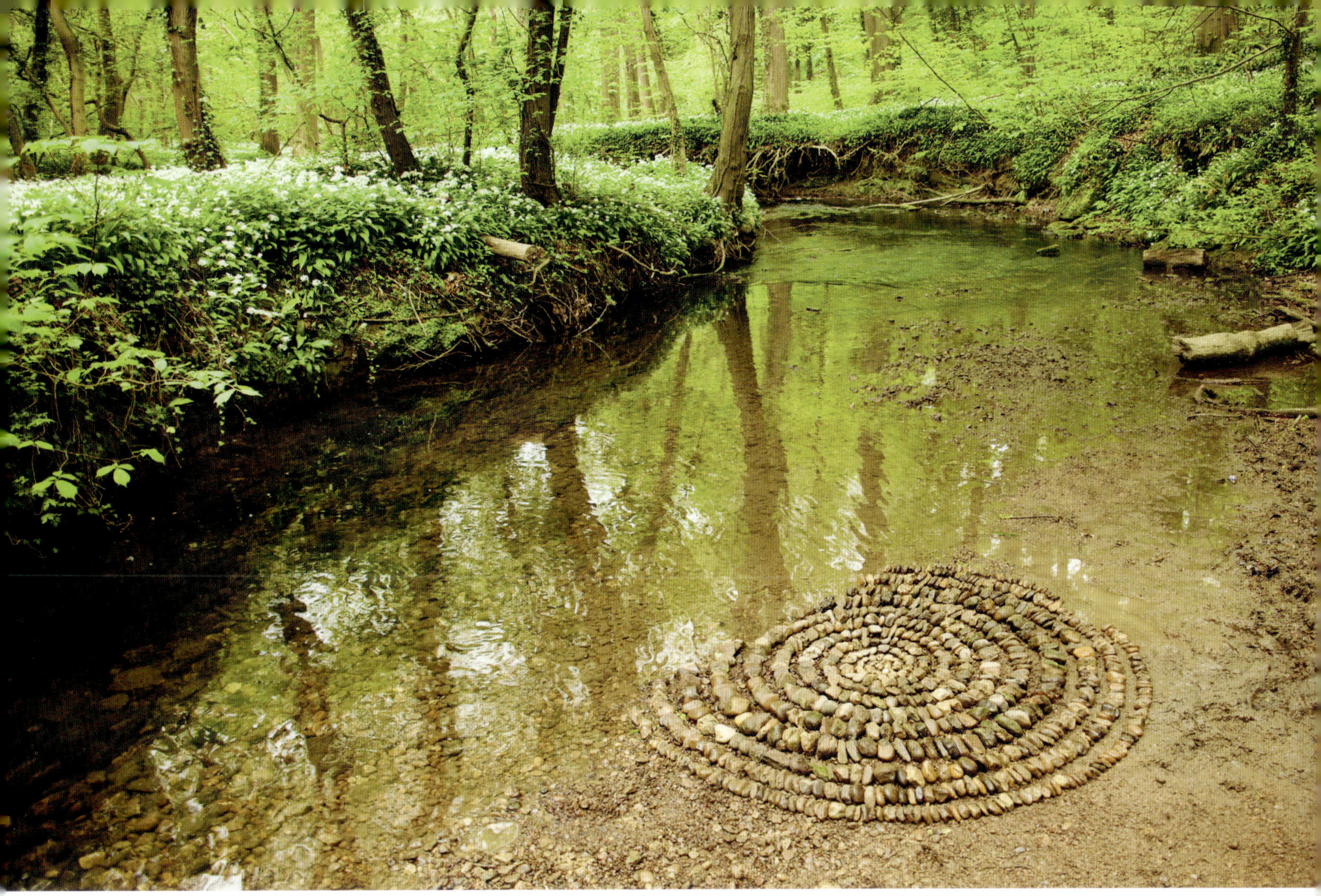

Above: *Low-water pebbles, Anston Stones. There's nothing more beautiful than the color palette of spring woodlands.*

On the second point of repetition within the body of work, while processes may be the same, each work is its own moment in time! The relationship with the natural environment around me was unique to that time, the locations spoke to me for many different reasons, and the wider elements of weather and time of year all add up to create its own story. Therefore, I don't feel repetition is a big issue for me to consider.

I tried to answer my friend's question with a concise version of the above, but ultimately there was no easier way to express it than "I just do what makes me happy." I'm in such a privileged position to have that time with nature, the last thing I want to do is overcomplicate it.

People often refer to the patience I must have to make the work I do, but again, I just don't see it. Patience to me suggests I'm waiting for something, and waiting for something is no fun. I try not to think about time and just *be*. Be part of the landscape around me; the birds will sing, the breeze will pass through the trees, the midges and mosquitoes will search for food, and the leaves, twigs, and natural litter will be rearranged. I'm always busy, busy looking, feeling, noticing, watching, and at the same time, my hands have a physical connection to the materials around me, so the concept of patience never truly resonates with me. A more accurate way to express the reaction people have to my work would be to question my focus; that feels more like what people are trying to say. Focus is a very different thing and a key player in all my works. Focus also has its own rules; for example, my focus is much longer when on a beach than it is when I'm in the woods or a forest. I have no idea why. I love both places equally, but as much as I try, it never changes.

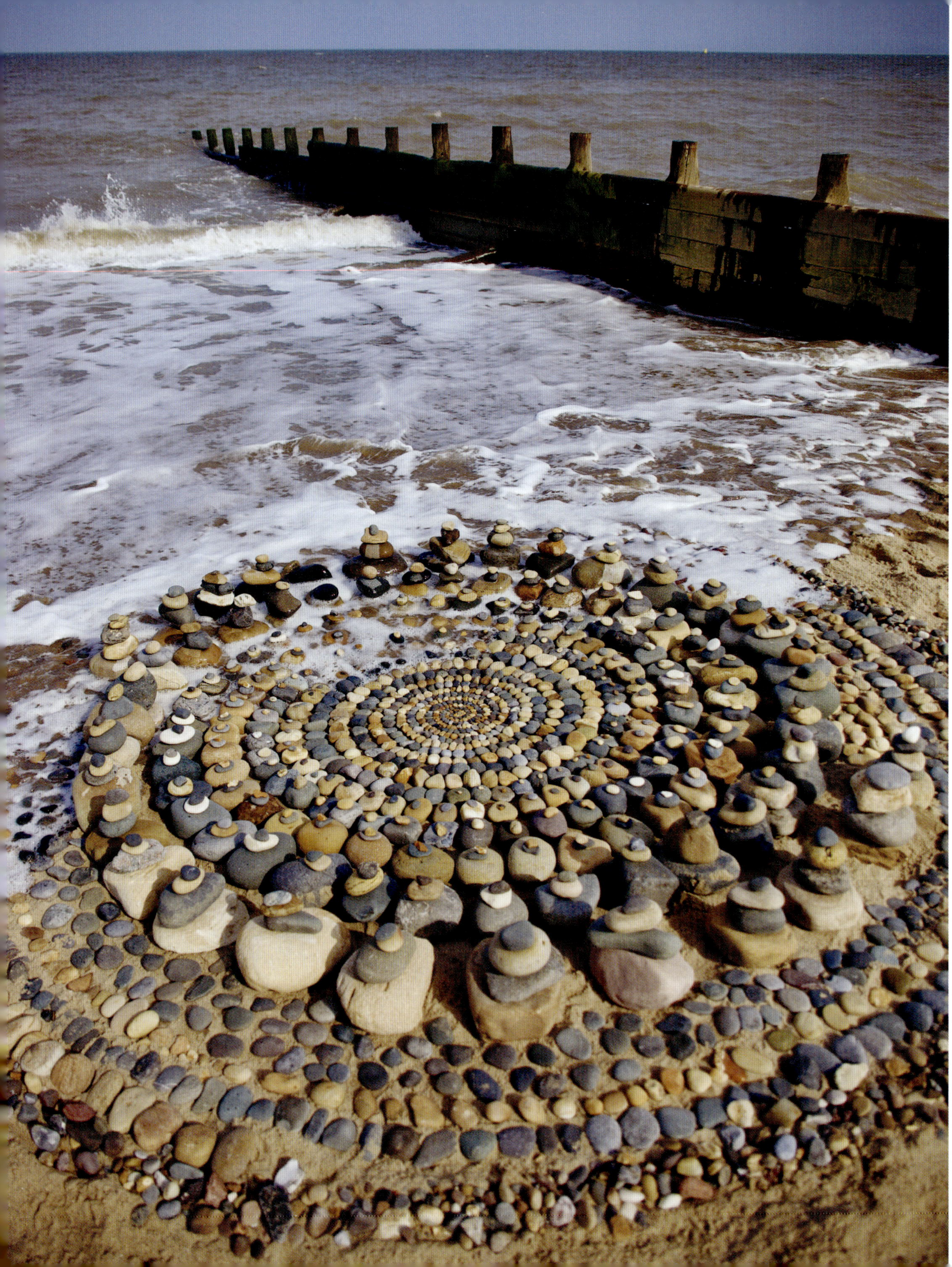

Confidence and contentment in my own working practice also play a part. Where I'm currently at with my working practice is part of a creative journey that molded who I am. I do remember a time when a less confident me did search for something different, feeling I had to find the next piece that would build on the last one. I don't think that was a healthy approach, and it certainly did not embody the desire to be at one with nature. So while this time was an important part of my creative learning, it also represents a time when I didn't feel a deep connection to a moment or place. Now, my own fulfillment is much more important than a need to improve. To visually represent this, I am very content with spirals!

Left: *In comes the tide, Hornsea beach. There's something very comforting about sitting back and watching nature begin the process of reclaiming the work.*

Below: *Boggle Hole spiraling. The fossil-like aspect of this work fit perfectly with the location, a regular haunt for fossil hunters.*

Being so close to nature has shaped who I am. In 2015, I trained to become a Forest School level 3 practitioner. Forest School is an alternative approach to education focusing on holistic learning and developing key life skills within an outdoor environment. Now a worldwide phenomenon, its origins formed in Scandinavia. I both love the ethos of what Forest Schools can offer children who really need it, but have issues with how it gets diluted in the real world. Here's what I mean. I was blown away by how inspirational my Forest School training was and by the impact it can have on children who may never excel within an academic environment. It provides crucial life skills and confidence to grow into an adult, which struggling in a classroom, feeling bad that you don't understand what happens in front of you, will never give you. But more and more, I see Forest Schools as outdoor time for entire classes. This should happen anyway; no teacher should need a Forest School certificate to transfer a lesson plan from indoors to outdoors. But as a result, we are letting down the children whose lives and futures could be greatly improved by the Forest School ethos.

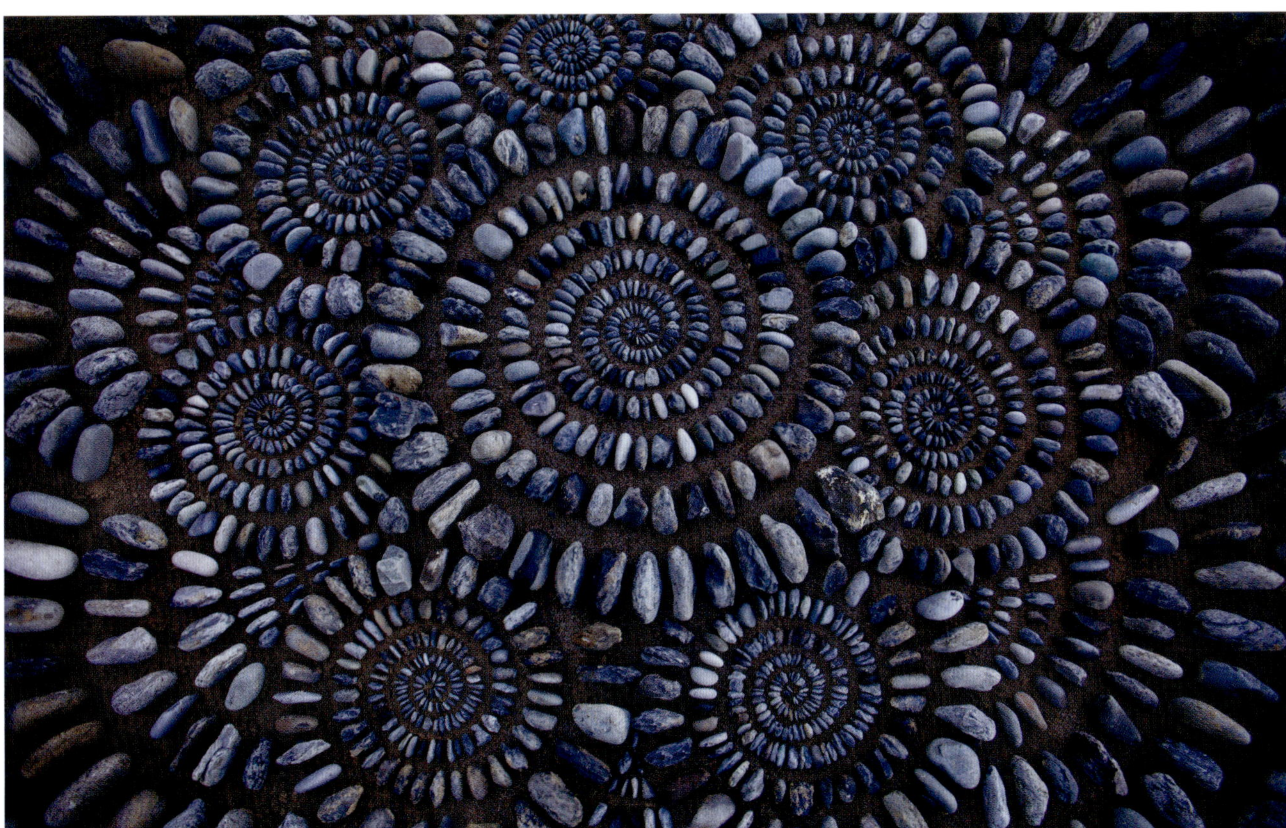

The biggest impact my Forest School training had on me was to awaken a thirst for an understanding of the natural world around me. I have very little time for any works I made before this time, since I don't see them as works created with all my senses open to the world around me. After 2015, I became much more conscious of working in harmony with the landscape and environment around me, as opposed to merely using it for artistic purposes. From this I started to make decisions about what I was happy and not happy to do, a working code started to develop (see page 20), and my work started to take a natural course to where it is today.

Every work I create is a result of this in-built understanding of my code, which leaves me content in the knowledge that any impact I have made on the environment is both minimal and short term.

Working in schools and with children often brings about the same question: "What's your favorite piece of work you've made?" They ask it because it's natural for them to approach images of my work in this way and have their own favorites. But for me, all my creations are incomparable. Work created on a windy day will look less "polished" than that created on a still, calm day, for example. There are so many factors that contribute to what a finished piece of work will look like: weather (which can change during), location, materials, my thoughts, the time I have, interactions with other people/dogs, all contributing to how a work plays out.

I do however have very memorable experiences; these are things that stand out. The real joy for me comes in the making of the work, the time immersed in natural surroundings, being—for a short time—part of that environment. Often when I look back over images of my work, I have no memory of the making process; others stimulate brief recollections of the experience that I'd forgotten, while others I remember every small detail of how that piece came about. What I find extremely interesting is that it's often these works, the ones that left a real impression on me, that others will cite as their favorite pieces.

Right: *Maple leaves, Anston Stones. On walks with my dog Foxy, it's often stumbling across the right opportunity that forms the starting point of a work.*

Below: *Pebbles on Bridlington beach. At first glance the beach was acres of golden sand, but when I looked a little closer there was plenty to find.*

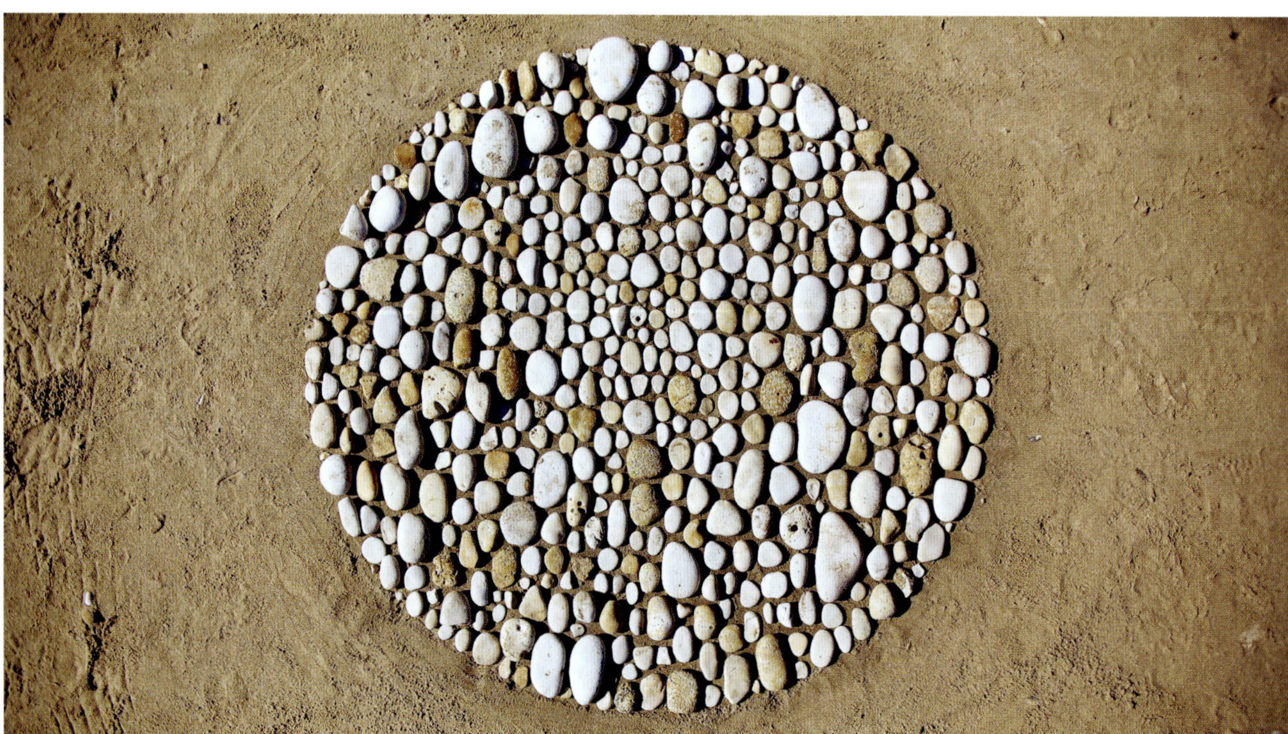

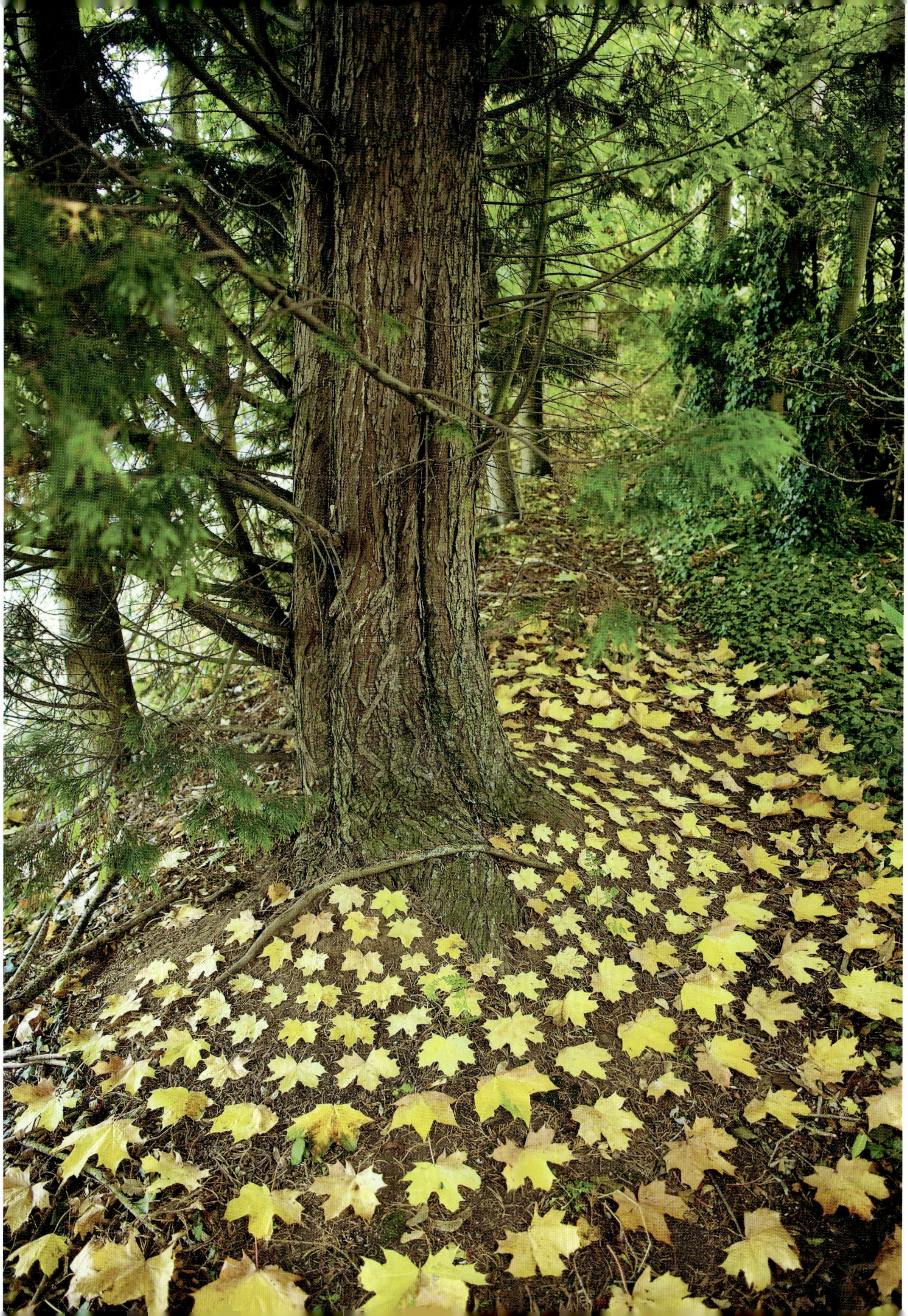

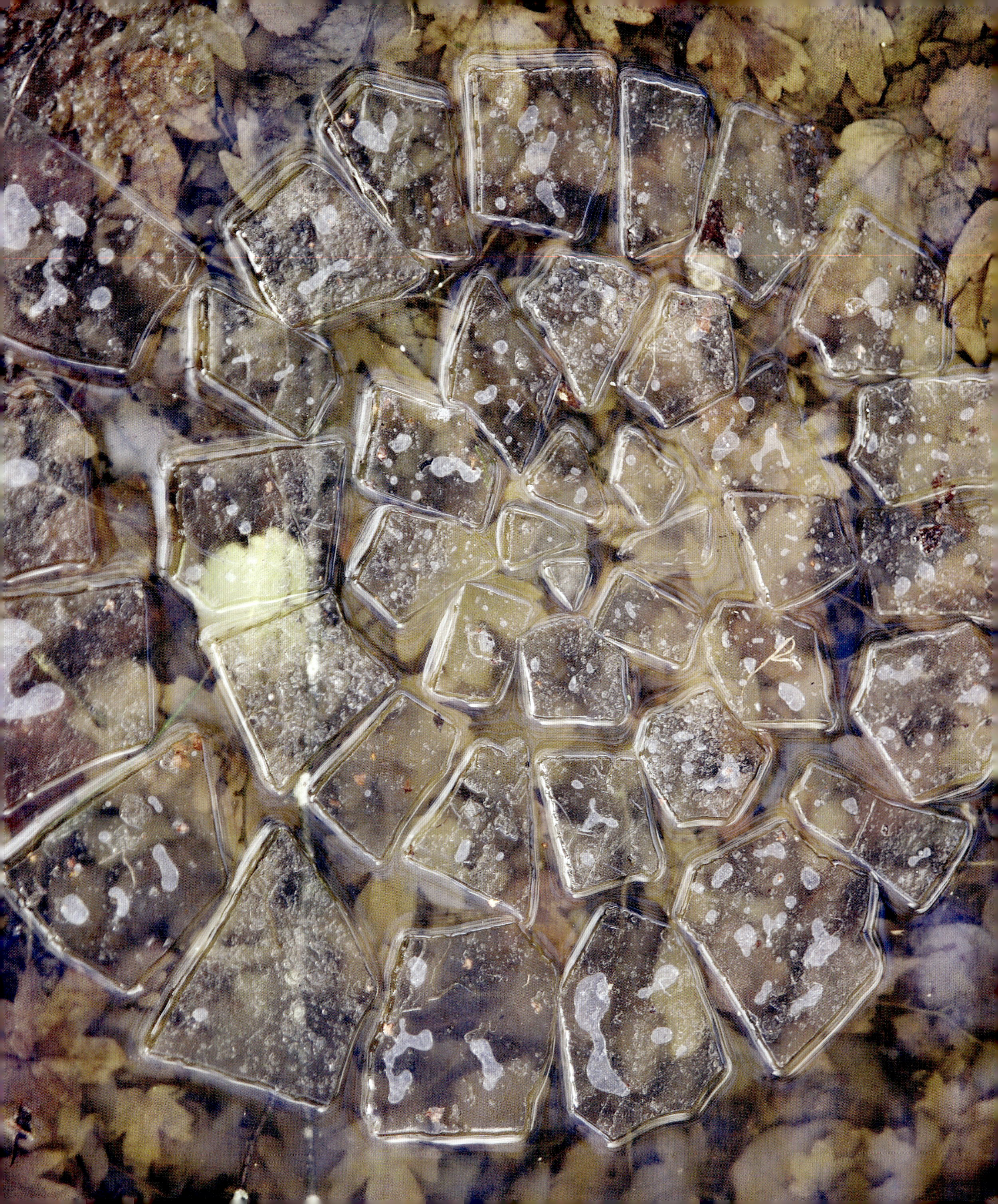

I've often said that I make work solely for myself, and the fact that many people seem to take pleasure in the work I make is very humbling, for which I'm eternally grateful. To this end, the capturing of work and production of photographs are necessary parts of the process of building awareness and a following for my work. But for me, the photography is a task that needs to be completed following the real pleasure of making. Having said that, clicking that shutter and capturing the work before it disappears is a poignant moment and marks the time when I hand over the work back to nature to do its thing! I sound like an expert; the truth is, I take many shots to—I hope—get a few decent images that I'm happy to share. I keep this aspect of the work extremely simple; I have a camera in a bag with a few extra lenses that I very rarely use. The idea of taking huge amounts of kit and setting up equipment to get *that* shot seems a burden that would get in the way of the real passion. For other artists I know, the reverse is true; all elements come into play when searching that optimum moment when the camera shutter is pressed. I find watching artists such as Richard Shilling and Michael Grab fascinating, since I know I will never share their technical prowess.

***Left:** Melting ice spiral at Weleda, Derbyshire. The weight of the ice placed on the frozen surface allowed water to seep over the top and begin to melt everything.*

***Below left:** The kit bag. I try to keep my work as simple as possible so take only a few things with me. Camera, tape, ruler, and the trusty fondue fork.*

***Below right:** Marking out a circle in the sand, and the fondue fork in action.*

The making process is a very simple and experiential one, so I try to keep all elements of what I do as simple as possible. In the same bag as my camera, there is a folding meter ruler, a 1-meter (3 foot) sewing tape measure, and an old fondue fork, all of which are used to mark out a circle within which to work. It's not something I do very much, since I prefer works that organically grow. That's the full extent of my kit.

When working, I try to abandon any thoughts of "artist at work" and enter a state of doing that fits into the environment. The process happening is just another constant in the world around me. Above me, the clouds slowly move, birds are calling and foraging, insects seek food and shelter, and in front of me the natural matter is rearranging. In this respect, I like the process to be purely about me and the material; no tools are used to prepare materials (not even the fondue fork!). The same can be said for my physical experience of creating; thoughts of blocking out any of the senses during the making process would stop me in my tracks—for example, no matter how cold, I could never wear gloves; the physical connection to the material as works evolve is crucial to my experience. Ditto for sound: sound is so important; it's my radio station as I work. The creak a tree makes when swaying in the wind, or water meandering along its course, the birds that edge ever closer, or the rustle from the undergrowth from an unknown source all add to the work's unique soundtrack and experience. A hood to protect against rain, if it in any way nullified the sounds around me, would be disorientating and have a huge impact on the process. Even a thick coat would create a barrier to experience; if it's cold, I want to feel it.

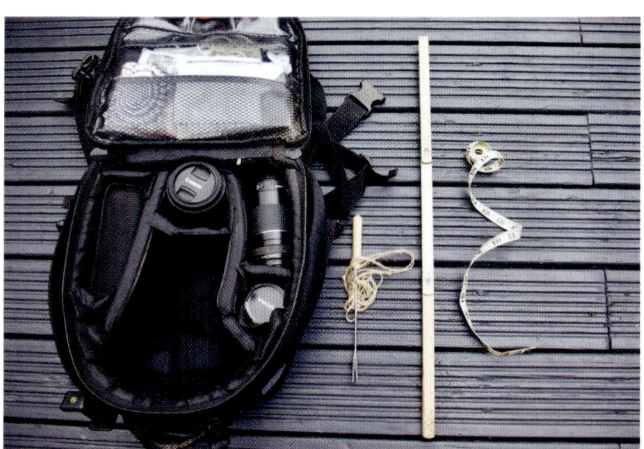

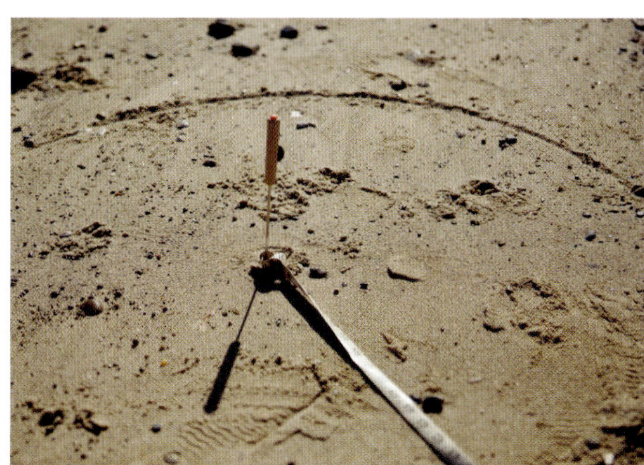

My Working Code

Over time, my relationship with the environments in which I work has developed through repetition and experience. Becoming more aware of the impact the moving natural matter has on the environment and ecosystems, it wasn't long into my journey before I began to notice things, small things like the evidence of life on upturned stones in a fresh flowing river, or on land for that matter; my natural response to moving a stone and seeing a spider disturbed from its web was always to apologize to the spider and return it immediately. But more than this, as my connection to space grew, it became increasingly important to ensure the impact I left behind was minimal.

So, a code began to develop organically, things I was happy or not happy to do in the making of work; it's an evolving process created out of experience and understanding, but here is my current code as it stands.

1. Simply put, I work with what nature gifts me, not what I can take from a natural environment. I try to emphasize this in all the work I do with others. Working only with what we can find on the floor, and not, tempting as it may be, to pick things from trees, shrubs, and wildflowers.

2. I don't take stones away from their natural habitat. In fact, beach works are made where the material is in abundance, so I never have to go searching far and wide for the right pebble. The material is never more than several yards away, meaning when the tide turns and reclaims the work, everything returns to the place it was found.

3. Beach works are created in popular resorts, resorts that welcome and rely on tourism. I don't seek out areas of natural untouched beauty to leave my mark in.

4. If I work in a more sensitive site, it will be through invite; in these cases I check with the relevant people about potential environmental concerns. For example, I love Spurn Point, a nature reserve on the east coast of the UK (and incidentally one the most atmospheric beaches I've worked on). But before visiting, I contacted the visitor center first to discuss any considerations regarding habitat and species that I should be aware of, and fully take on board the advice I get. I would happily not work in a place if I was asked not to.

5. In woodlands, if you look at my work you'll see that the majority of pieces I make are created directly on existing paths or natural clearings. I don't want to go trampling flora in the pursuit of making work. This presents all sorts of potential hazards, but I'd rather lose a few works to roaming dogs than me causing harm to the woodland flora.

6. I don't (I have in the past) work in fresh flowing water. It's a personal thing, but I can see the impact on displacement in these situations and don't particularly see the benefit in me doing so. Okay, so this one is an interesting one, since I know many artists who do work in rivers and streams and do so with no less integrity than I. These artists have the same love of their surroundings and natural environment as I do. My decision was purely based on my own experience and how it influenced me.

7. I don't overpopulate environments with loads of installations. I make a piece of work that often, when finished, will last no longer than a couple of hours (often less), taken by natural and nonnatural interventions such as wind, tides, and footfall.

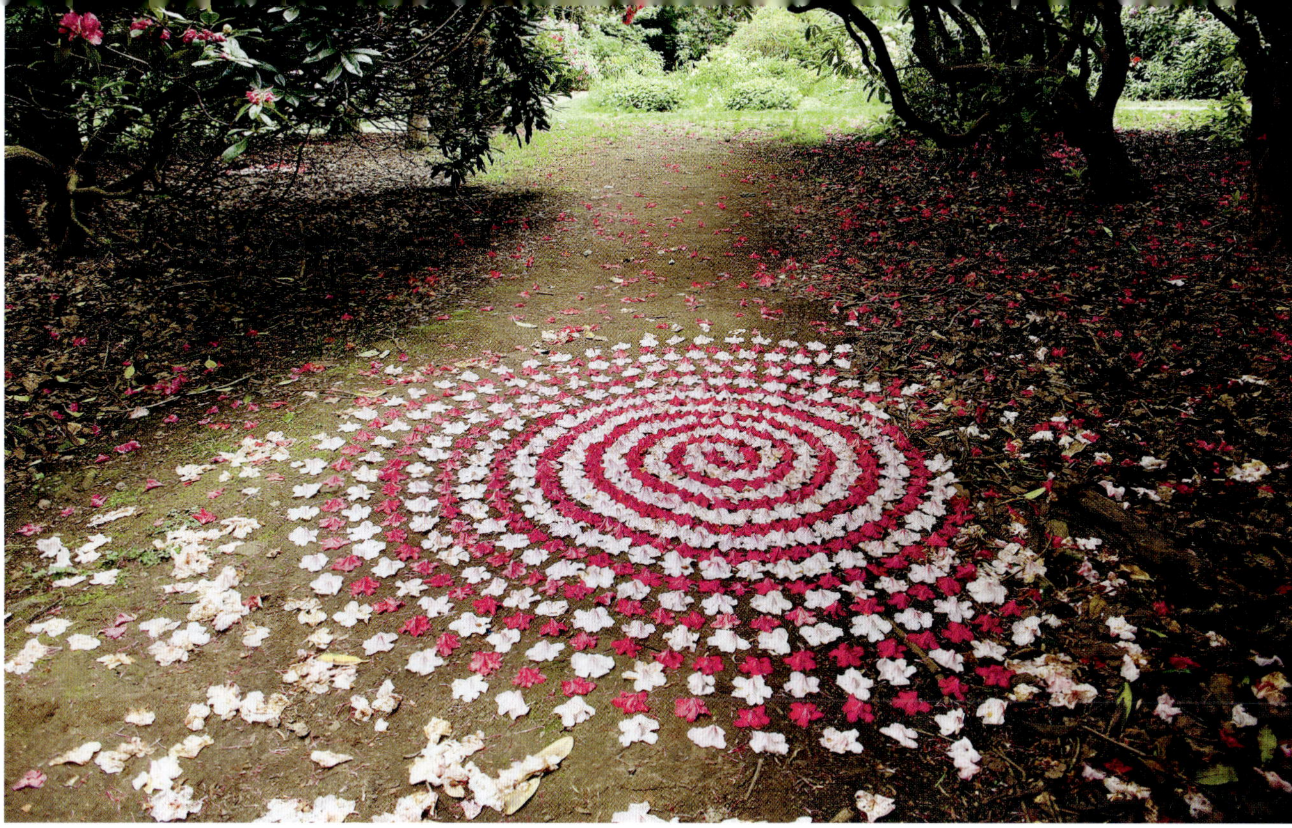

Above: *Rhododendron blossom, Cannon Hall. The year is bookmarked by key events: fall's leaf harvest and the blossom season in late spring / early summer.*

I can't tell you enough how much caring for and respecting the environments I work in means to me; in all aspects of my work, I try not to harm any living thing. I don't eat animals, I don't swat flies in the house, and I will gently usher along midges and mosquitoes feeding on me in the woods! We are all just trying to survive on this rock of ours, and I certainly don't have any authority to decide if something lives or dies; I'm merely getting by, just like every other living thing on the planet. How we choose to live that life is ultimately what will define us.

I like to consider my working practice as a new layer that temporarily slots into an environment. An experience that is often rewarded by wonderful natural encounters with the wildlife around me, wildlife that seems to accept my presence within the woodlands or wherever I may be working.

There are, and always will be, people who vocally share their dislike of what I do. It is, I'm afraid, the way of things; for all the positive aspects of social media and its impact on my career, there is a negative side: people will do their best to make others feel bad. I've not encountered anyone in person who has objected to what I do; online, however, I and other artists I know do receive our fair share of negative comments, from objections to our "messing" with nature that is already beautiful (no arguments here), to quite vindictive attacks and accusations of natural vandalism. I would be lying if I said this doesn't get to me; it does! But equally, only I hold the knowledge of how I work and the care I take within the landscapes I work.

Obviously the positive response to my work far outweighs that of the negative, but like many artists, I don't take on board praise very well, and I do let it wash over me, but the negative stuff I tend to hold on to. But my code grounds me and ultimately allows me to face any negativity with an inner knowledge of my own truth. And more importantly, it enables me to work side by side with the world around me, knowing the impact my work has is minimal, with very short-term effect on the environment.

Much of this code has developed during time spent in one of my favorite places, Anston Stones Wood, which I call my studio; in fact it's been my studio, college, teacher, and refuge.

Invitations to Play

I don't want you to approach this book as you, the reader, merely reading about me, the artist. Every one of us deserves to make time to stop what we are doing and allow ourselves time to go out and play. I truly believe we are all artists until we tell ourselves we are not, so throughout the book I will be inviting you, the reader, to get outside and play! From my experience of working with people of all ages, I know this can be a daunting task for many, like being faced with a blank piece of paper and asked to draw a picture; people often don't know where to start. Add to this that you may be going out into a public arena, and embarrassment can become a factor (I still sometimes feel fear of public scrutiny). So I hope that these little prompts will take away the nerves to begin something and allow you to just create, and if you are met by inquisitive passersby, introduce what you've been up to; you never know, you may inspire someone else. I hope these prompts provide a good insight into how I go about making work; I try not to think about designs or how I want something to look, and I rely much more on the process of repetition.

If you accept these invitations (please do), I'd love to see what you create! Share any of your lovely creations by connecting with me on any of my social media pages (see page 128 for details) and title your works "invitation to play" along with either 1, 2, 3, or 4, depending on the invitation.

I'm already looking forward to seeing your works.

So let's get started.

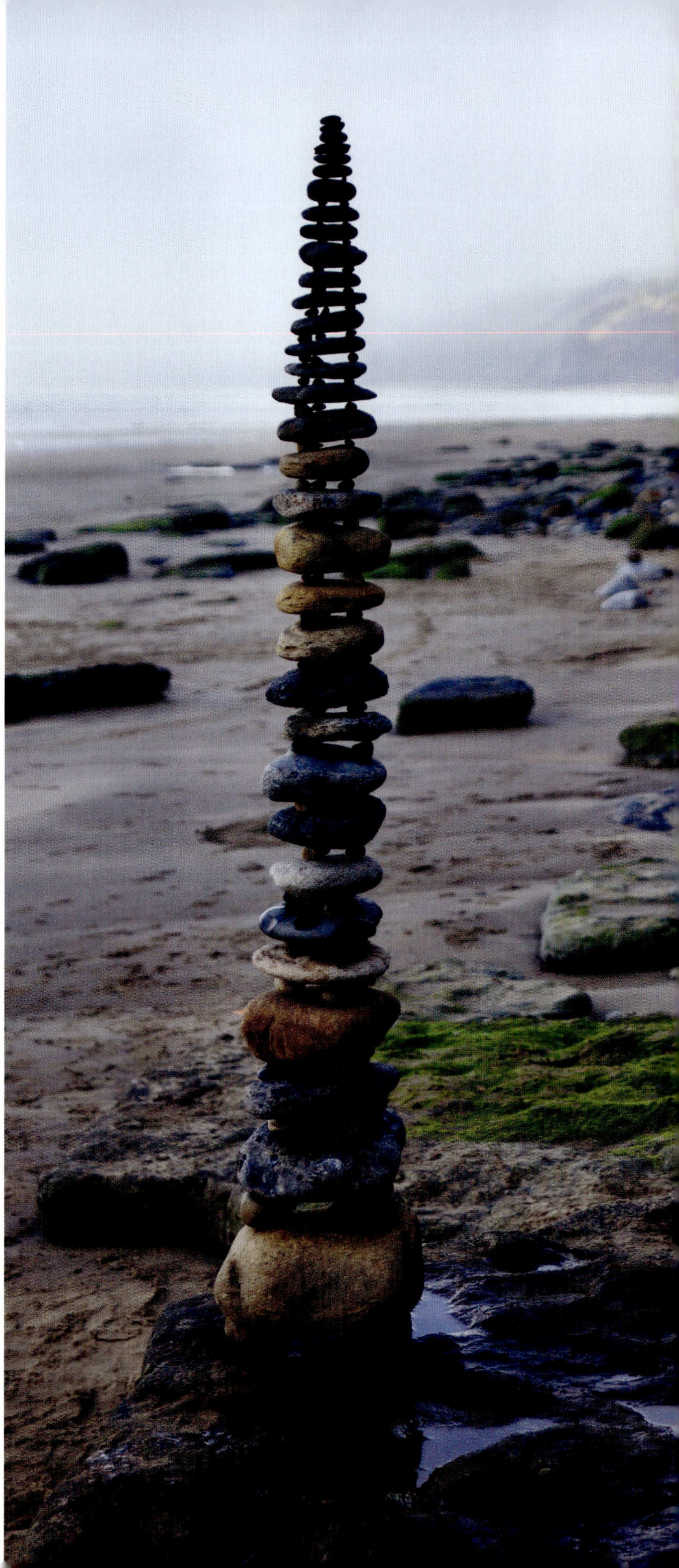

Invitation to Play 1 *(The Spiral)*

If you know my work, you will know I often create spirals of natural materials. I've always explained the creation of spirals as "wanting to get lost in a simple process," a process that requires nothing of me other than focus over a period of time. The only decision is where to start, how the spiral will interact with its surroundings, and what it will be created with, and this is often presented to you by nature itself. So, this invitation aims to take away the fear of starting something or of not knowing what to create.

- Step 1—enjoy your walk and surroundings (always do this).
- Step 2—as you walk, be aware of what materials are presenting themselves.
- Step 3—remove any loose materials from your chosen area (you don't need to dig stuff out or pull out living plants; just work around them).
- Step 4—make a start, work from the middle, and spiral outward.
- Step 5—enjoy what's going on around you; what birds can you see/hear?
- Step 6—don't rush; it's not a race.
- Step 7—finish when you've finished. The joy of something like a spiral is that you're not dictated by a given size; it doesn't have to be big.
- Step 8—sit back and have a moment with your creation.
- Step 9—walk away and leave it for others to find and enjoy.

Note: The images that accompany this invitation to play do not follow the steps above. They are here to serve as inspiration and to show the creation of one of my works in stages.

Tip: Work with the weather, not against it. If it's windy, choose materials wisely (e.g., sticks, acorns, conkers, or conker shells work well in windy conditions). If you are determined to use leaves, consider weighing them down with something. Little sticks are great, but make sure you place them consistently so the viewer sees them as part of the spiral.

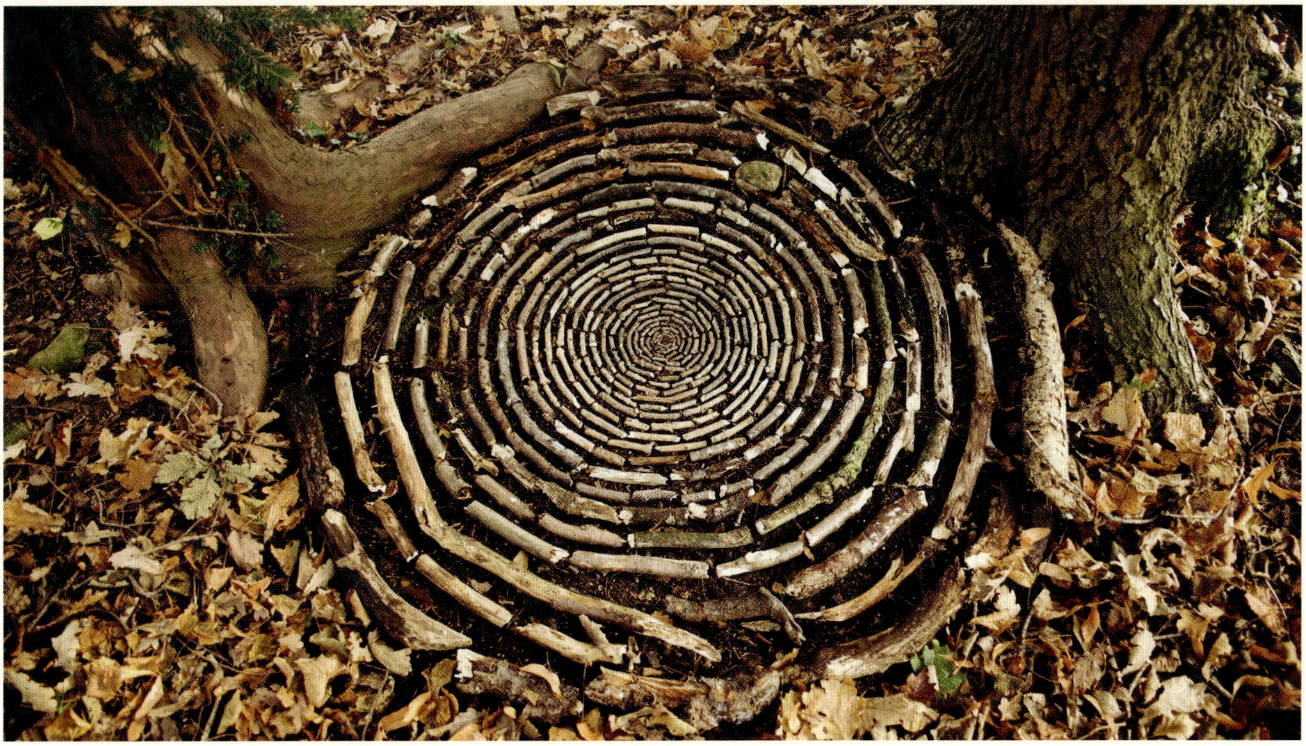

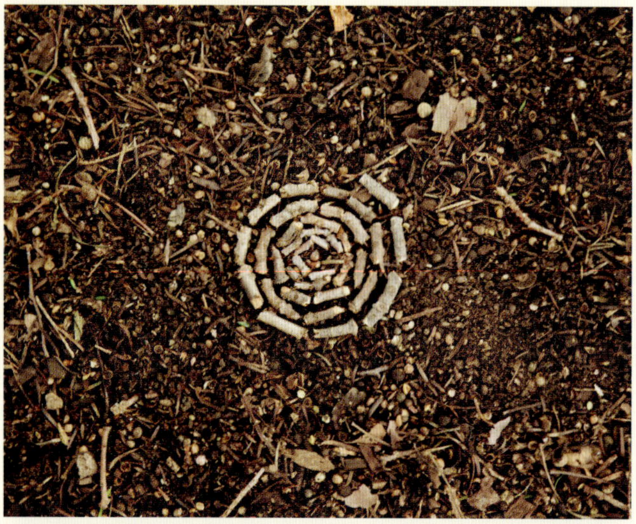
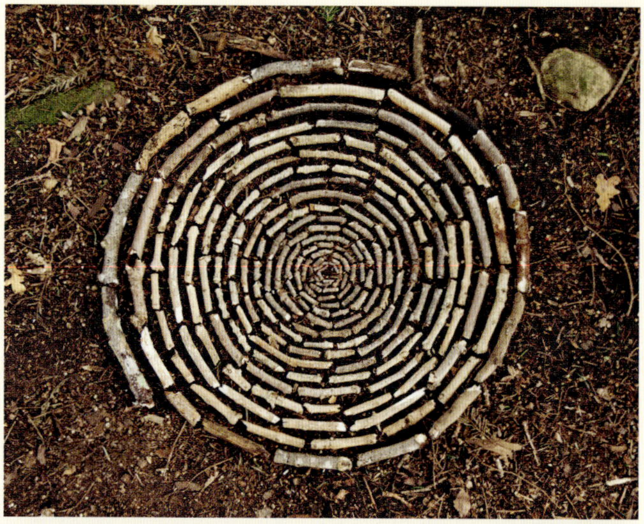
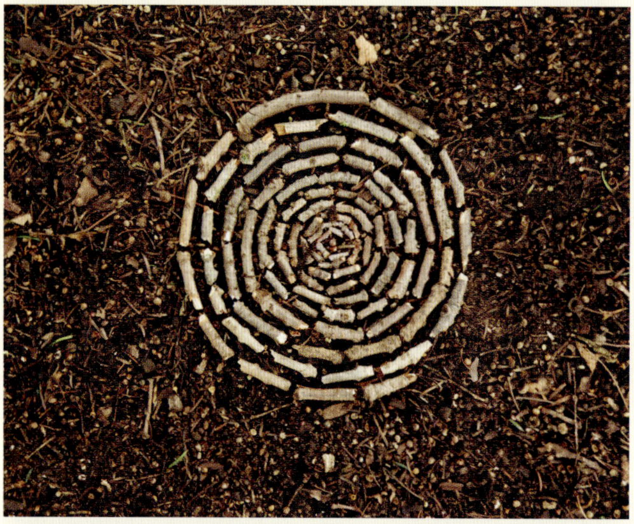
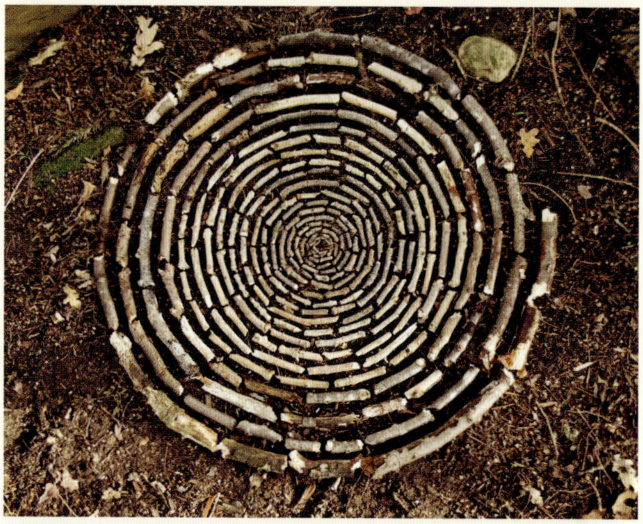
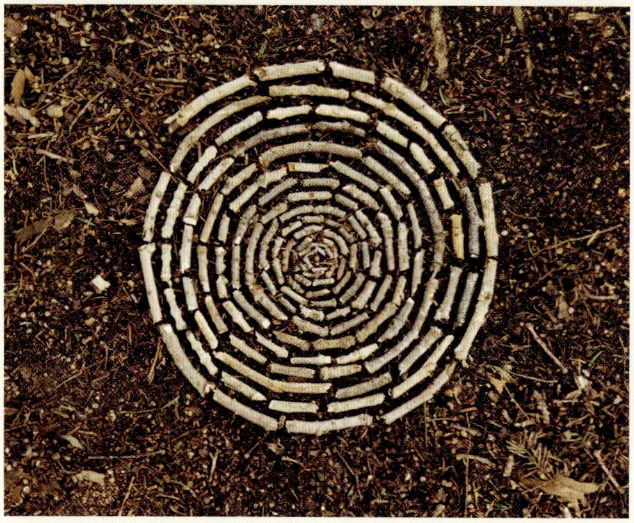
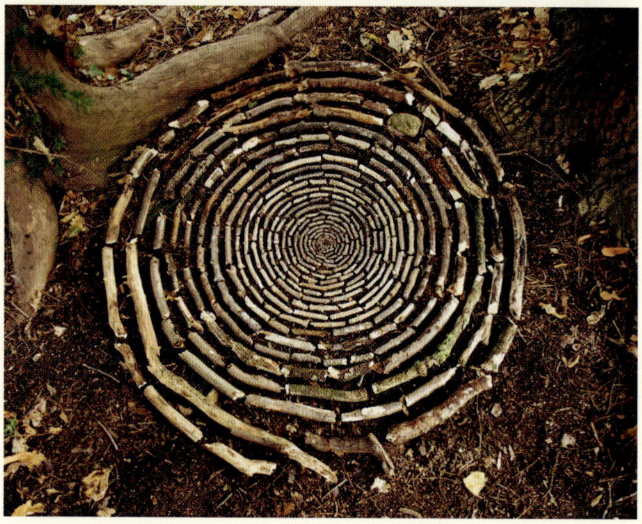

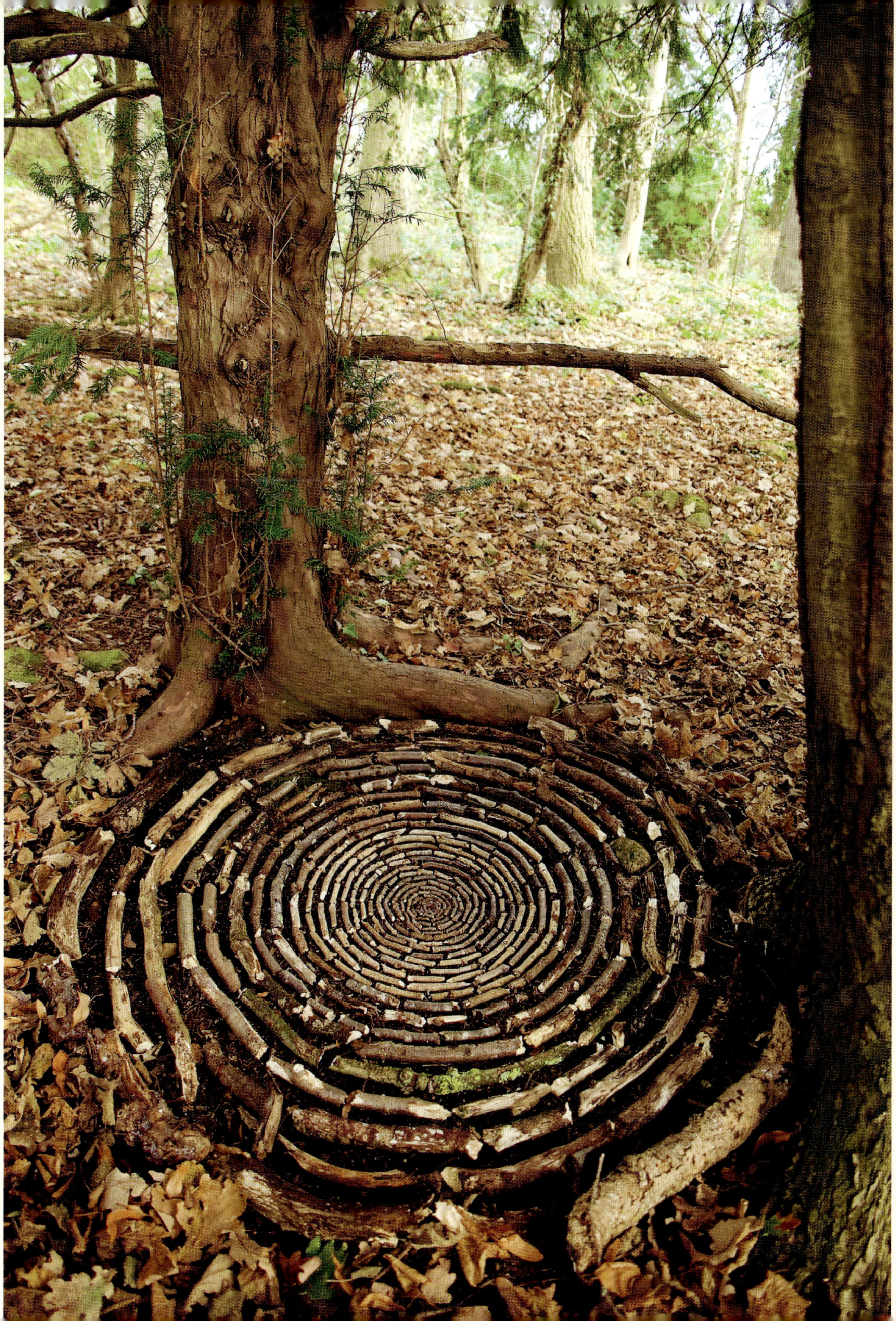

My Studio—Anston Stones Wood, South Yorkshire

Take a walk with me.

From the front door, I can go either left or right.

Across the A57, always busy, always facilitating the rush to get somewhere.

Depending on which way we go, either under or over the old colliery railway line.

Two minutes from home, enter the woods.

Anston Stones Wood.

My studio.

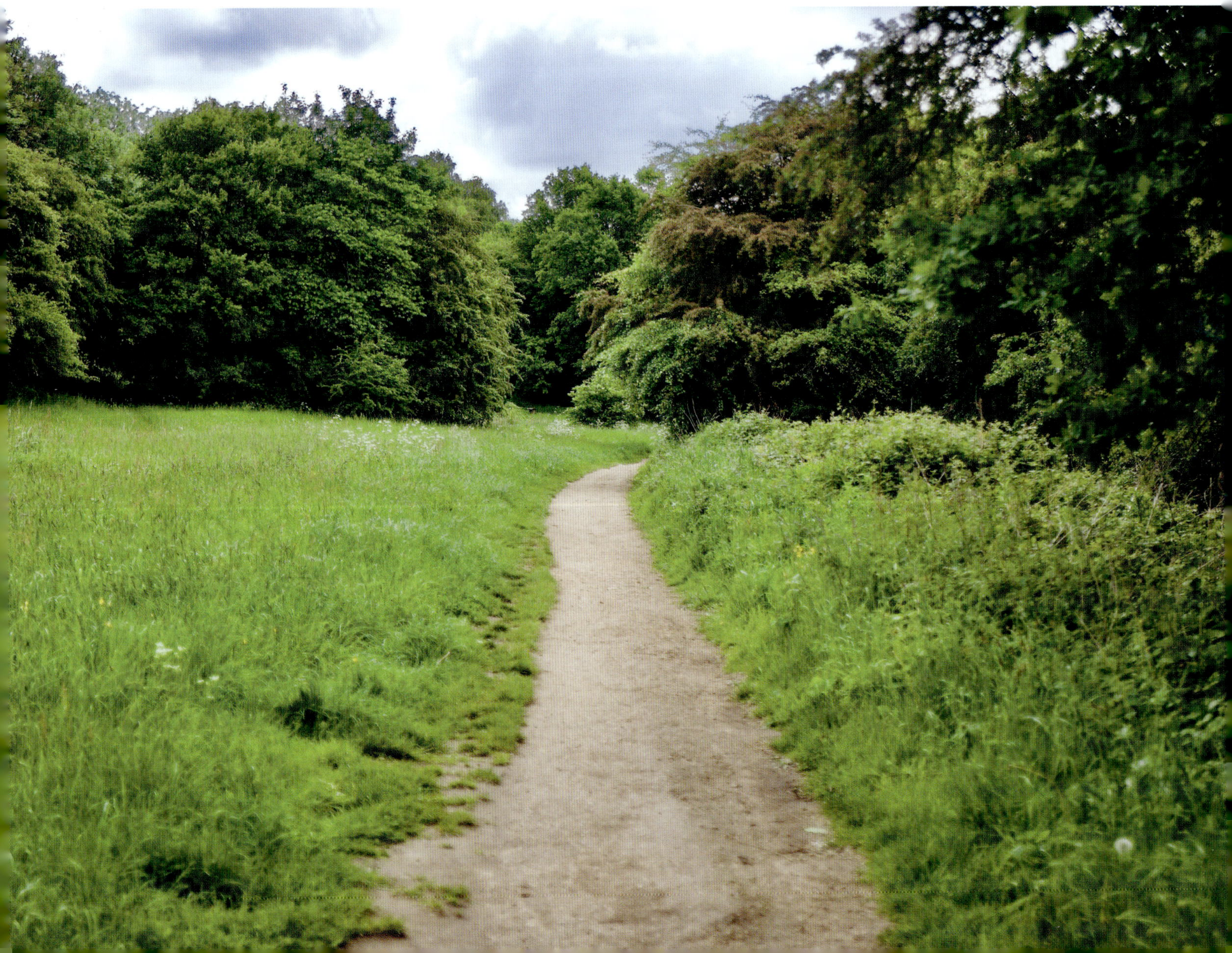

I can't really write this book without a huge shout-out to Anston Stones Wood; it's a place I have a huge connection to. A narrow limestone gorge and woodland in Rotherham, South Yorkshire. This is not a "drive to family day out" location, but more of a dog walk hotspot for locals and residents. A place of adventure (and misadventure) for children and teens, but beautiful nonetheless and, crucially, a two-minute walk from my house.

It runs alongside a busy road, heading toward the county of Nottinghamshire, with a rail track and a stream running through it, splitting it into a series of parallel paths, rocky limestone cliffs, and mixed deciduous woodland.

On entering Anston Stones, it's no exaggeration that I immediately relax; any stresses or worries seem to melt away. I have the dog (Foxy) with me; there's no expectation to create anything, but often I will. An opportunity will present itself: a location I've passed a hundred times or more will, on this day, seem different; it will capture my curiosity, will invite me to closer inspect, and will wait as I figure out the connection. Then I begin.

Below left: *Heading down "the Stones" during the lush greens of summer.*

Below: *Limestone woodland, the second best in Yorkshire, but definitely my favorite.*

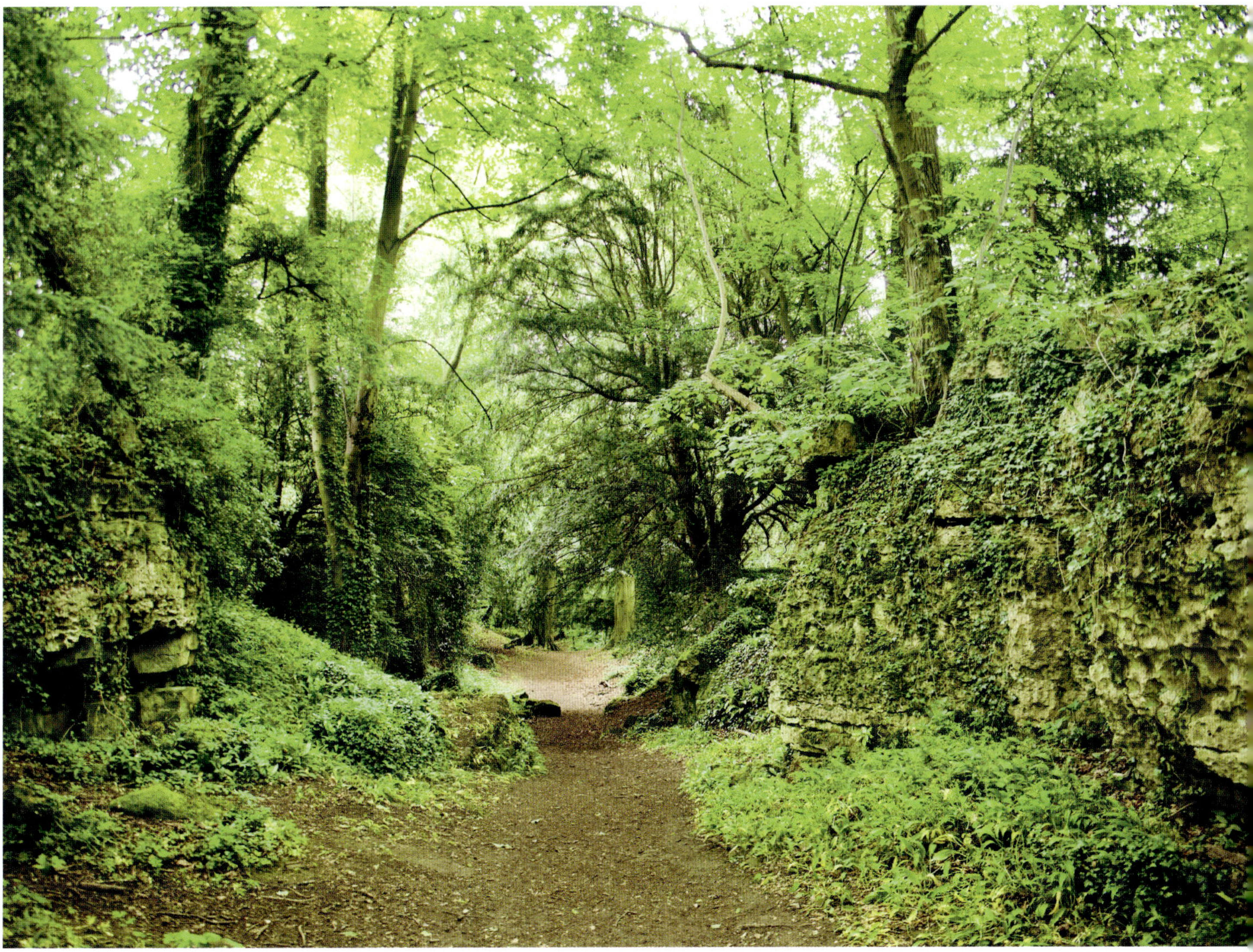

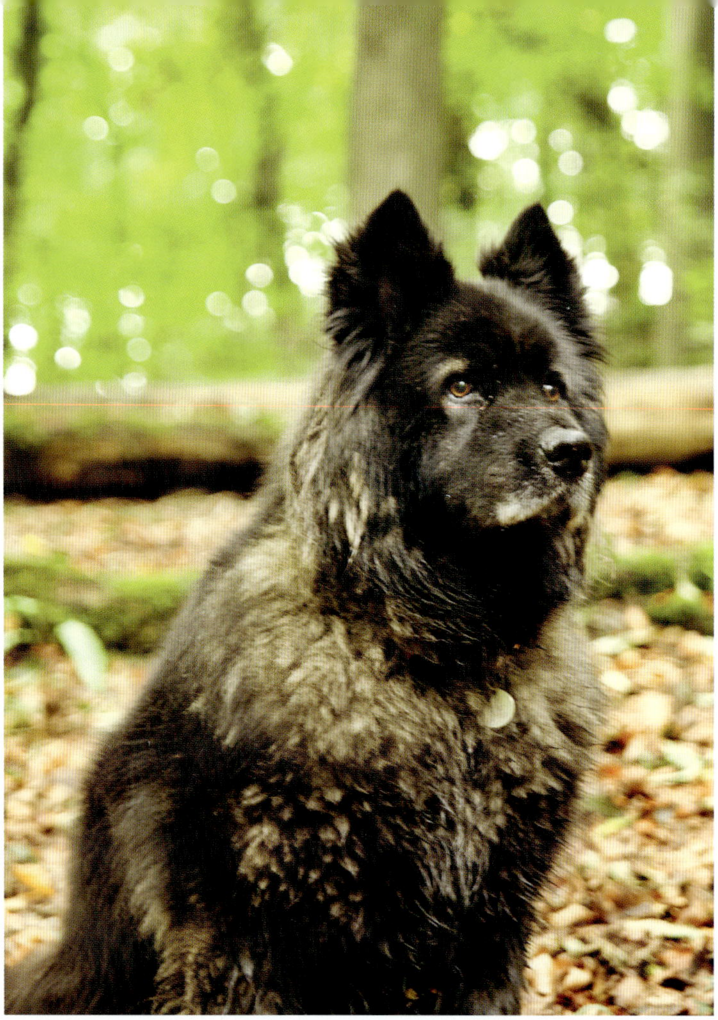

I mentioned the dog. We rescued Foxy from a local animal sanctuary in 2014, and she quickly became a regular assistant to my creative-learning journey in Anston Stones. Calm and gentle by nature, she's quite happy to curl up and snooze as I work, stirring only to greet other dogs, and often being the perfect distraction to avoid dogs walking all over work in progress.

A couple of years ago, I was invited to write a piece for a national newspaper on "favorite walks," and, not being a regular walker, I chose to write about the only place I truly know, Anston Stones Wood. Reading through it now, it still seems so relevant to my work and creative development, so I thought I'd include it for you.

Left: *Foxy, the artist's assistant. We recently had a DNA test done to find out exactly what she is—50 percent Akita, then a heady mix of German shepherd, Swiss white shepherd, Siberian husky, and golden retriever.*

Below: *Heading down one of the many paths, the woodland changes as you get closer to the brook.*

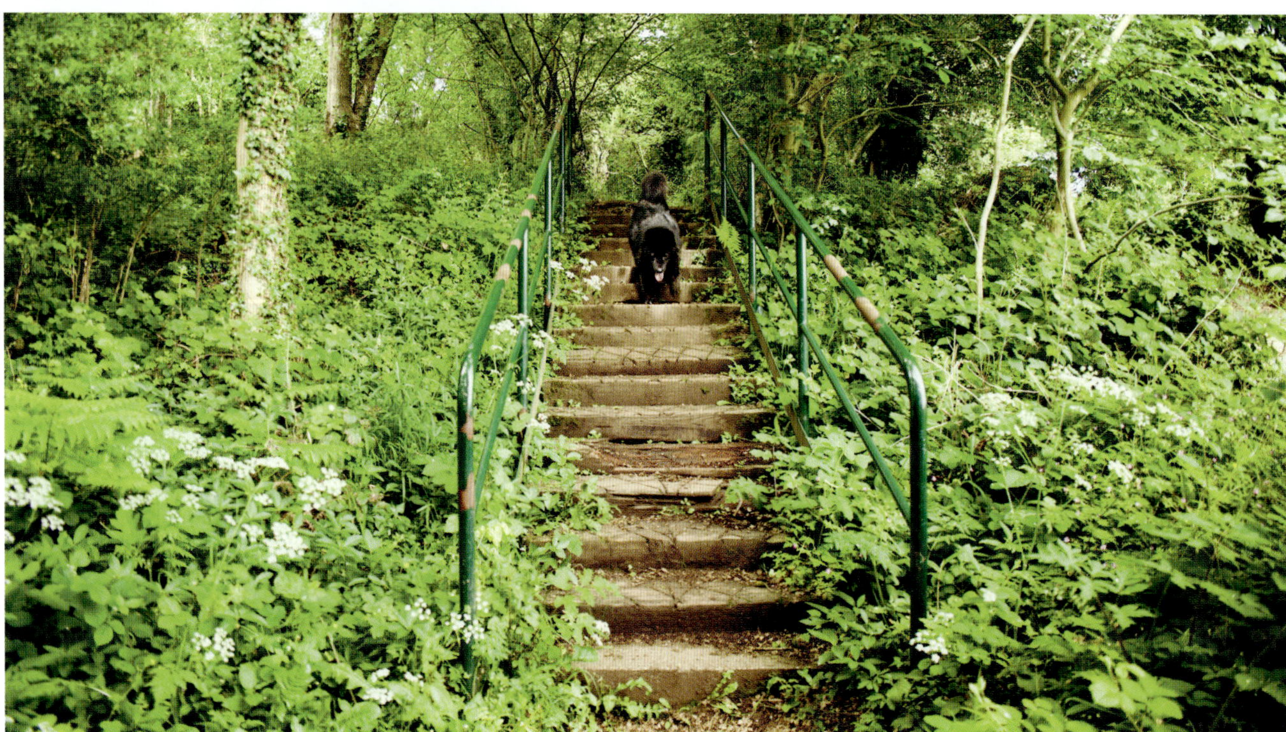

About 10 miles east of Sheffield, hidden away from the more popular and well-trodden destinations of the High Peak that border the city, is a hidden gem. Known mainly to the locals who live close by, Anston Stones Wood follows a natural limestone gorge close to South Yorkshire's border with Nottinghamshire. Situated within a small, thin, but richly diverse strip of land, it has a lot to offer walkers: limestone cliff faces, caves, stunning woodland, and a network of paths to explore a variety of habitats. It also boasts the claim to fame of producing quarried stone for the rebuilding of the Houses of Parliament following a fire in the 1830s.

As an artist, this 3-mile walk and its many subsidiary paths are the closest thing I have to a studio, two minutes from where I live, a place to play, create, and share a deep connection to the natural environment, right on my doorstep. Walks with Foxy (my Akita / German shepherd / husky cross) often include two-hour stops to create a temporary natural artwork for those following my path to stumble upon. It is also my daily connection to all things natural and a healthy dose of well-being. The path from the cricket ground follows Anston Brook at the base of the gorge for 1⅓ miles, before cutting back and retracing its steps along the higher slopes of the northern bank, taking in a pleasing array of changing habitats. From alder along the banks of the brook, to beech-and-ash-dominant woodland on the southern banks, to birch, yew, grassland meadows, and some rather splendid broadleaf lime, with root systems that battle dramatically with limestone cliffs that they perch on, along the higher paths.

In spring, the woods come alive, the drumming of woodpeckers fills the air, pockets of bluebells stand proud among the carpet of wild garlic, and, for the last two years, a resident pair of kingfishers offer a stunning flash of blue along the brook, probably hunting the increasing numbers of brown trout seen recently. Fellow dog walkers tell stories of deer sightings in the early hours of the morning, but I've yet to see them. If spring is the most welcome of seasonal changes, for me it's the least productive time artistically. After the color palette of autumn and naturally littered woodland floors of winter, spring is the pressing of the refresh button, a chance to restock my studio for the coming year. The budding awakening of life in the woods takes center stage, and more often than not, I simply enjoy the walk for its glorious backdrop of the lushest greens I've ever seen.

You cannot walk in Anston Stones Wood without searching for Dead Man's Cave (obviously haunted), a "rite of passage" camping spot when I was a teenager growing up in the area, but more significant for the 12,000-year-old flint tools and Ice Age animal bones found there during archeological excavations in the '60s. It's situated off the main path, but ask any of the local dog walkers and they'll point you in the right direction. Part of the walk's charm is also the never-too-faraway railway line that cuts through the gorge, a rarely used freight line now, but a monument to the region's mining heritage, which once thrived with the transportation of coal from the region's long-since-closed colliery sites.

A place to picnic is the Little Stones, a rocky outcrop on the higher slopes of the gorge after 2 miles of walking. Here the woodland opens up, offering views across to the village of South Anston and ultimately the walk's final destination of the village pub, the Loyal Trooper.

My relationship with Anston Stones Wood and its network of paths is always evolving; the more I create there, the deeper my awareness of the natural world around me and the impact of what I do has on the landscape. My working code of practice has developed out of this relationship and steers the direction of my work. Quick online searches will tell you that Anston Stones Wood is the second-best example of limestone woodland in South Yorkshire! Well, not for me. For me, it's by far the best.

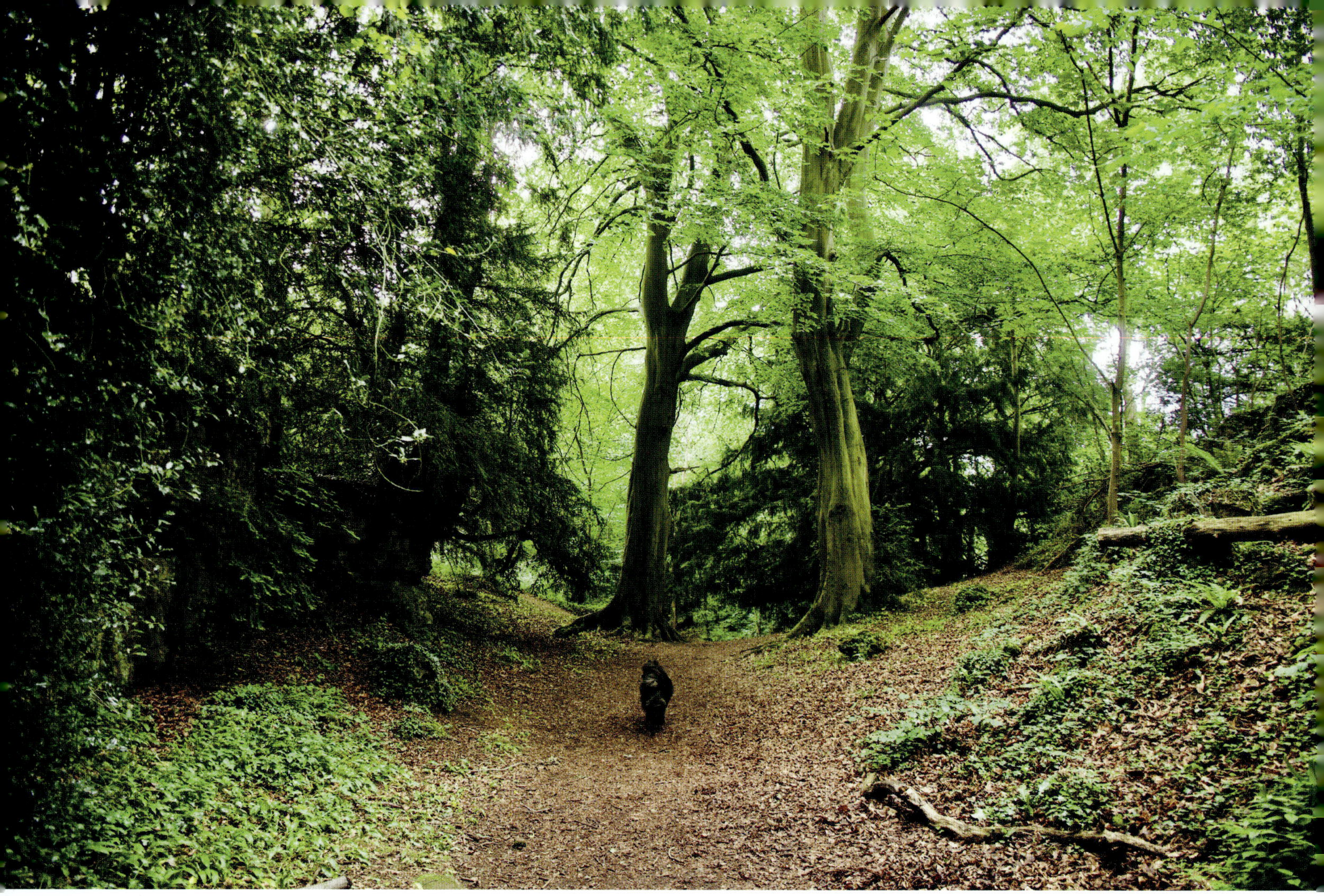

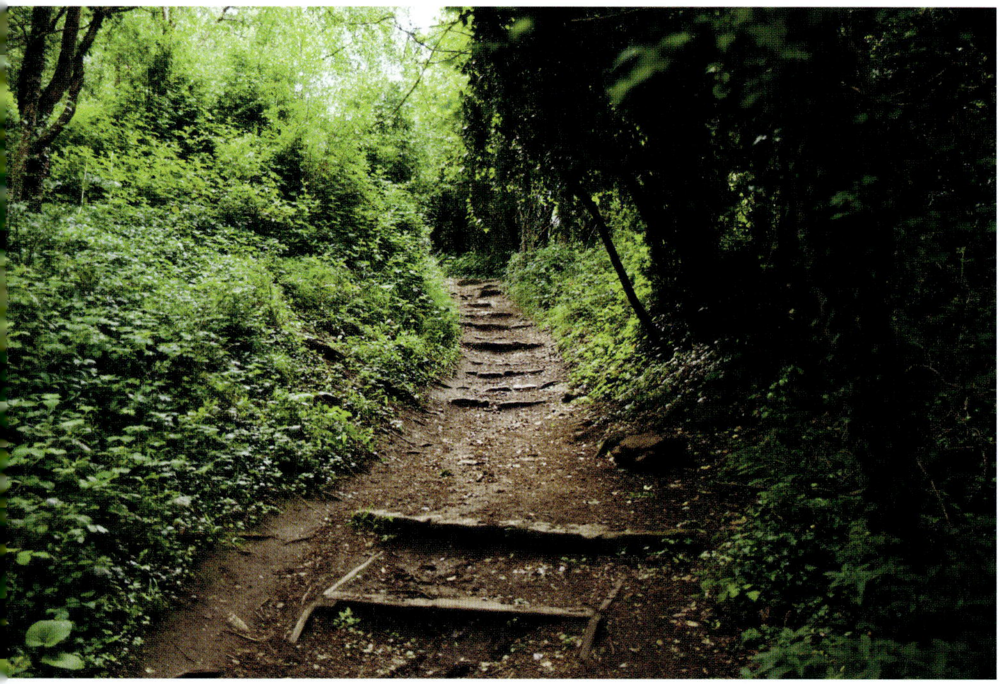

Above: *Foxy leading the way. Recognize the two big beech trunks Foxy is heading toward?* *See page 107.*

Left: *Exploring the quieter paths, I often seek out the quieter spots to work.*

Right: *Dead Man's Cave, historically important for flint tools found there and bones from Ice Age animals. Now home to some very impressive cave spiders.*

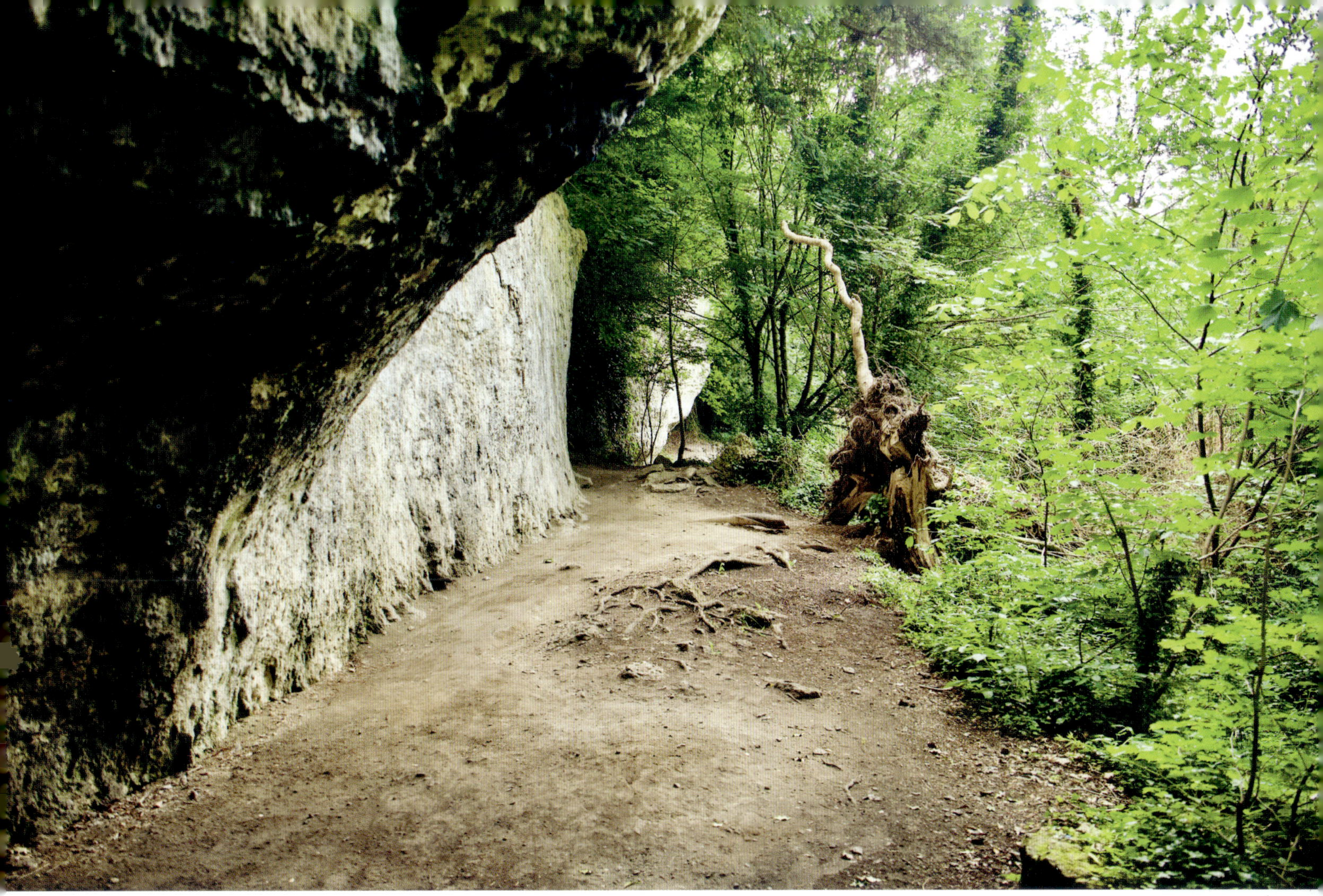

***Above:** The cliff sides are well used locations for my work. Providing shelter, material, and interesting environment to respond too.*

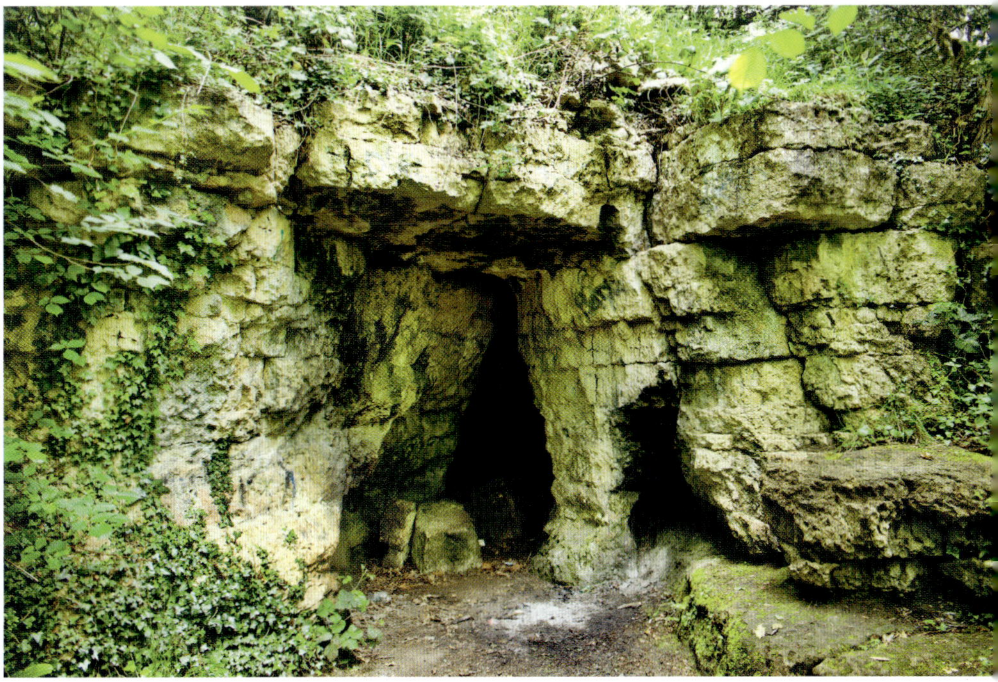

Anston Stones Wood has and always will be a place of play for me—familiar yet always surprising, refreshing and reviving, and while I say I know it like the back of my hand, it still reveals new paths and places to explore. I'm sure you will have your own "Anston Stones Wood"; spend as much time there as possible—sit, watch, listen, feel, and play.

And on that note...

Invitation to Play 2 *(Repetitions)*

The second of my little prompts, to get you out exploring your creative side, is another simple one: repeated patterns. There is something very pleasing about reordering natural matter, and a wonderfully simple way to do it is through a repeated pattern. These works don't rely on having long periods of time; they can fit in with your schedule and be as small or as large as you want. Some of my most striking images are repeated patterns that may not have taken more than an hour to create. The smallest section of order, within a wider landscape of disorder (a carpet of leaves, a beach of pebbles, for example), creates a visually conflicting story that draws the eye in.

- Step 1—like before, enjoy your walk and surroundings.
- Step 2—again as you walk, be aware of what materials are presenting themselves.
- Step 3—once you have selected the material, familiarize yourself with it; with leaves, for example, do the two sides of the leaf have different colors or textures? These nuances can be useful to create contrast.
- Step 4—select an area to work and remove surface litter.
- Step 5—begin your process; this can be as simple as a grid, but remember the contrasts within the material.
- Step 6—don't rush; it's still not a race.
- Step 7—consider how your work fits with the wider space; for example, I often try to make the work appear to have been revealed when the surface litter was removed, and that underneath the leaf carpet, the whole woodland floor is covered with the repeated pattern.
- Step 8—sit back and have a moment with your creation.
- Step 9—walk away and leave it for others to find and enjoy.

Note: The images that accompany this invitation to play do not follow the steps above. They are here to serve as inspiration and to show a couple of variations on the theme of repetition.

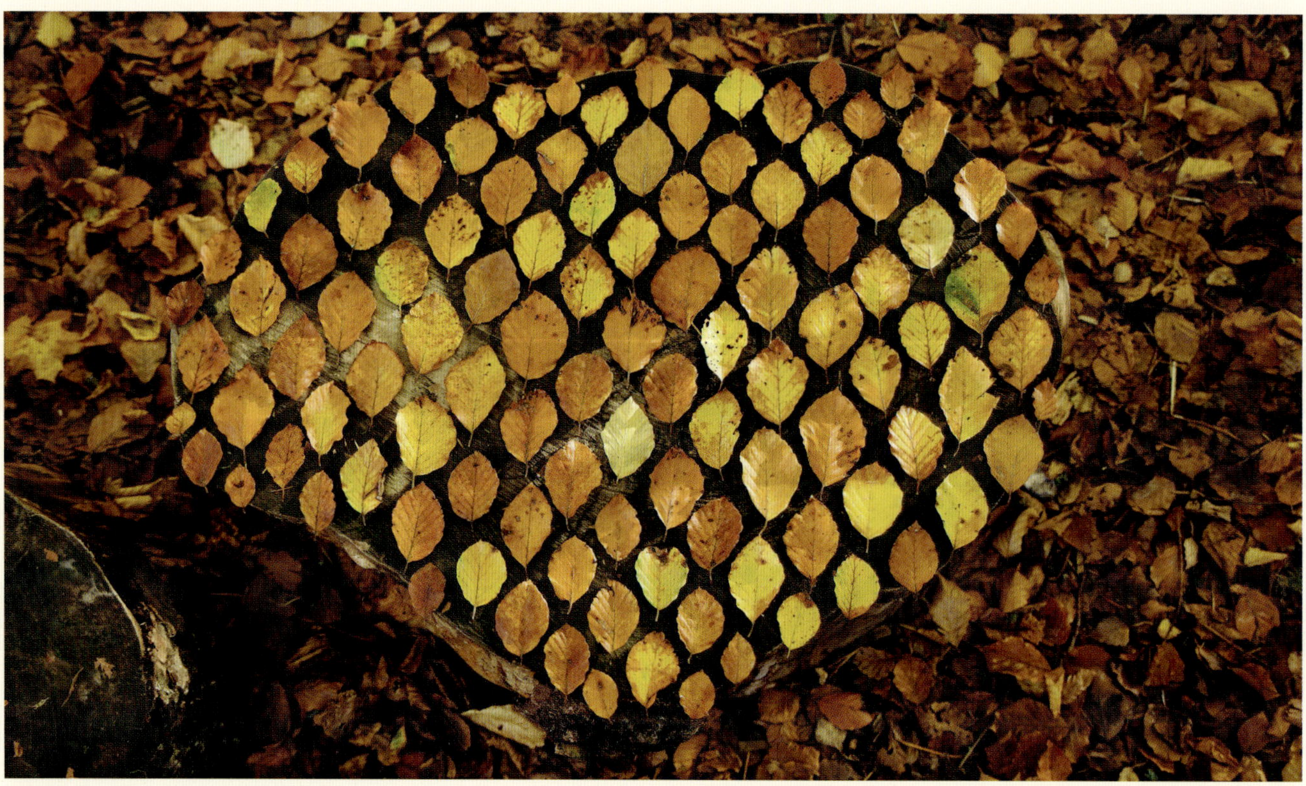

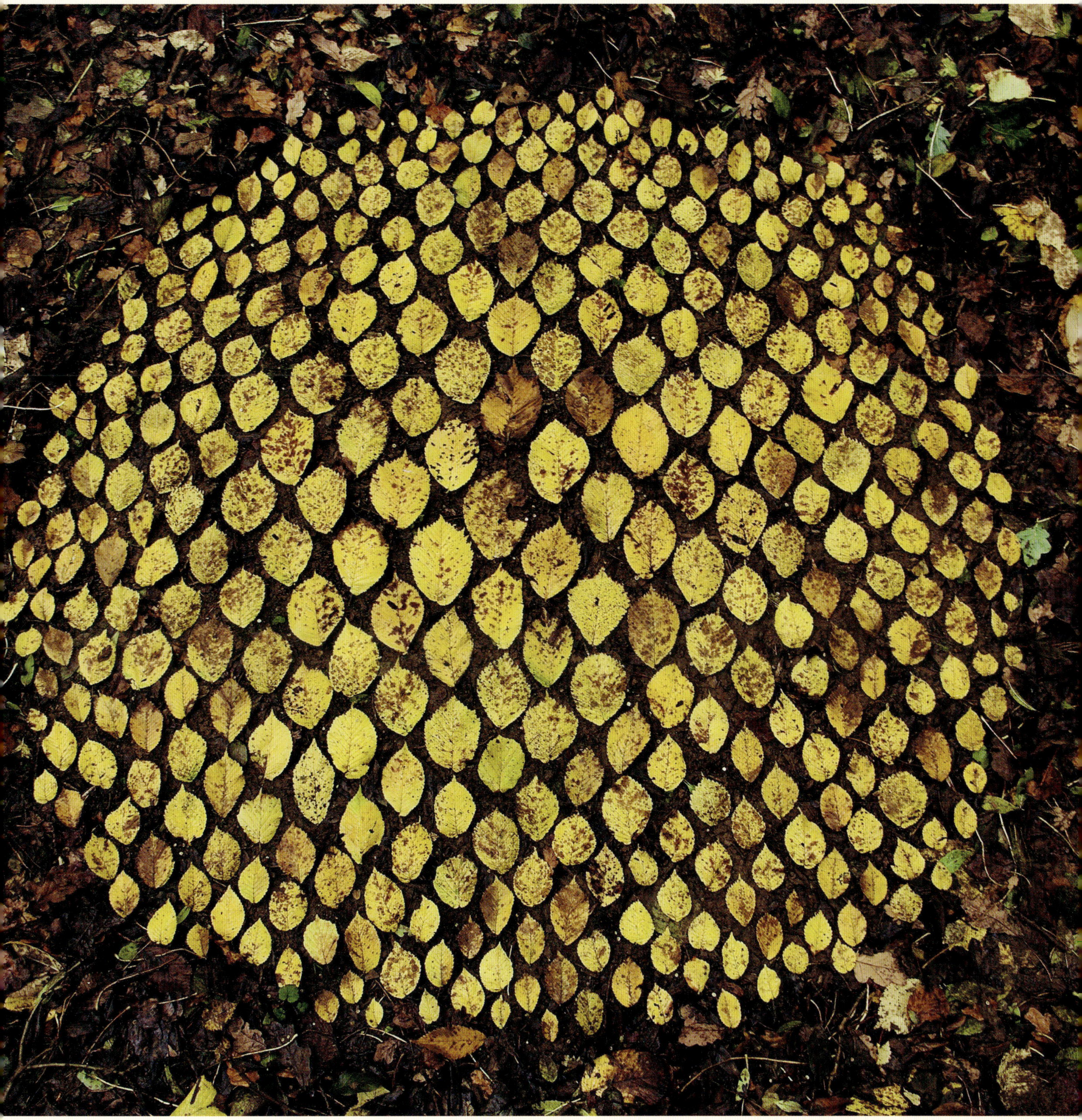

Connections to Place

I've already spoken about my relationship with Anston Stones Wood, but there are many places farther afield that I have a similar connection to, places key to my creative development.

Everyone feels some sort of connections to specific places, whether connections associated with fond childhood memories such as holiday destinations or shared experience, or the familiar, comforting spaces embedded in our consciousness through repetition. I'm no different; I'm drawn to the Yorkshire coastline for exactly these reasons, familiarity honed over many years of good memories and shared family experiences. It has become a place that as I approach, I feel its comfort immediately wash over me. As a result of this connected history, specific locations and places become an intrinsic part of my creative journey. The beach at Filey, a North Yorkshire coastal town and holiday resort. A sweeping bay of sand, with the famous Brigg, a rocky outcrop heading out into the North Sea on its northern point, and the lighthouse of Flamborough Head to the south. The town of Filey itself retains its quiet charm, despite it being an up-and-coming location for second-home seekers.

Below: *A well-known landscape, Filey beach looking toward the Brigg. This was one of my first trips to the beach after COVID lockdowns; I can't tell you how much I needed it.*

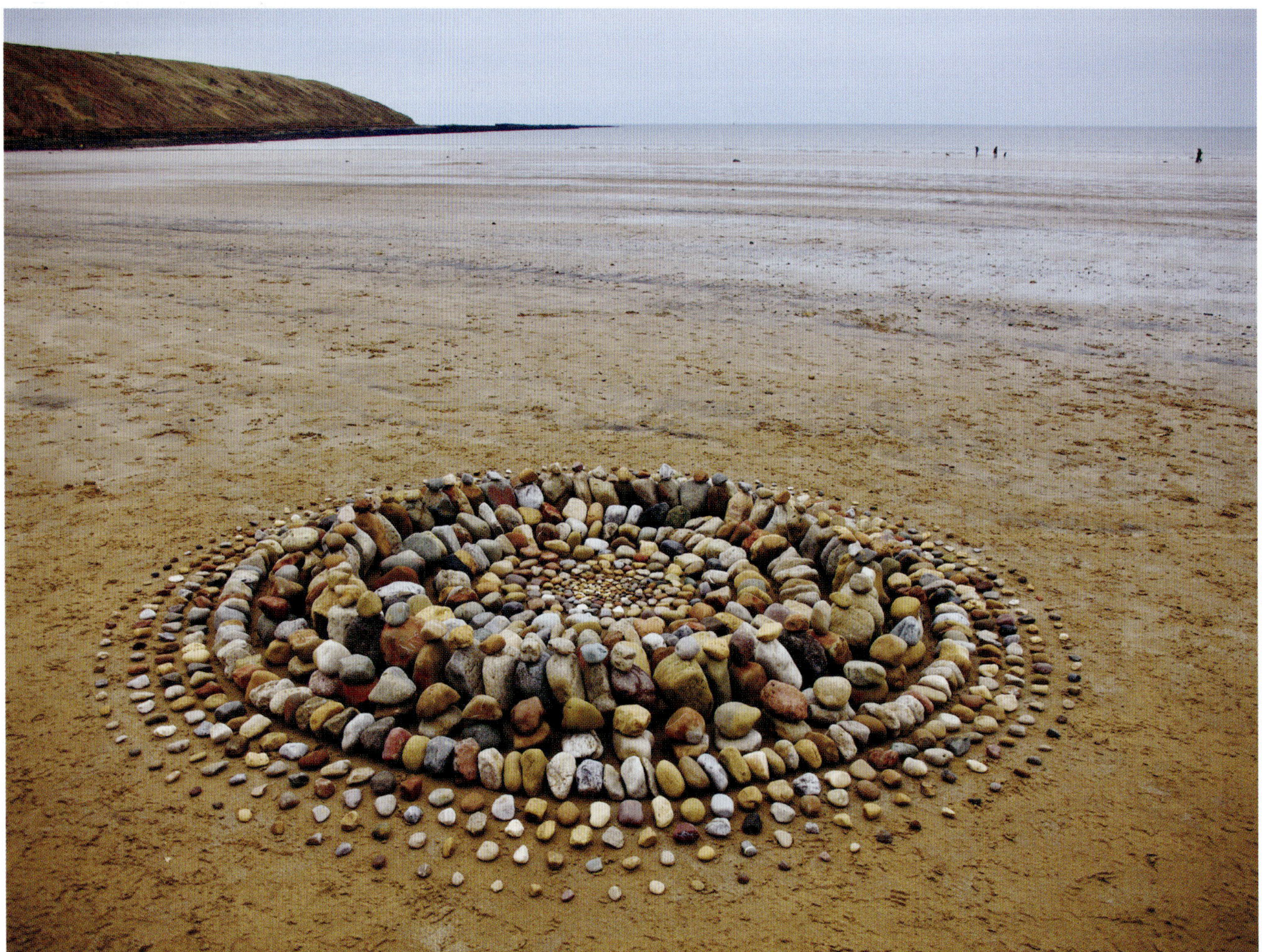

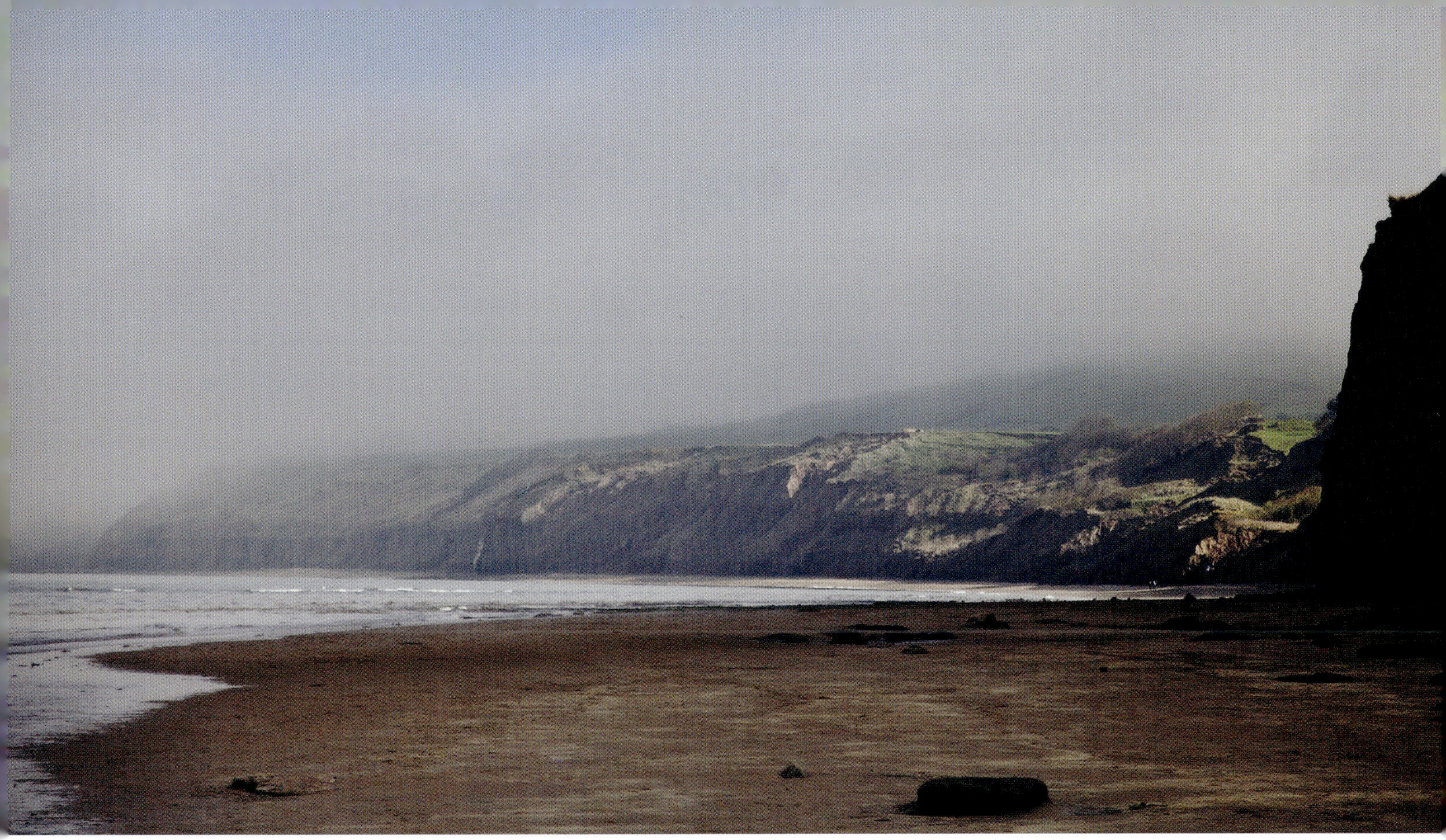

***Above:** The rugged coastline of Robin Hood's Bay, on the Heritage Coast of the North York Moors.*

From Filey, let's head north first. Heading up the North Yorkshire coast, it's dotted with places that all ooze familiarity and comfort. Scarborough, Robin Hood's Bay, Whitby, Sandsend up to Staithes the farthest north; all places filled with memories, and the connections run deep to my childhood.

Truth be told, Whitby should be the place I'm talking about before Filey; that's where most of my childhood holidays were based, but it's a further hour up the coast, and the beaches at Filey snare me in its grasp before I get there.

South of Filey, my relationship with the coastline is much more linked to my creative journey. North and South Landing at Flamborough, Danes Dyke, Bridlington, Hornsea, and Withernsea, where my connection has been built over many years of summer workshops, all the way down to Spurn Point, possibly the most atmospheric beach I've worked on in the UK.

***Below:** I just loved the colors of these pebbles where Sandsend Beck meets the North Sea in the beautiful village of Sandsend near Whitby.*

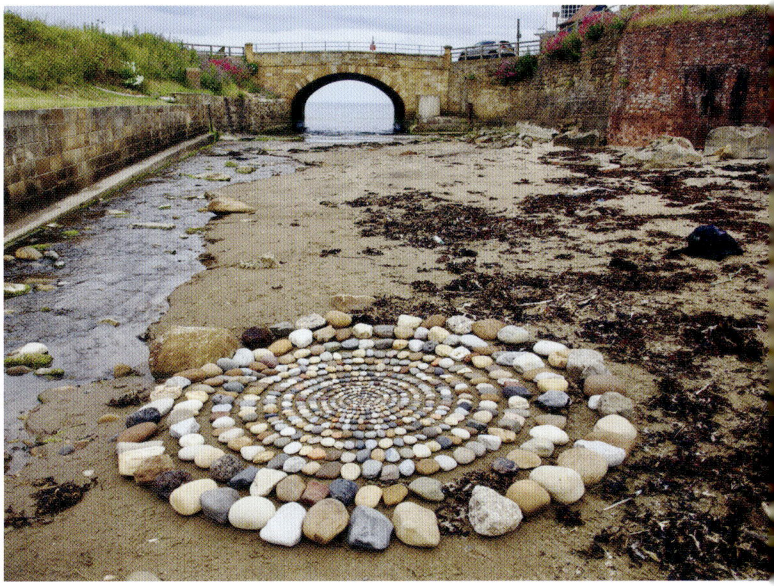

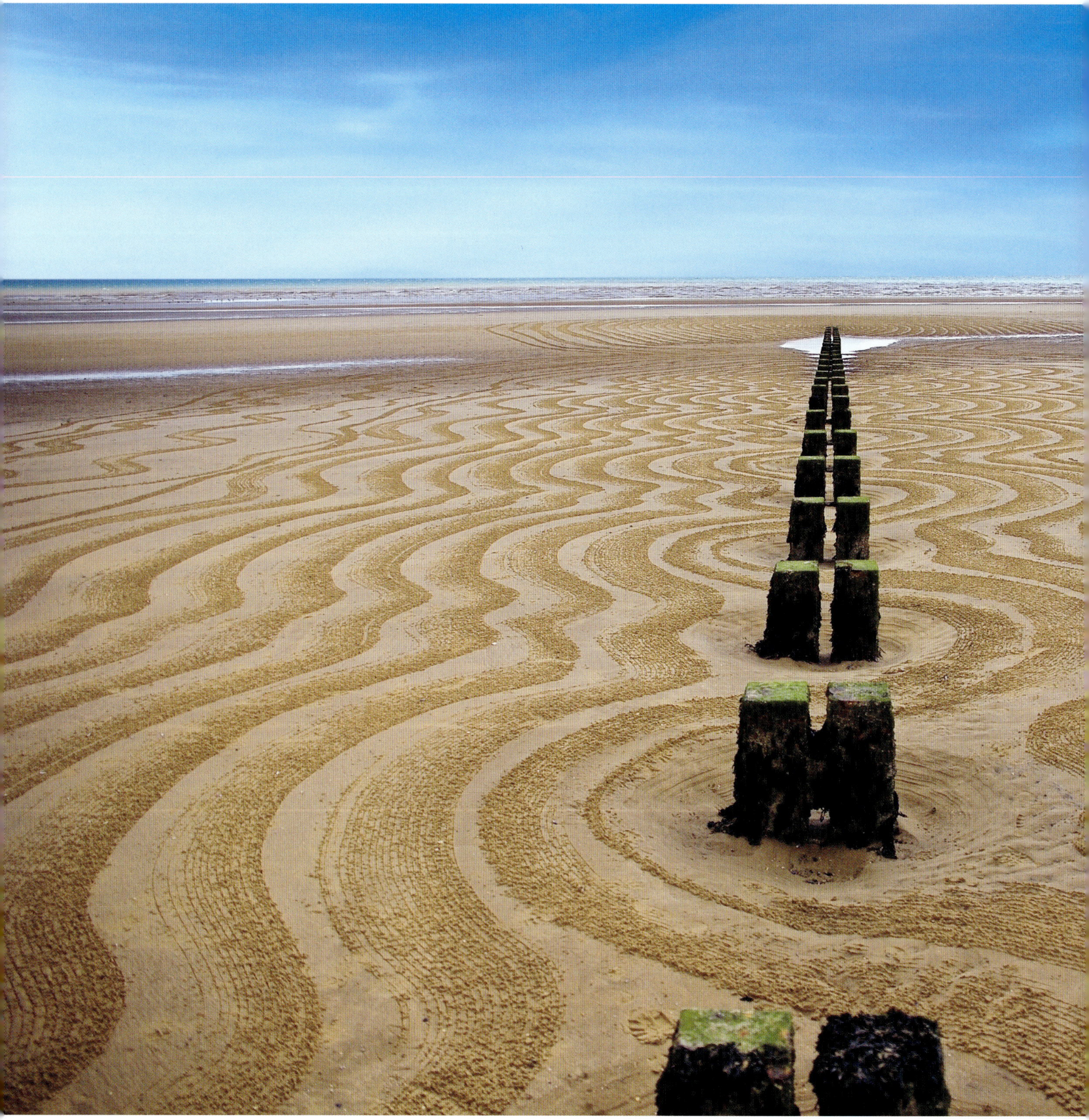

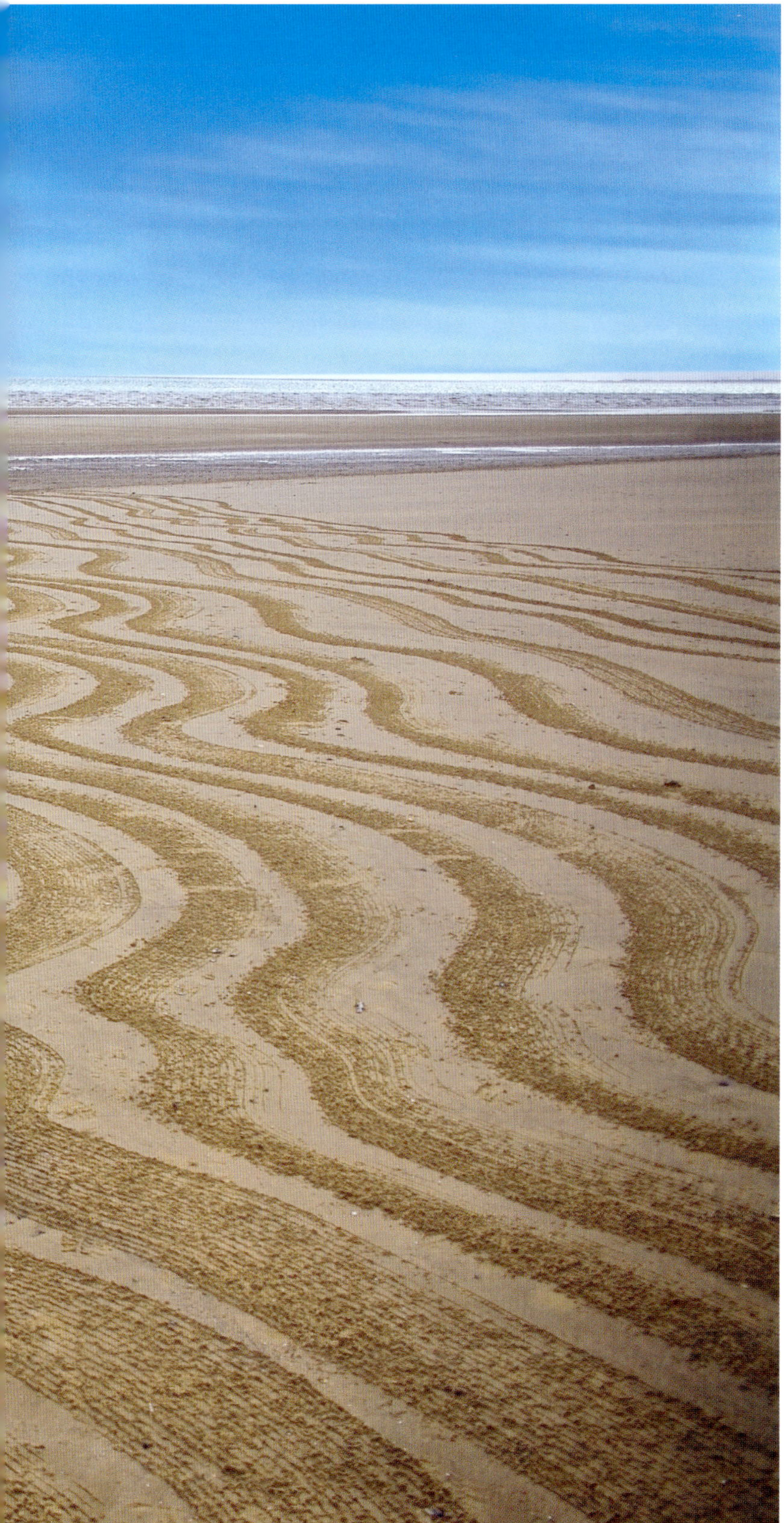

Water, the ocean, plays a huge role in the pull of the coast. I've yet to meet anyone who doesn't feel uplifted by water, and I'm no different. A first glimpse of the ocean, and a weight immediately lifts off my shoulders. I've always credited the ocean with my enhanced attention span when working on beaches, where I can happily stay focused on a repetitive task for the six hours between tides. In woodlands, however, my focus starts to wander after three hours maximum. I know when this time is approaching when I start talking to the work. The ocean is wonderfully grounding, the tide ever regular: in and out, in and out, not caring for my plans and endeavors; working in knowledge that sure as ever the tide creeps closer, I respect its repetitive constant and see the connection to the repetitions in my work. The power of nature ever reminds me of how small an impact I have on it.

But there is something more intricate at play here. Developing a deep-level connection to a place, through regular, almost daily contact, builds intimate relationships with specific views, vistas, and spots within a landscape. Often for me, this can be a small patch of land, the base of a tree, or the negative space between two branches; it begins simply as recognizing a particular composition or frame in which a work will sit. But with every week and seasonal variance, that same spot or composition will change and offer up new creative opportunities. I have several areas in Anston Stones Wood that I revisit and repeatedly create work in, developing series of work that highlight seasonal change. Additionally, I can notice a place of interest that I know, one day, the right time will come to create there. I can walk past it hundreds of times, look but not stop, until one day all the elements are right and I will look, stop, take in what is different this time, and, more often than not, make the work that that place had been waiting for.

Left: *Sand drawing on Bridlington Beach. Some of the outer lines were drawn by a family who joined me to help.*

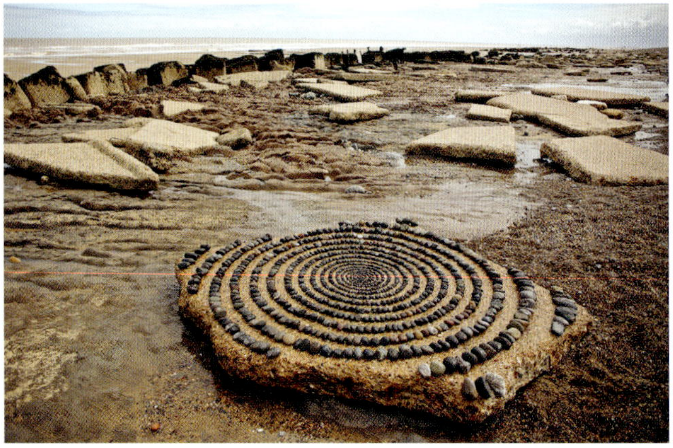

Above: This piece was created at Spurn Point, a narrow sand tidal island located off the tip of the coast of the East Riding of Yorkshire. It is one of the most atmospheric places I know.

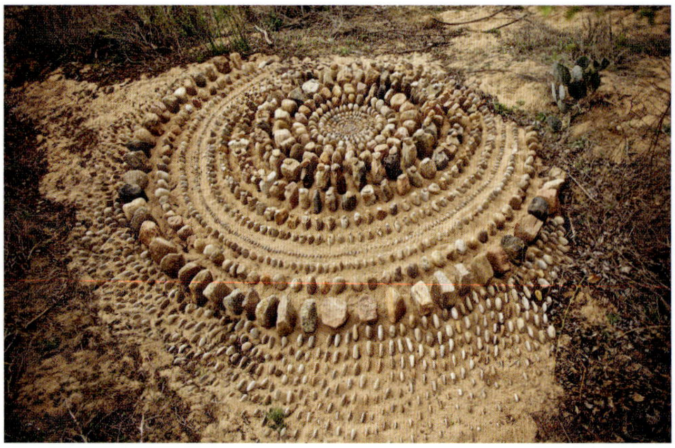

Above: My first work in Texas, at the Llano Earth Art Fest; I worked on it over three days.

A lovely example of how much a small piece of land can affect me was my second time in Llano, Texas, for LEAF or the Llano Earth Art Festival (more about this wonderful event on page 54). My first year had been all about meeting other artists, whom I knew online but had never met. But my second year, 2019, was all about the landscape. Several months before, heavy rain had caused severe flooding across Texas, and the river rose by several meters, decimating the trees and shrubbery from the riverbed. Walking around the festival site, which was so different from my first year, I came across a fallen willow, horizontal to the sandy riverbed. At first, it appeared arid and dry, no signs of life, but right there beginning to protrude out of the water-washed gray bark were these tiny green buds. The more I looked, the more evidence I saw that this and much of the seemingly dead trees around me were not dead at all, just altered, and that a new landscape would grow again, and again after the next flood, and so on. I repeatedly returned to that tree for the whole festival, each day making a new piece of work around it. Each work linked together to form my little celebration of that tree and the new chapter in its turbulent life. In 2020, my third LEAF, the first thing I did on-site was to visit my friend, almost unrecognizable now amid all the new-growing shrubland. But it was there, thriving now, as were the remnants of my gift to my friend the willow.

My creative year is connected to the following seasonal highlights, moments I await with anticipation and can feel getting closer.

Spring
Bluebells and wild garlic
Cherry blossom falling
If I'm lucky (it's happened only once), beech blossom on a path
Maples and sycamore discard young keys
In my garden the catkins fall from the goat willow

Summer
Rhododendron flower and fall
Trees will drop their first leaves
On the coast, beach workshops
A summer of engagement
Foxy covered in seeds and buds

Fall
The trees turn
Palette changes
Immersed in color
The goat willow transforms my garden again
Texture
Season of schools

Winter
Beauty in decay
Work changes to adapt
I feel the pull of the ocean
A bleak winter's beach
Alone with the ocean
Fingers numb with dirt under nails

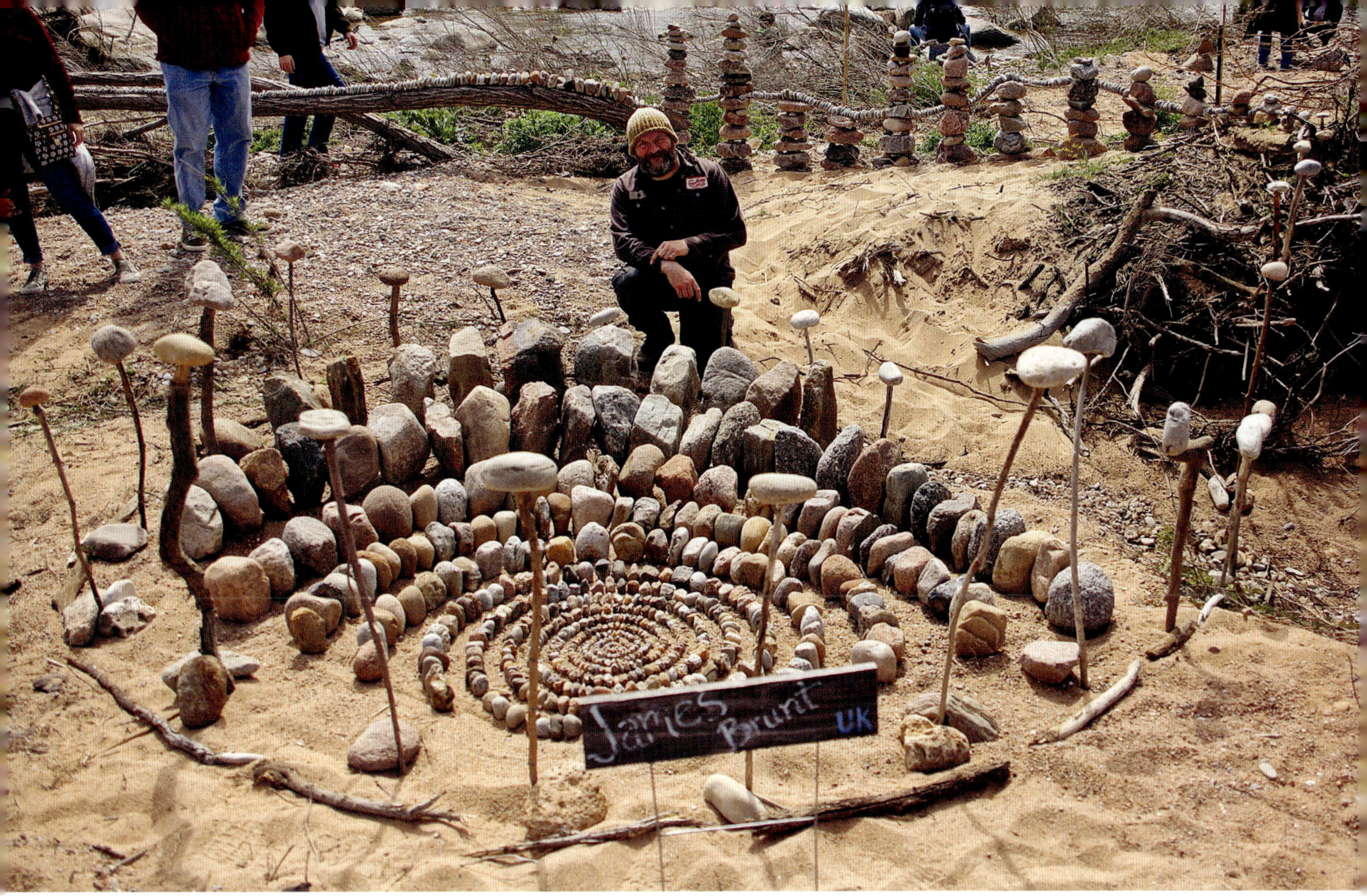

Above: *Me at the Llano Earth Art Fest in 2019 after completing my "gift to the tree".*

Below: *After the floods. "My" tree in Llano. The following year it was hidden with new growth and life.*

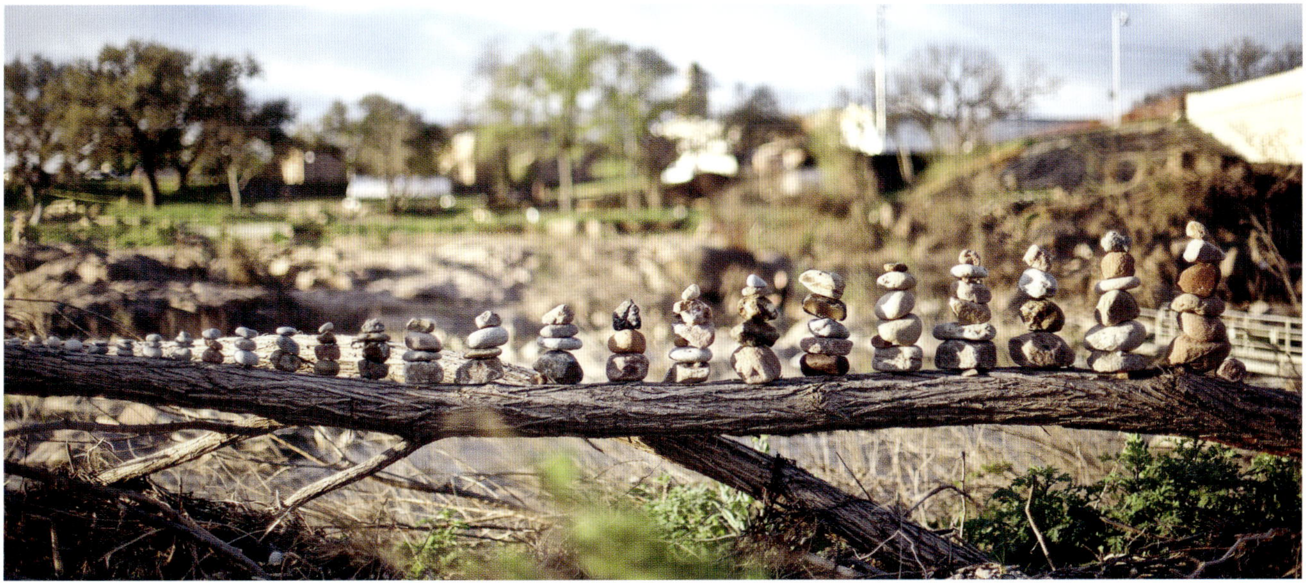

The Importance of Play

For anyone who has attended any of my schools or community sessions, you will probably have heard me introduce myself as a "professional child." Now, before we go any further, I want to say, this is not my own term; I borrowed/stole/embraced it after hearing it for the first time when I watched a short film by a friend and fellow artist, Michael Grab (check him out; you will not be disappointed). It just seems to sum up perfectly how I feel about my work. I get up in the morning, head out to make work, and feel like I'm off out to play!

When I tell children (and their teachers) the "professional child" line, it always gets a little laugh. I then tell them I'm deadly serious and that if they take one thing away from spending the day with me, it's to never stop playing, no matter how old you are. It's so important! Life throws so much at us, and we've created a stressful existence for ourselves, it's so easy to forget or, worse, grow out of playing. Now your play may be totally different from mine; we don't all like the same things—believe me, enough people tell me online that they don't like what I do. But find what makes you happy, find your play, and do it whenever you can; even better, try to make a career out of it.

Having worked across the whole education system, from preschool- to college-age children and young people, what seems to be glaringly obvious is that as we grow older, the less confident, the less gregarious, the less open to try and fail we become. It's so disheartening to work with young adults on an art-and-design course who hardly speak to you, who have a fear of trying something new, and who don't seem to have the same passion I had (or hope I had) when I was their age.

***Right:** Workshop cat. Young artist unknown, but a young artist in the making with a big future.*

***Below:** All hands-on deck at St Ann's School in Knowsley. Creating work as a group is so very rewarding for me, and, I hope, the children.*

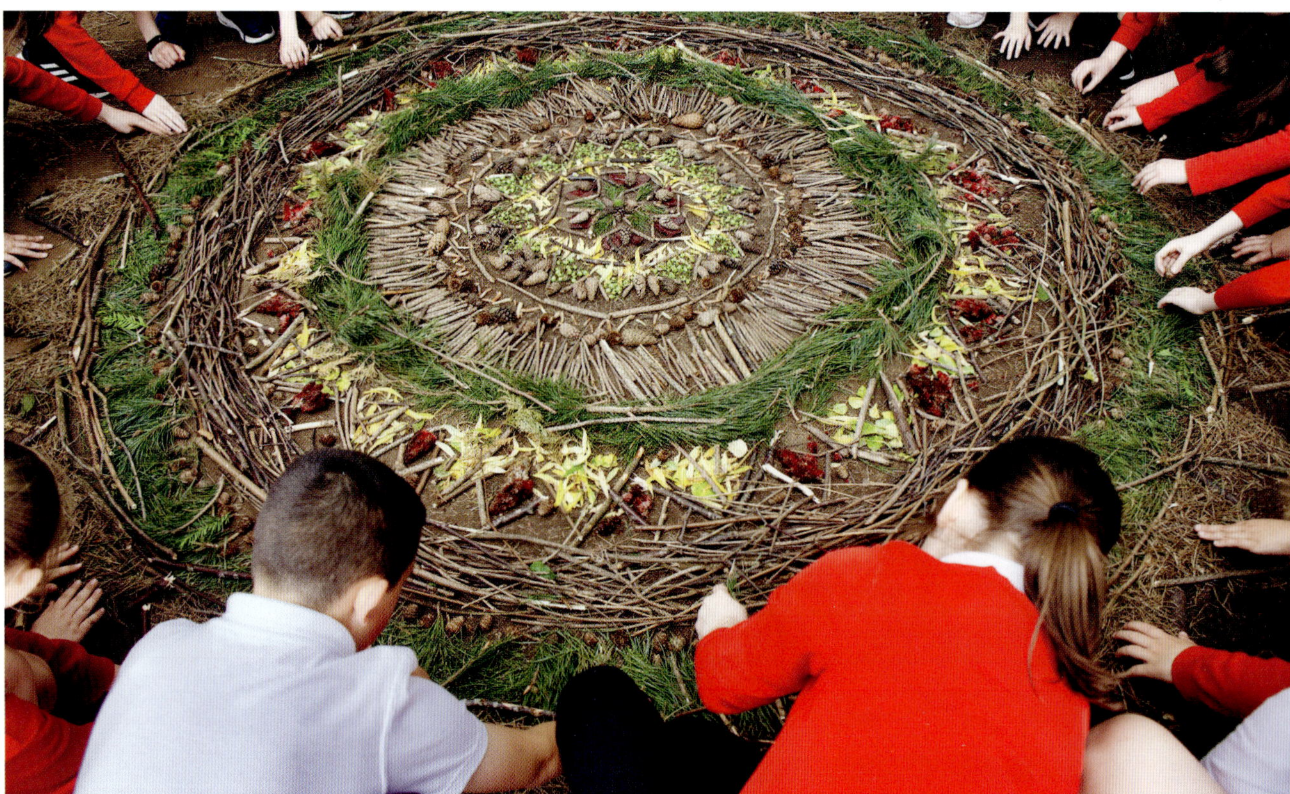

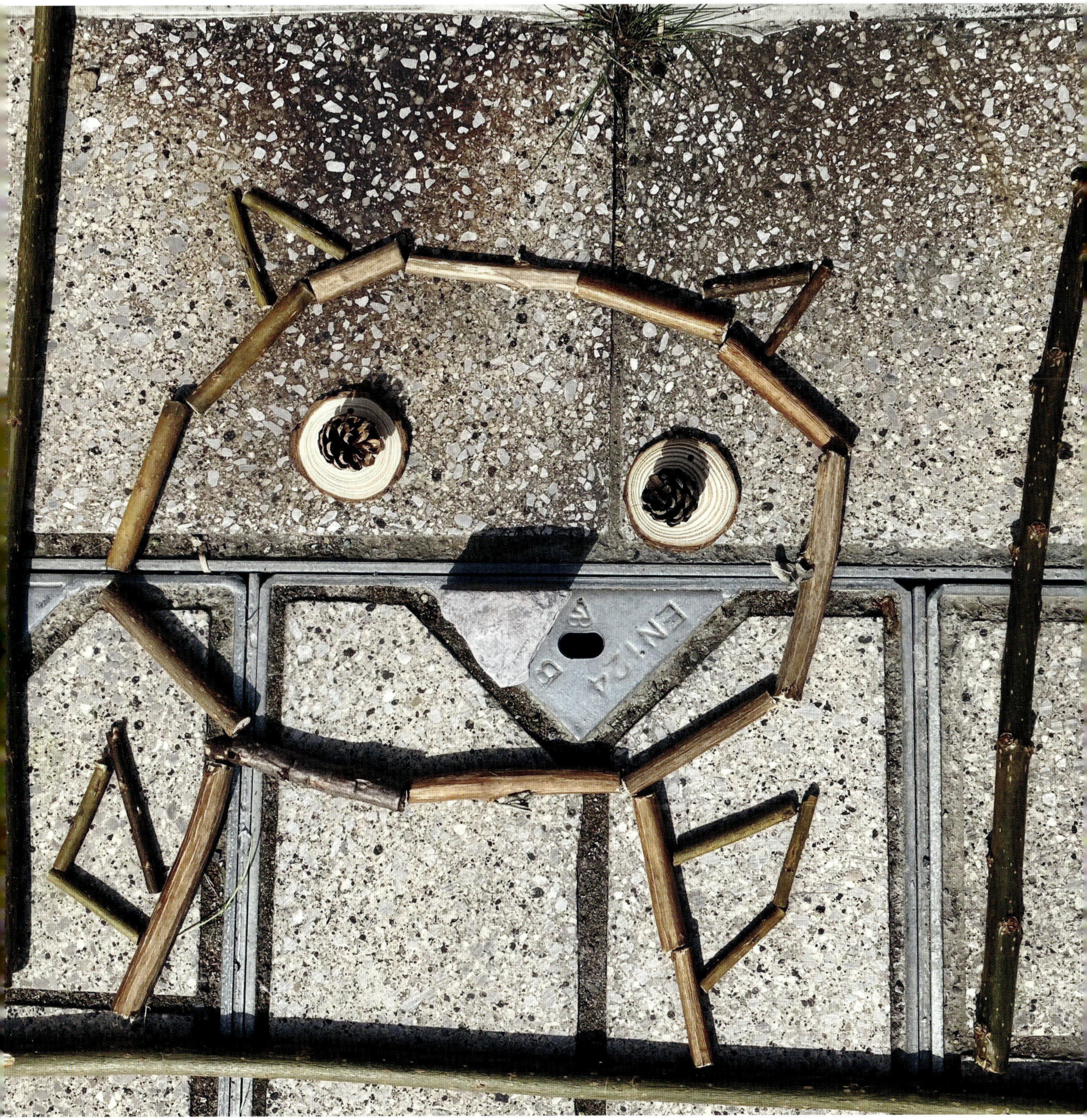

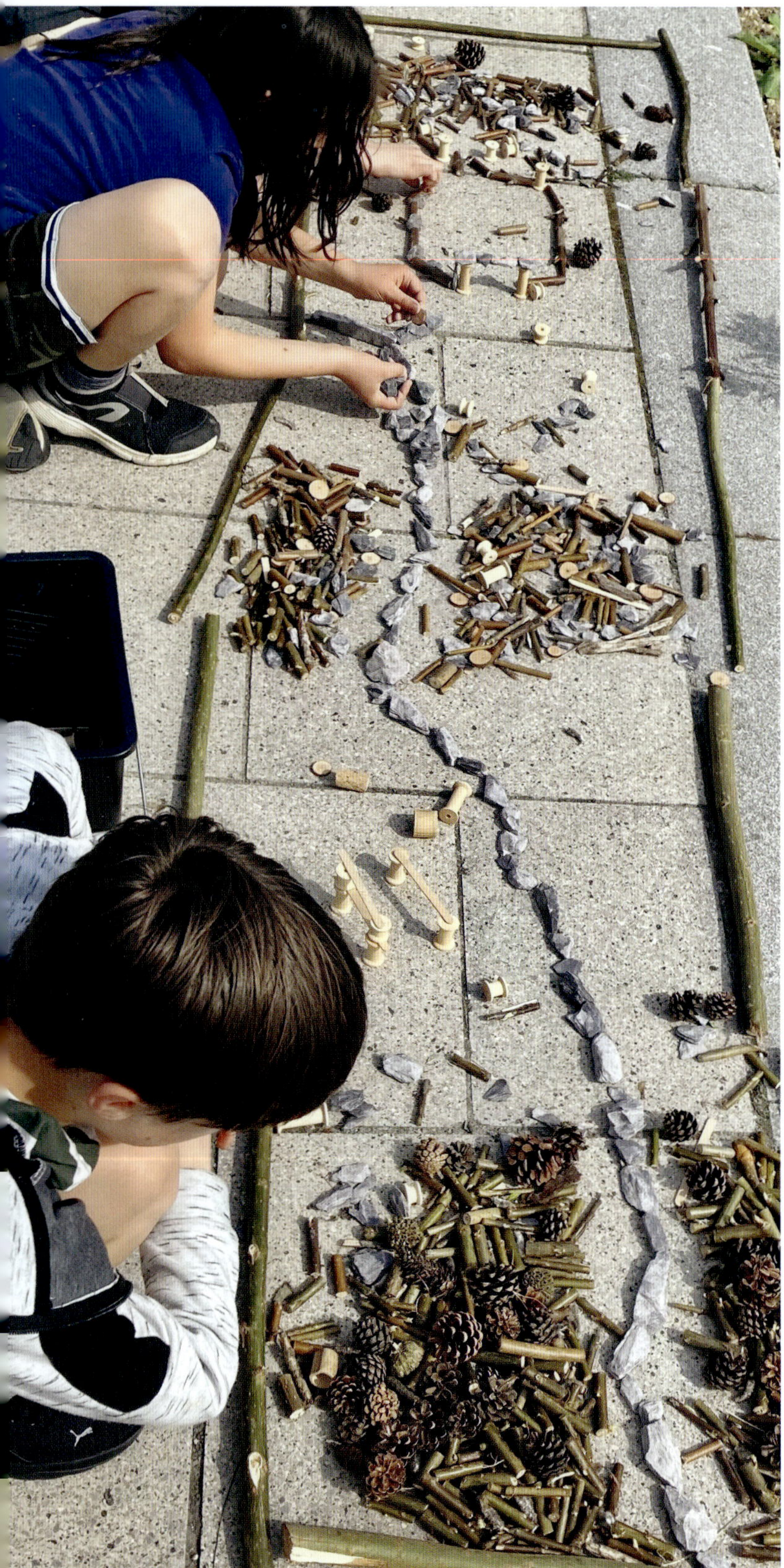

Switch that to an early-years-education setting; their environments are full of stuff, but not expensive stuff. Old pots, pans, planks of wood, crates, you name it—children will play, transform, and reappropriate objects to meet their imaginative needs. If we know that encouraging learning through play is so important at this age, why do we think it becomes less important as we grow older? A simple example of this is a primary (elementary) school, which starts with nursery- and reception-age children at age four to five and has classes up to year 6, so ten-to-eleven-year-olds. The outdoor space of the four-to-five-year-olds will be just as I've described. Loads of stuff to move, collect, stack, build, transform. By the time they leave school at ten to eleven years old, the outdoor play space is fairly sparse; yes, there may be some fixed play equipment, to climb on and such, but nothing to move, reappropriate, or encourage imaginative play.

It's no surprise to me, then, when we jump forward a few more years and our budding artists are now in college, that they struggle to express themselves. It seems to me that we are slowly teaching our children to play less, and when we give them the opportunity to play more, they are too self-conscious to do so.

I've rambled. Sorry; I do it because I truly believe we are getting it wrong. But this is in no way a dig at teachers, whom I have so much respect for. I could not do their job; they are the real heroes. But the system is set up to achieve certain outcomes, and happy, well-rounded, confident, inquisitive, playful adults is not high on the priority list.

With that little rant over, it seems the perfect time for you to play again.

Left: *The importance of loose-parts play, allowing children, no matter how old, to further their development.*

Right: *Who lives here? Young artist unknown. I love the variety of approaches children bring to creating, when invited to make something.*

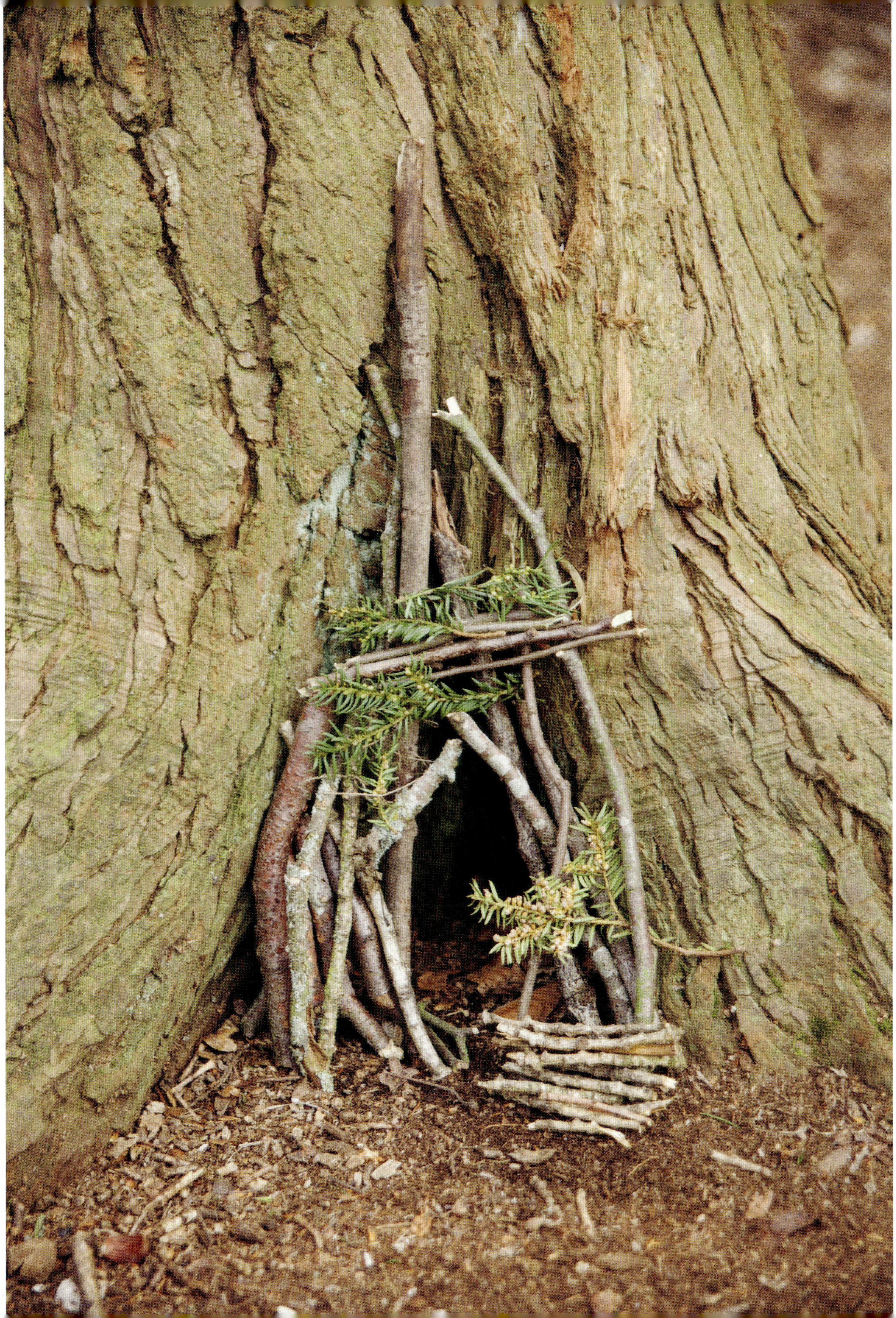

Invitation to Play 3 *(Natural Frames)*

This little prompt is all about considering how your natural intervention works within its own environment. I personally really enjoy works that have this kind of interaction with location and relationship with space, so much more than simply clearing space in which to create a design. It can also provide you with an achievable-sized space to work in, and allows you to see an achievable end point.

- Step 1—enjoy your walk and surroundings (again).
- Step 2—as you walk around, look for small spaces created within the environment that make natural areas (frames) to work in; these don't need to be large or uniform in shape (see examples). Tree roots often work a treat.
- Step 3—tidy up the space and remove loose materials from the surface of your chosen space (you don't need to dig stuff out or pull out living plants; just work around them).
- Step 4—look around you; what are the loose materials around that area that you can use to create?
- Step 5—what are you going to make? This is all down to you, but personally I like to keep things simple, begin a process, and continue until the frame is filled.
- Step 6—sit back and enjoy your creation, chat to people who may wander by, and listen to the birds.

Note: The images that accompany this invitation to play do not follow the steps above. They are here to serve as inspiration and to show the creation of one of my works in stages.

I often "get to know" these frames and return to them again and again. Each time the materials are slightly different, and each work contributes to building up a picture of that space over the seasons.

The examples on the following pages are from an oak tree near me in Anston Stones Wood. All the materials are from that tree, at different points in the year.

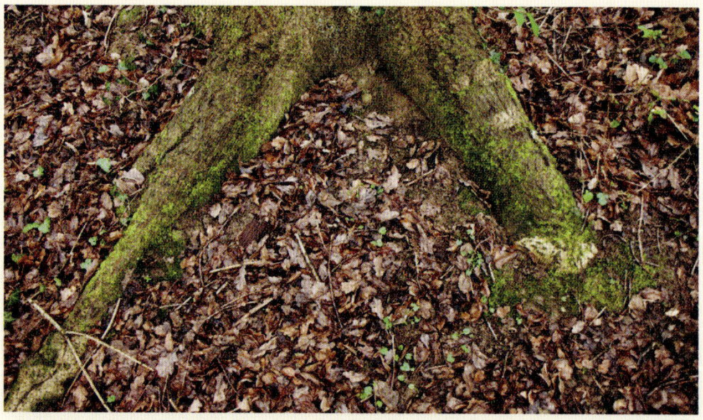

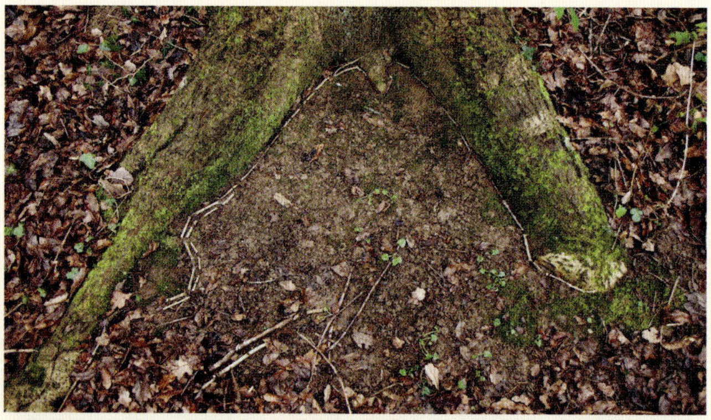

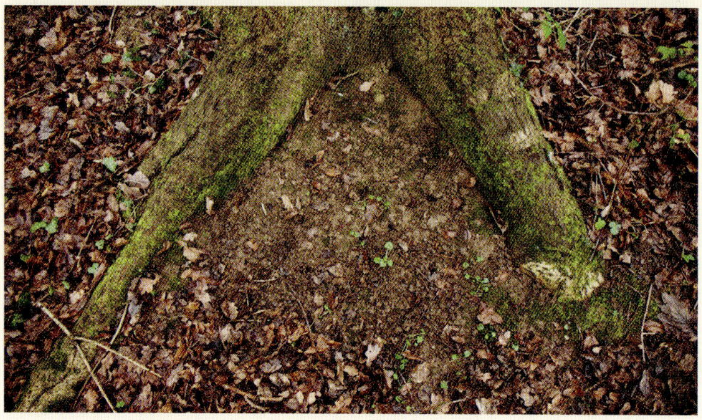

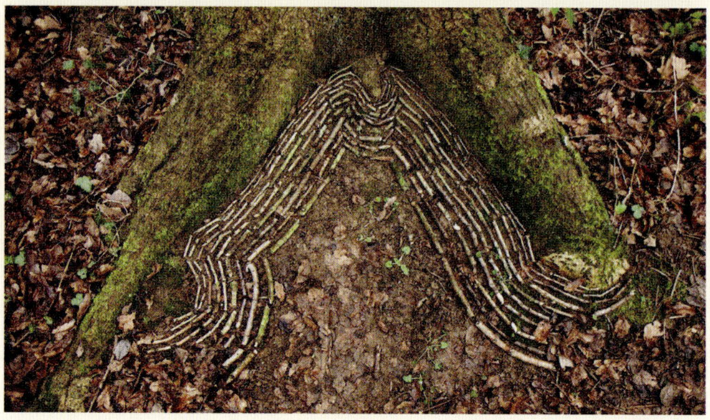

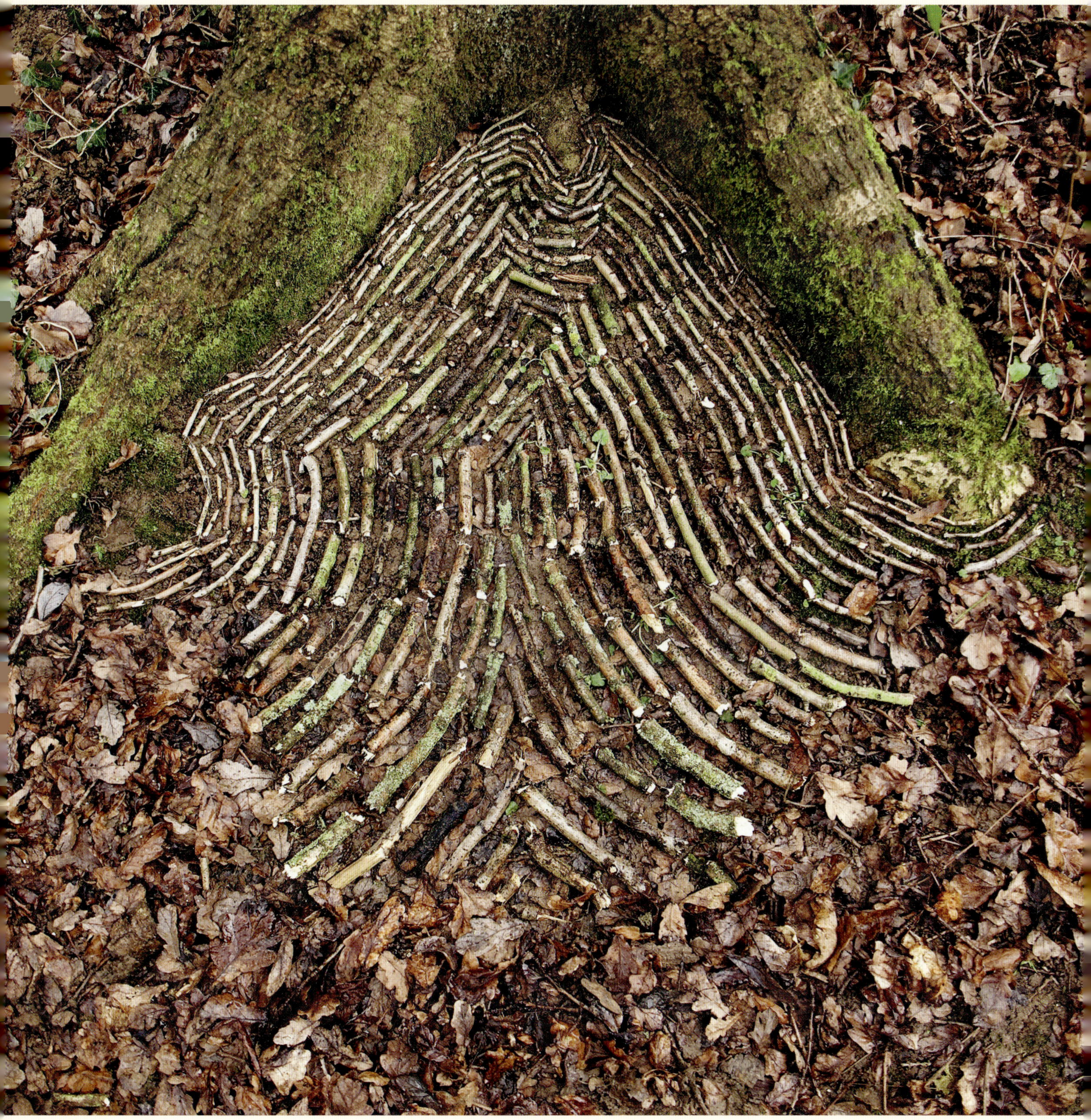

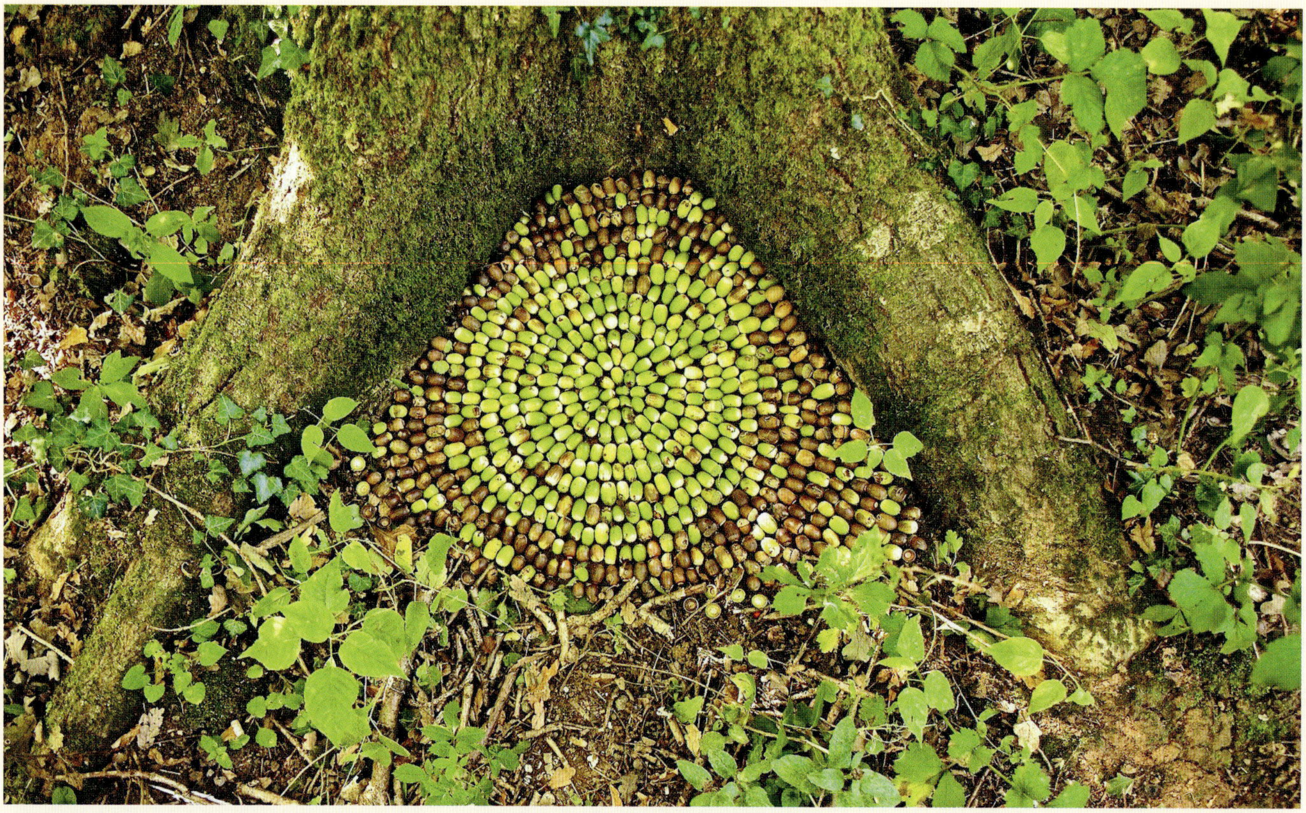

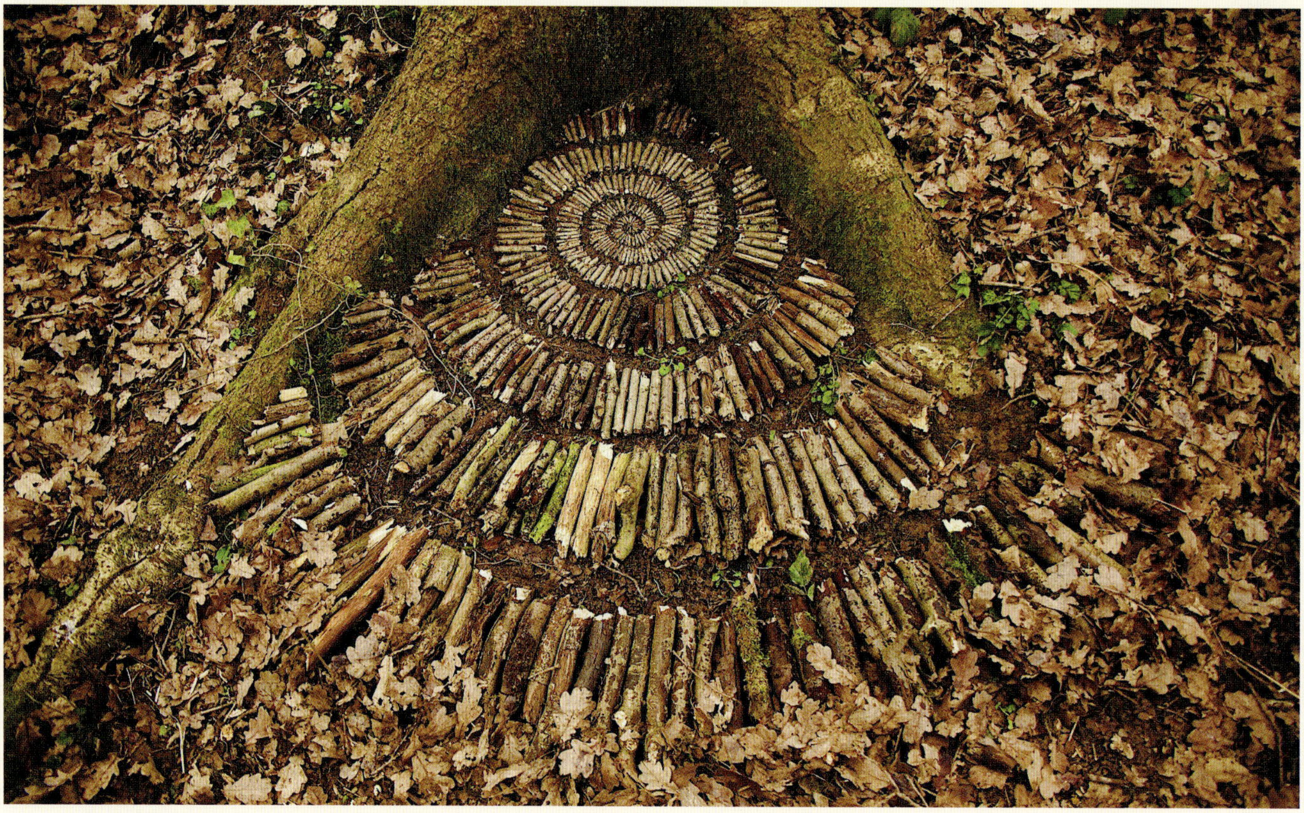

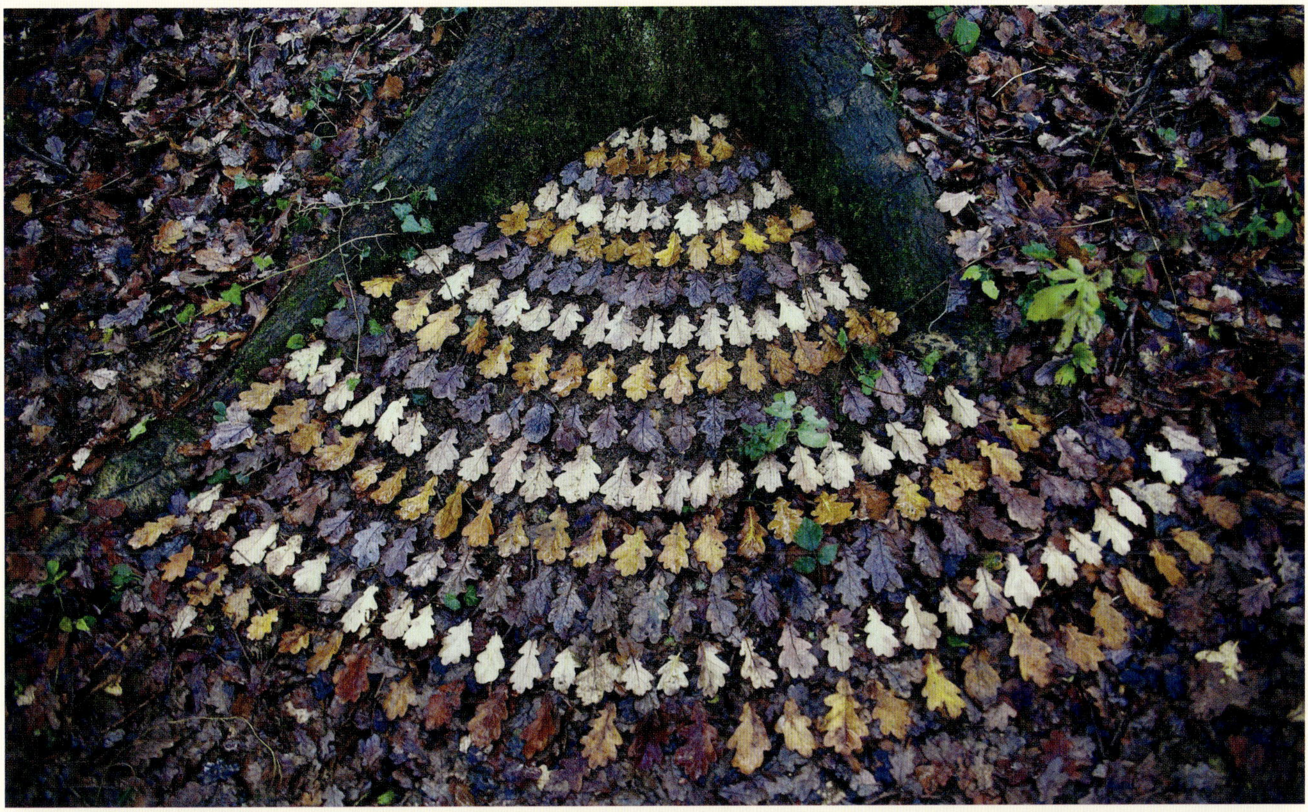

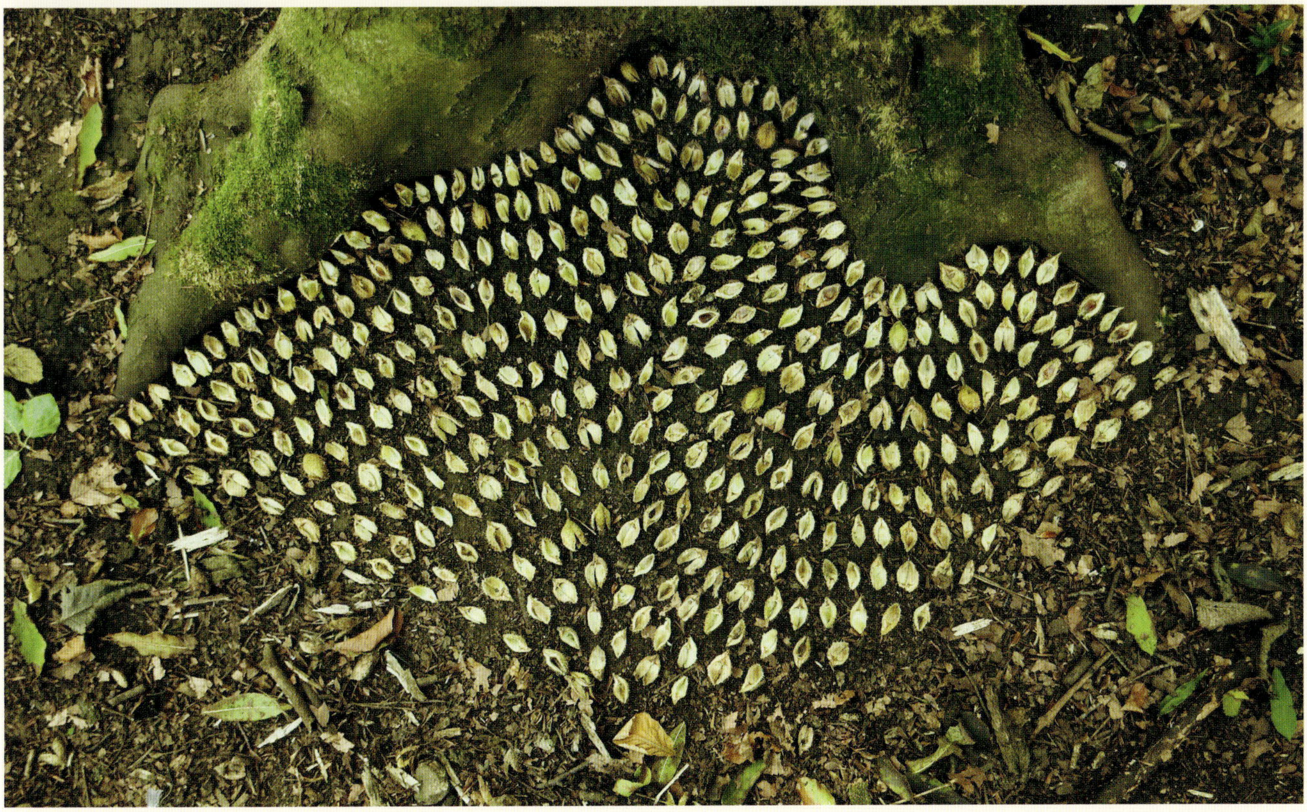

Engagement—Sharing and Learning

Early on in my creative journey (and still today, to be honest), financial stability came through delivering workshops and natural-art activities for schools, festivals, and events. This has never been a means to an end. I love it! I get so much from sharing and working with other people, particularly children, who constantly surprise me with their approach and unique thinking. That said, I work with people of all ages, in such a wide variety of settings it makes for an interesting and rewarding existence. As I sit just thinking ahead to the coming year, I will be working in schools all around the country, in disused buildings bringing to life lost industry and heritage, in stunning woodlands, on beaches, along a sandy riverbed in Texas, developing new audiences for reclaimed green spaces in urban areas—the list goes on. Wherever I work, the idea of sharing what I do is always with me; whether a planned workshop or a chance meeting while I'm out working, I will always share an experience with others.

I'm not naturally the most social of creatures. I shrink into myself among socialites, am a quiet introvert around extroverts, and struggle to be part of conversations. I'm definitely not the life and soul of the party, but I do come alive when working with others. I guess it comes from doing the thing you love and believe in. And to share that with people is a pleasure.

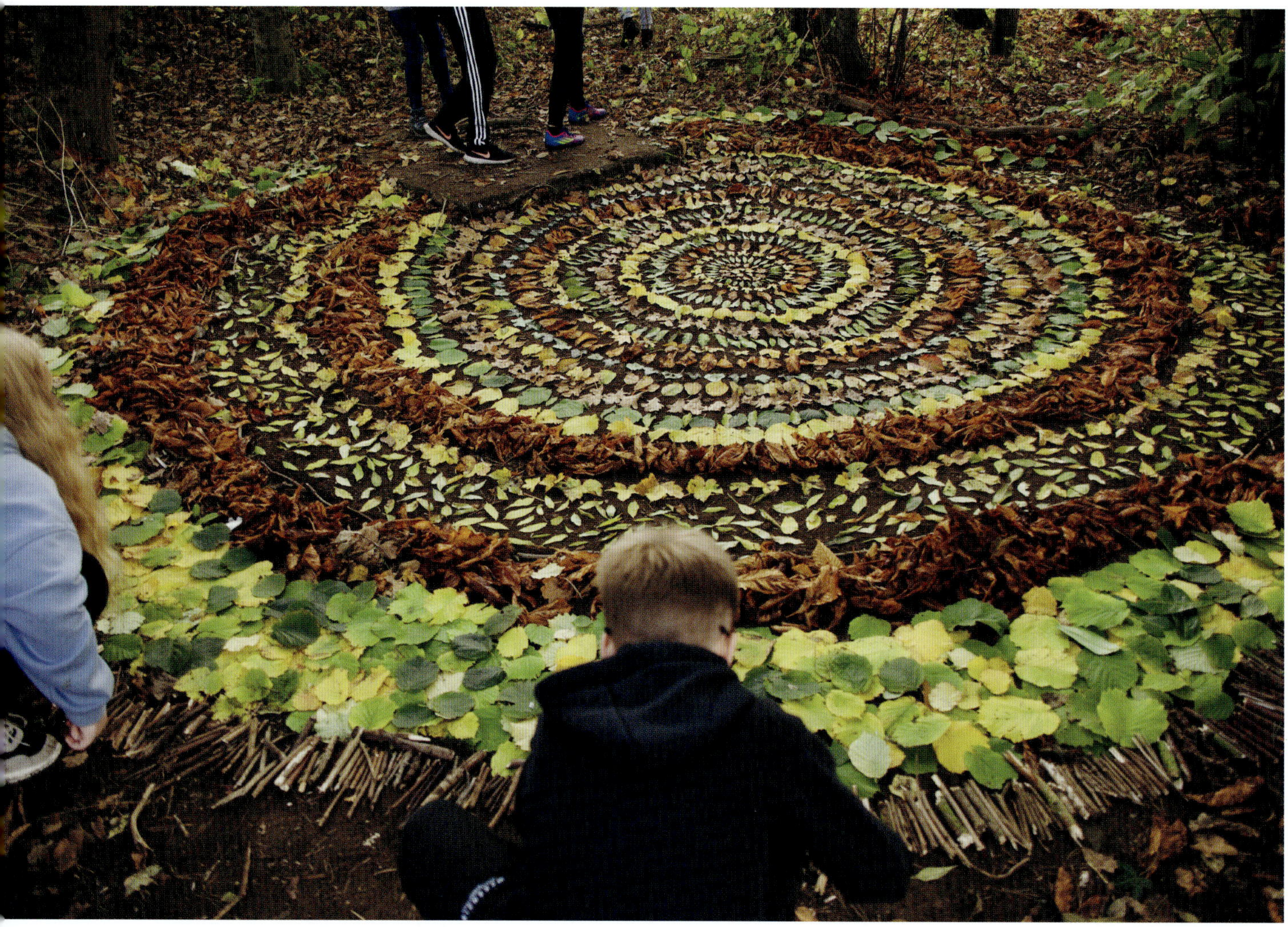

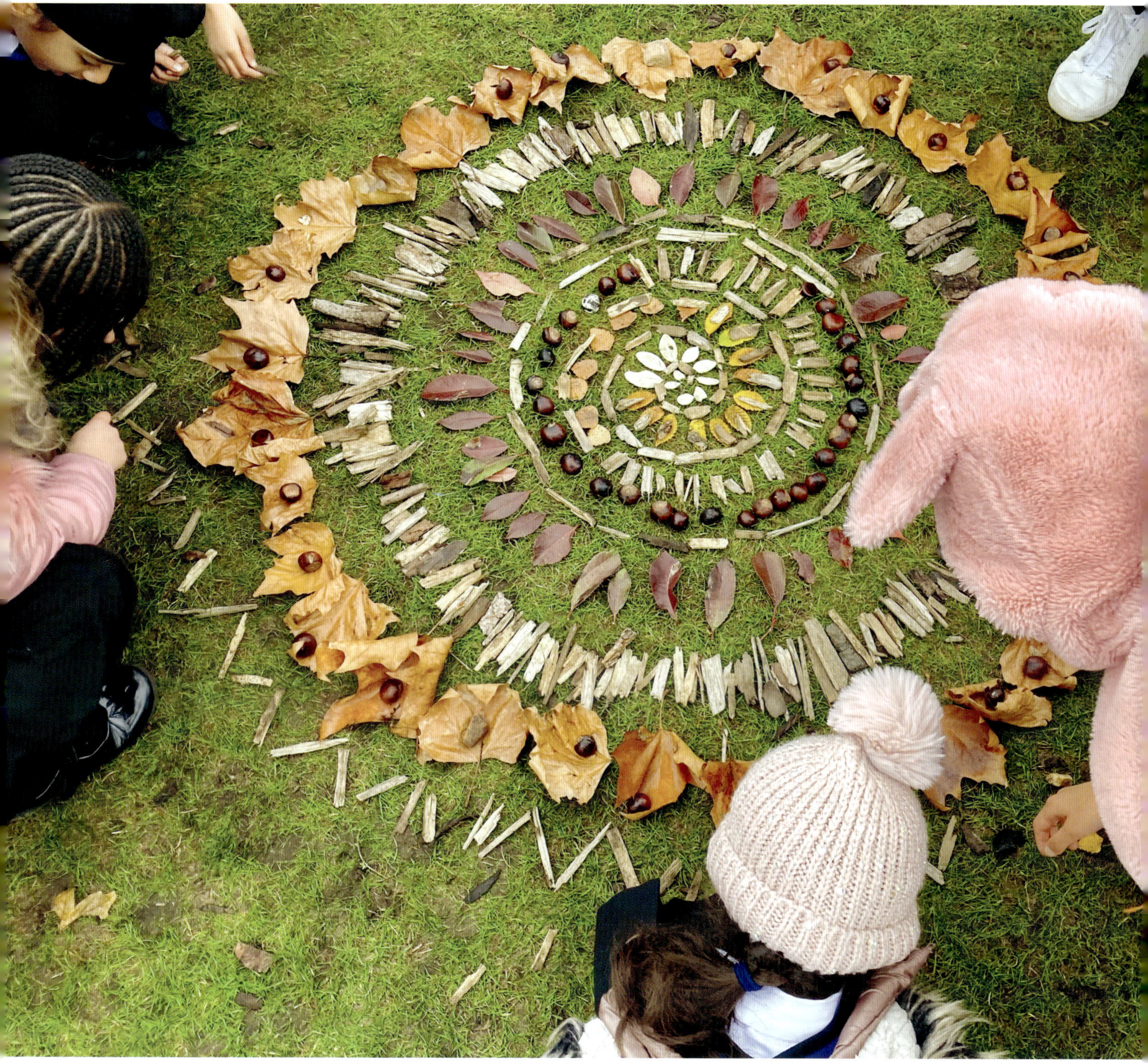

Left: *Many hands make light work. Full-school collaborations bring all the children together in one large-scale work and make something to show their grown-ups at the end of the day.*

Above: *Fun whatever the weather. Creating in adverse weather conditions builds resilience and is a key part of a child's development.*

Schools have been a major source of inspiration and financial security for several years now. During this time, I've developed and adapted what I believe to be an amazing experience for the children and indeed myself. Basically, using what we can find on the school grounds, we make a piece of work together, the whole school and I; class by class they join me and we work on a growing artwork that by the end of the day will have involved all the children. It's evolved over many years of delivering and fine-tuning and recognizing the elements that are important to the children's experience. These are the things that I think are crucial.

1. Although I've been booked to share my artistic practice, the most important element of my time in the school is that the children have fun.
2. I like to quickly establish equality; that I'm not an artist come to teach them, more that from the moment we start working we are all artists, working collectively to create a piece of work.
3. When working individually or in small groups, the least important part of that experience is the outcome. No matter how simple a child's work is, it's crucial to reinforce positive experience. I've seen teachers and teaching assistants look uncomfortable or even intervene when a child shows me and explains to me what they have created, often with a face full of joy and pride. It breaks my heart. In an education system full of right and wrongs, art is surely the subject where a child's expression cannot be wrong.

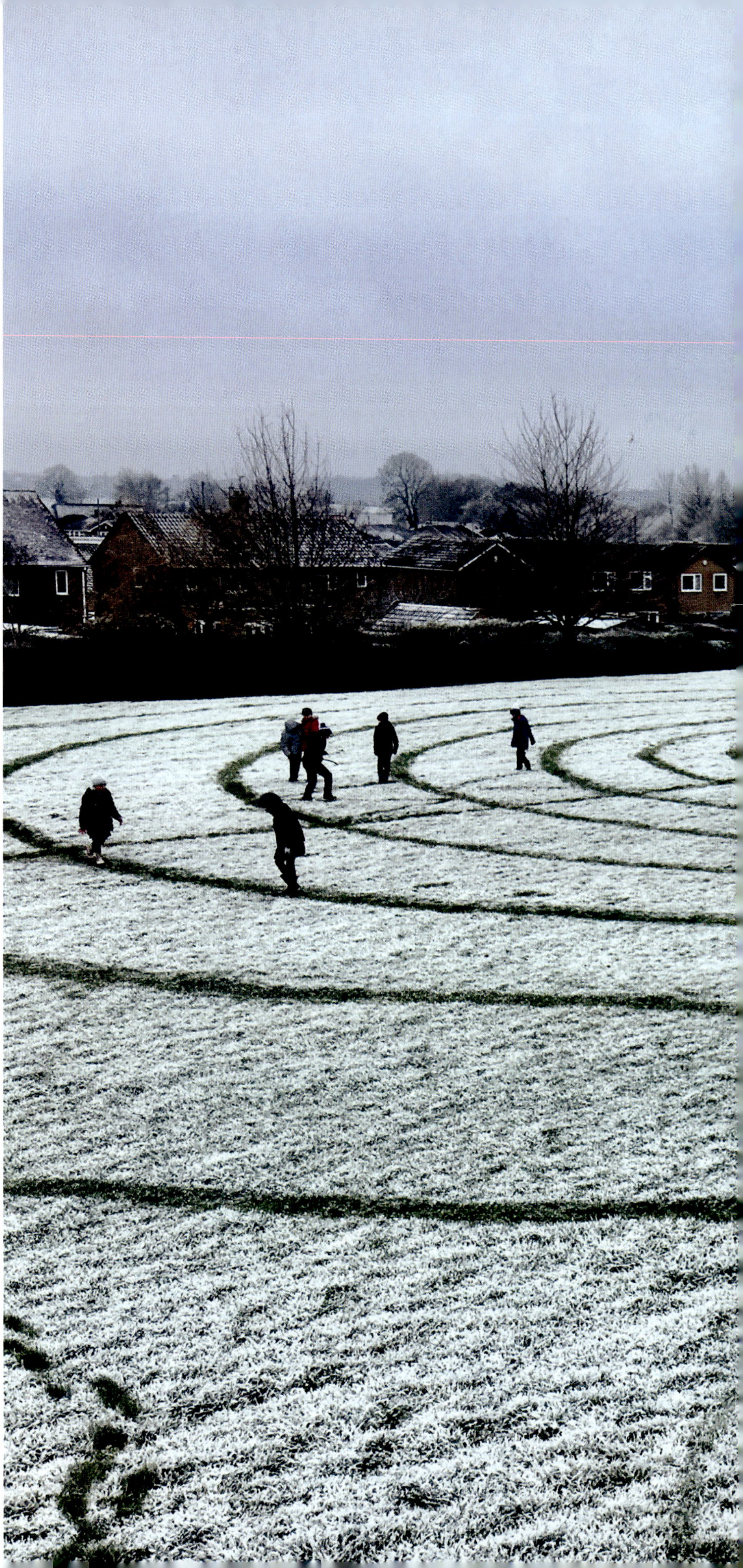

Right: *Walked frost drawing at Todwick Primary School. A very memorable day; the frosty field was an opportunity too good to be missed.*

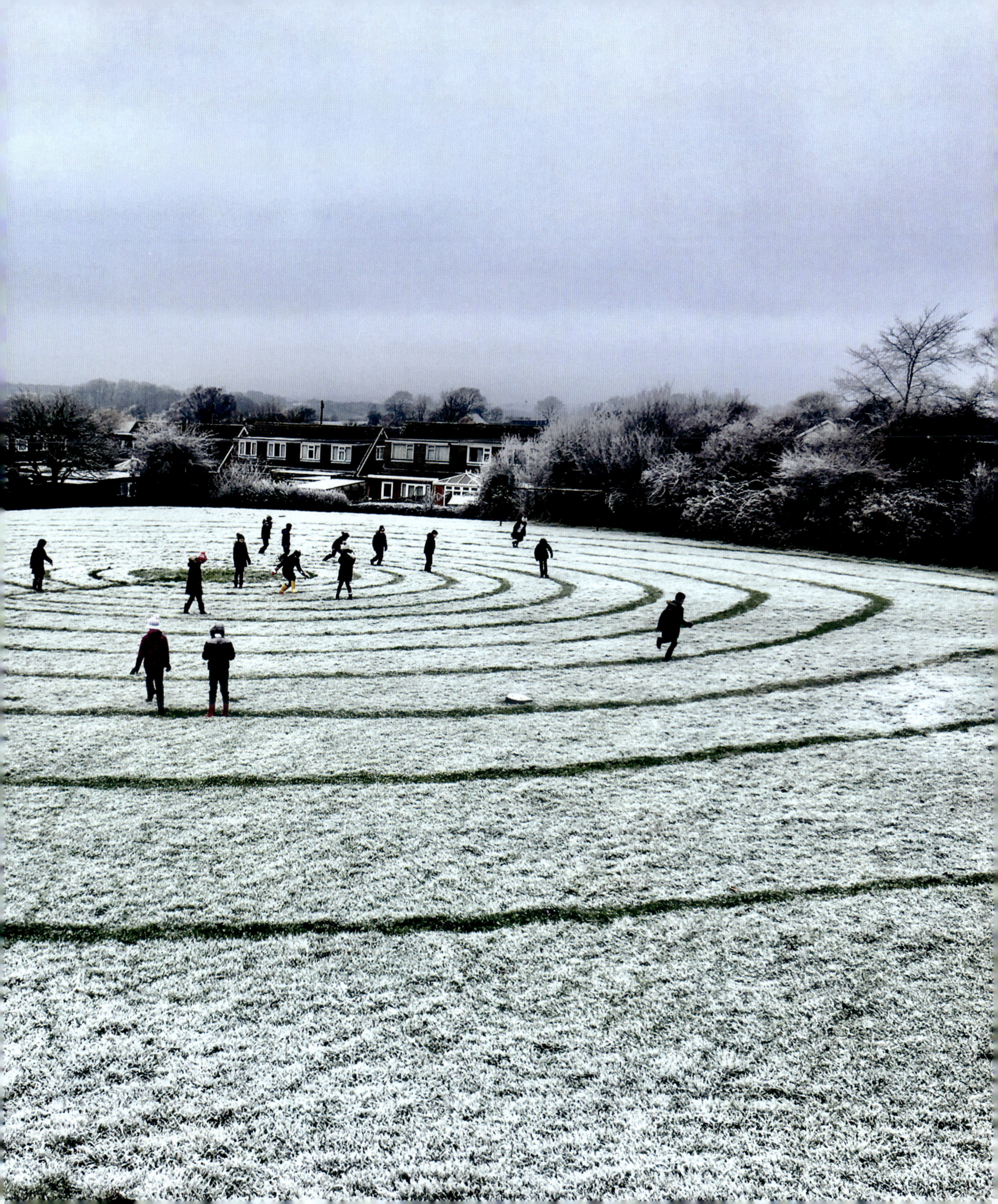

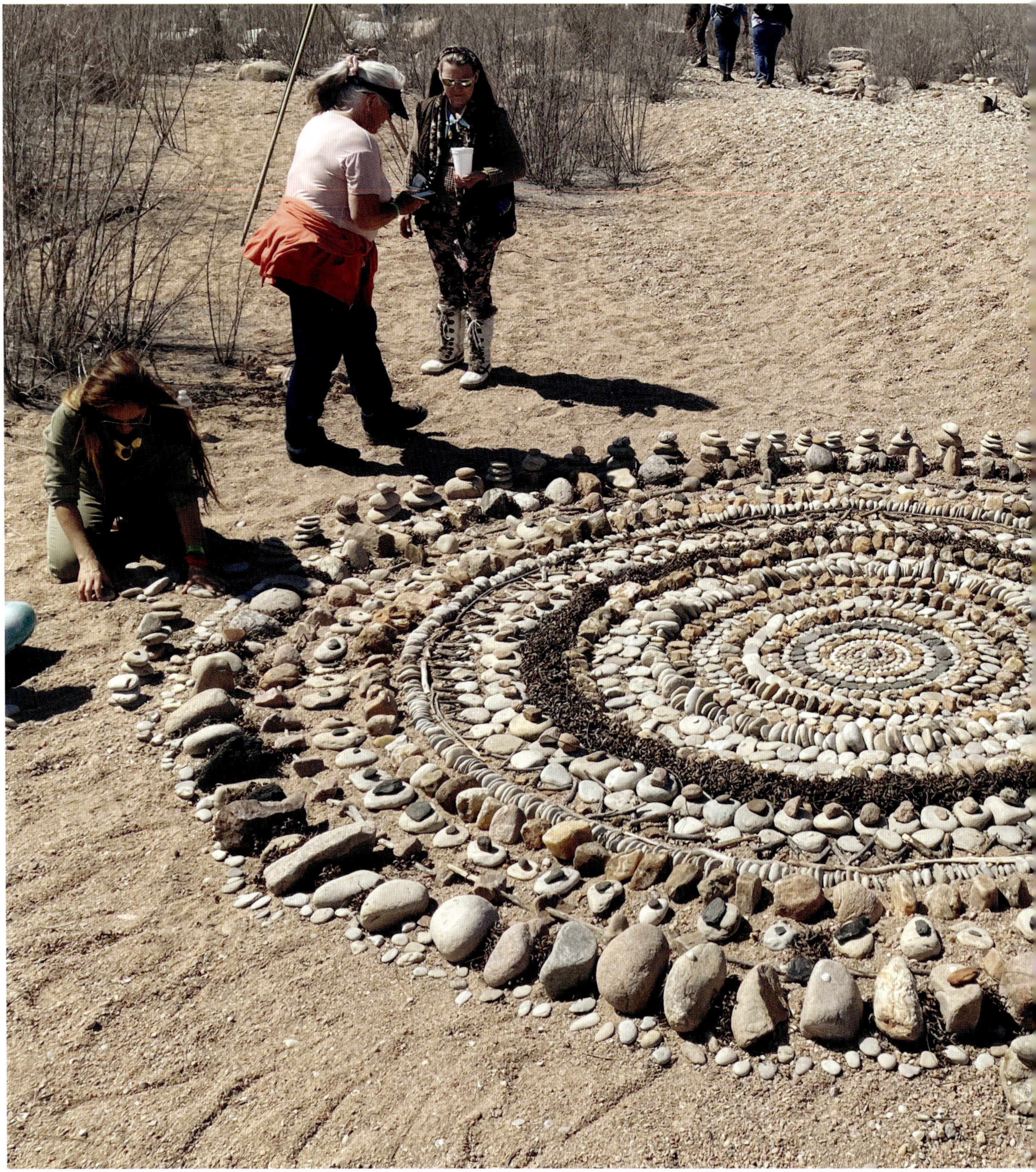

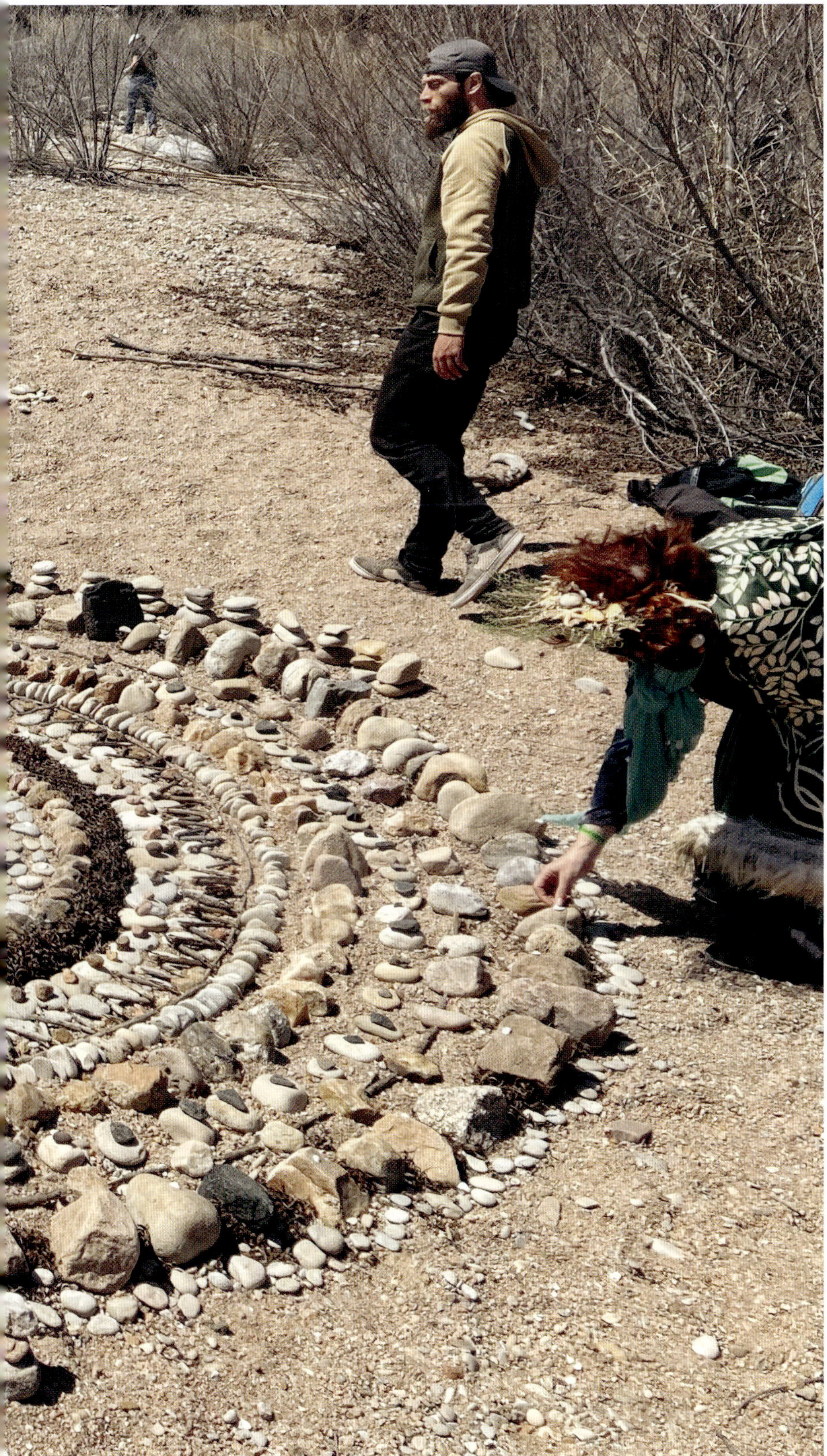

> “It always amazes me how many times I hear a child say, “Best school day ever,” after a day with me. I don’t say this with any kind of gloating, but with a sense of deep satisfaction that my work has such an impact.”

Whatever your passion is, or whatever you excel at, do yourself a favor and share it with someone else—teach. There is no greater thing than to spread joy through the sharing of your skills and experience. And no easier time to pass on and share your knowledge with others.

I always ask the children if anyone wants to be an artist when they grow up. Hands will always go up. To those budding artists, I say, why wait? Be an artist now and don’t stop! My favorite children book is *The Dot* by Peter H. Reynolds. It’s a beautiful story about a child who doesn’t think they are good at art. It should be staple reading for all schools, although I imagine there would be a lot of dot paintings in schools as a result, which is no bad thing.

***Left:** Llano community collaboration. Note artist Jon Foreman in the cap, getting involved.*

Collaborations and Connectivity through Global Accessibility

Land art, environmental art, or natural art, whichever is your preferred term, is going through a period of regeneration at the moment, and I'm a small part of that happening. Not through any relationship with current trends within the art scene, but more fueled by the digital, global connectivity that has become such a huge part of our lives. Social media has opened the floodgates for new audiences to a whole manner of stuff—good stuff, bad stuff, and the silly stuff. Within that landfill of available information are millions of like-minded people finding cause, purpose, and comfort in connecting with others who share the same passions as you, and finding people who like and appreciate what you do.

For me personally, social media began as a platform to share images of what I'd been doing, I don't think I ever saw it as a "work tool," but the more I posted, the more inquiries for paid work I got and the more I saw what other artists were doing, and soon the connection of like-minded artists, event organizers, and, importantly, new art audiences began to appear out of the craziness that is "online." Audiences who, without having to justify or back up their reasonings, can show appreciation for what they like (and don't like) by the simple click of a button.

This bond between people got stronger the deeper the connections became; "online" became "in person" with festivals and events—such as the Llano Earth Art Festival in Texas, various meet-ups between stone balancers in Italy, and the European Stone Stacking Championships in Dunbar—thankfully all taking advantage of the connections being made online.

It took a trip to Texas, to LEAF as it is known, to meet for the first time UK-based artists Richard Shilling and Julia Brooklyn (Lancashire), Jon Foreman (Pembrokeshire), Mark and Rebecca Ford (West Sussex), Tim Pugh (Flintshire), Brioney McClean (Wales), and James Craig Page (East Lothian), who also happens to organize the European Stone Stacking Championships in "Sunny Dunny." Not to mention many more artists from around the world, all making their own impact on this new Land Art family, all enabled by the connectivity of the internet.

***Below:** Regular collaborator Tim Haywood. Tim and I have worked together for a few years now, working on a series of Star Wars- and Marvel-based works.*

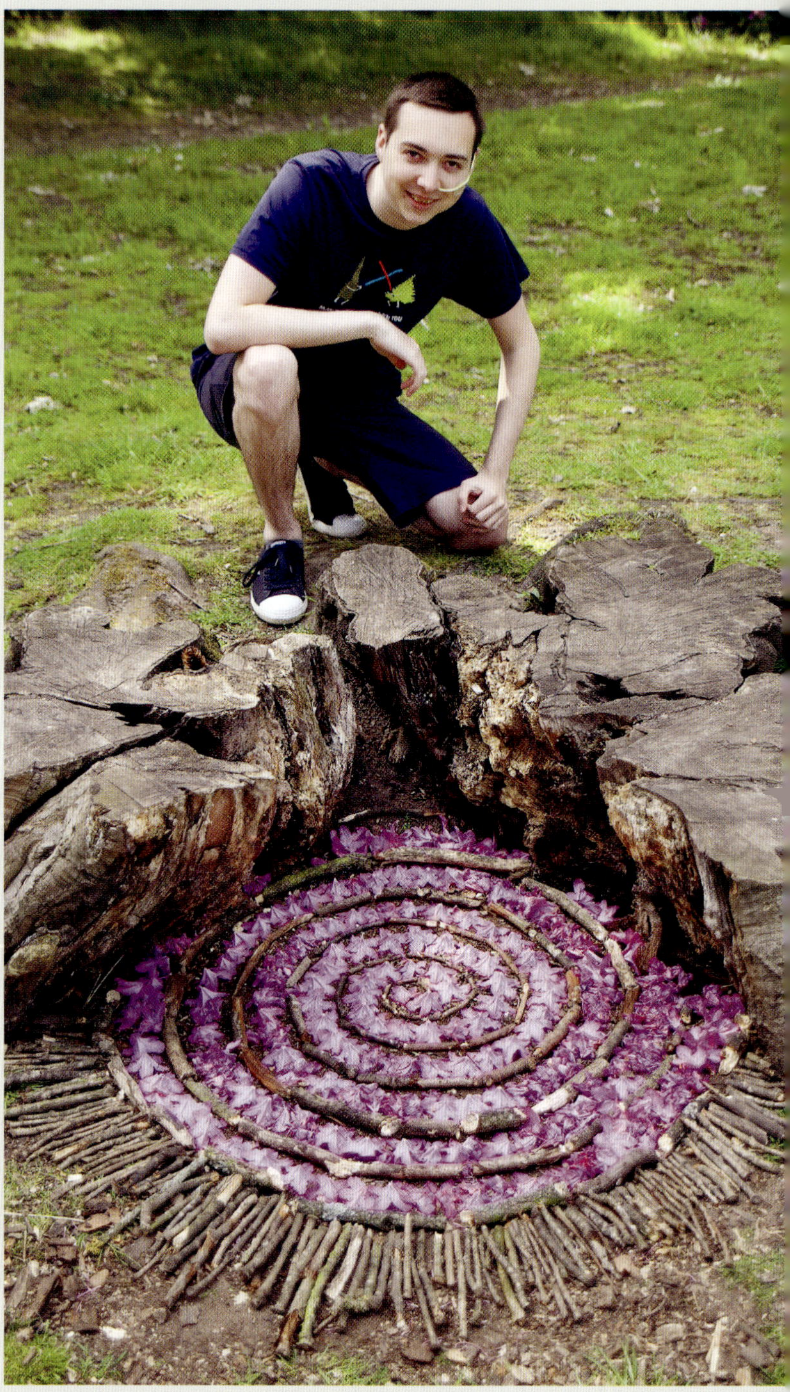

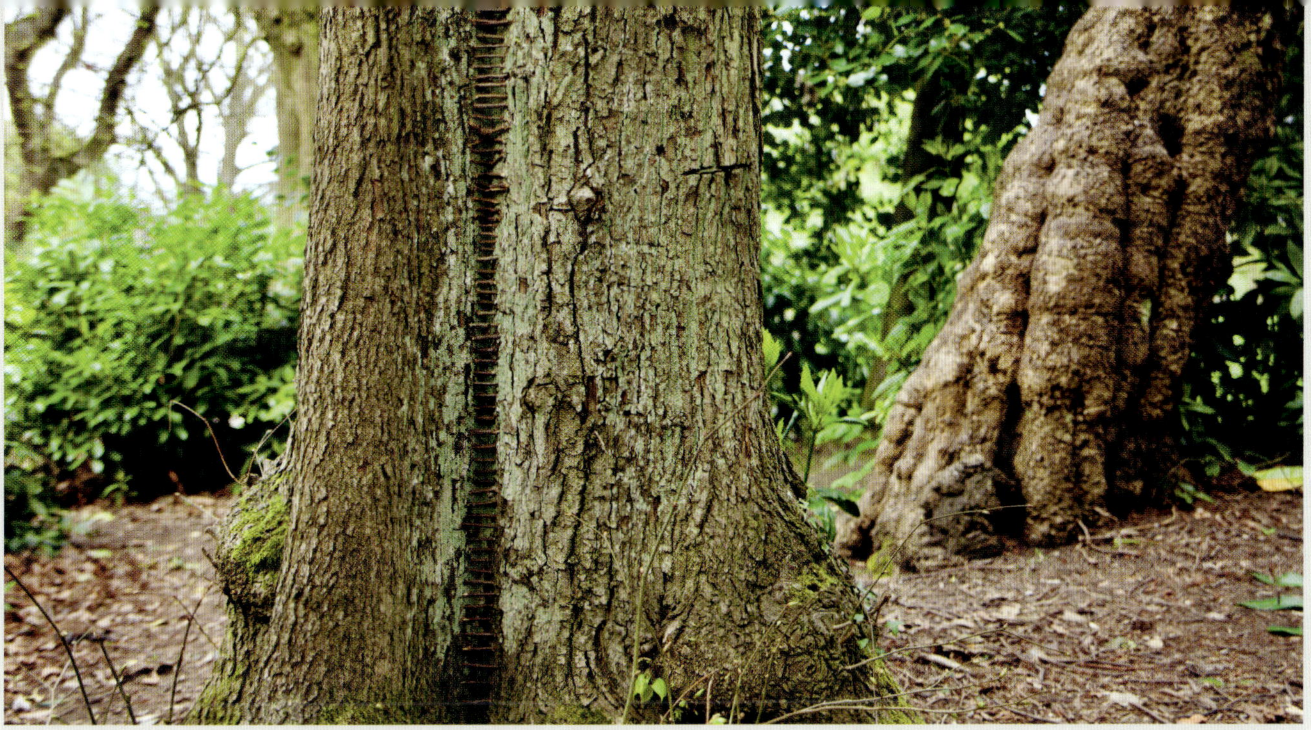

Above: *I made this during a workshop with a group of adults from a Barnsley-based charity, Creative Recovery. They are a lovely group who quickly find their own place to make work, and it's a pleasure to be able to work alongside them, nattering away, laughing, and joking in a lovely warm environment.*

Gatherings became celebrations of shared passions, friendships formed, and collaborations became a thing! Artists bringing their own approach to collaborative pieces between artists seemed a unique progression born out of the equally unique circumstances that had brought us all together. Sit around a fire with us with a few beers and listen to all the stories of how we first got to know each other, and you'll see there's a whole other book there waiting to be written.

The Llano Earth Art Festival must take a huge amount of credit in the ongoing story of the success of global land art connectivity. It was established in 2015 by the wonderful Binky la Faye, who wanted both to showcase her hometown and the Llano River that runs through it and also to put on an event to commemorate her father, who had passed away and who loved the river. That first year, Binky invited artists Michael Grab, Tim Anderson, and David Allen to attend the festival and showcase their work to visitors, with little knowledge of just what the festival would become. In my first year—2018, LEAF's fourth year—I joined around thirty invited artists from across the world; it was life changing. While there I collaborated for the first time, creating a large stone piece with Pembrokeshire-based artist Jon Foreman. It was an interesting and thoroughly enjoyable experience, and as I continued this trend, working with various other artists, what I've learned during these joint efforts is that while we are all working within the same genre, within each of us there are many small differences in how we think and approach work.

Following 2021's pandemic-hit online festival, which widened the LEAF family to an even-larger worldwide audience, I was delighted to attend the 2022 edition in person once again. I went with my partner, Caroline; youngest son, Sonny; friends Sam and Timm; and their daughter, Maddie—this family affair really sharing the magic of what LEAF is about. I met old and new friends and watched Sonny and Maddie getting stuck in, volunteering and helping out. The artists, organizers, volunteers, and visitors all combining to create something so positive for the planet. Sharing goodness and equality—one family, one planet, the citizens of Earth. As a friend of mine, Barry, says, "forever upgrading."

Since that first foray into collaborating, I've regularly created work with other artists, and I wanted to include some of these images and tell the story of how they came about. Not all the works are with "professional" artists; some are with community groups and schools, but all are with creative, inquisitive, and artistic people, and I see these works as equally valuable collaborations.

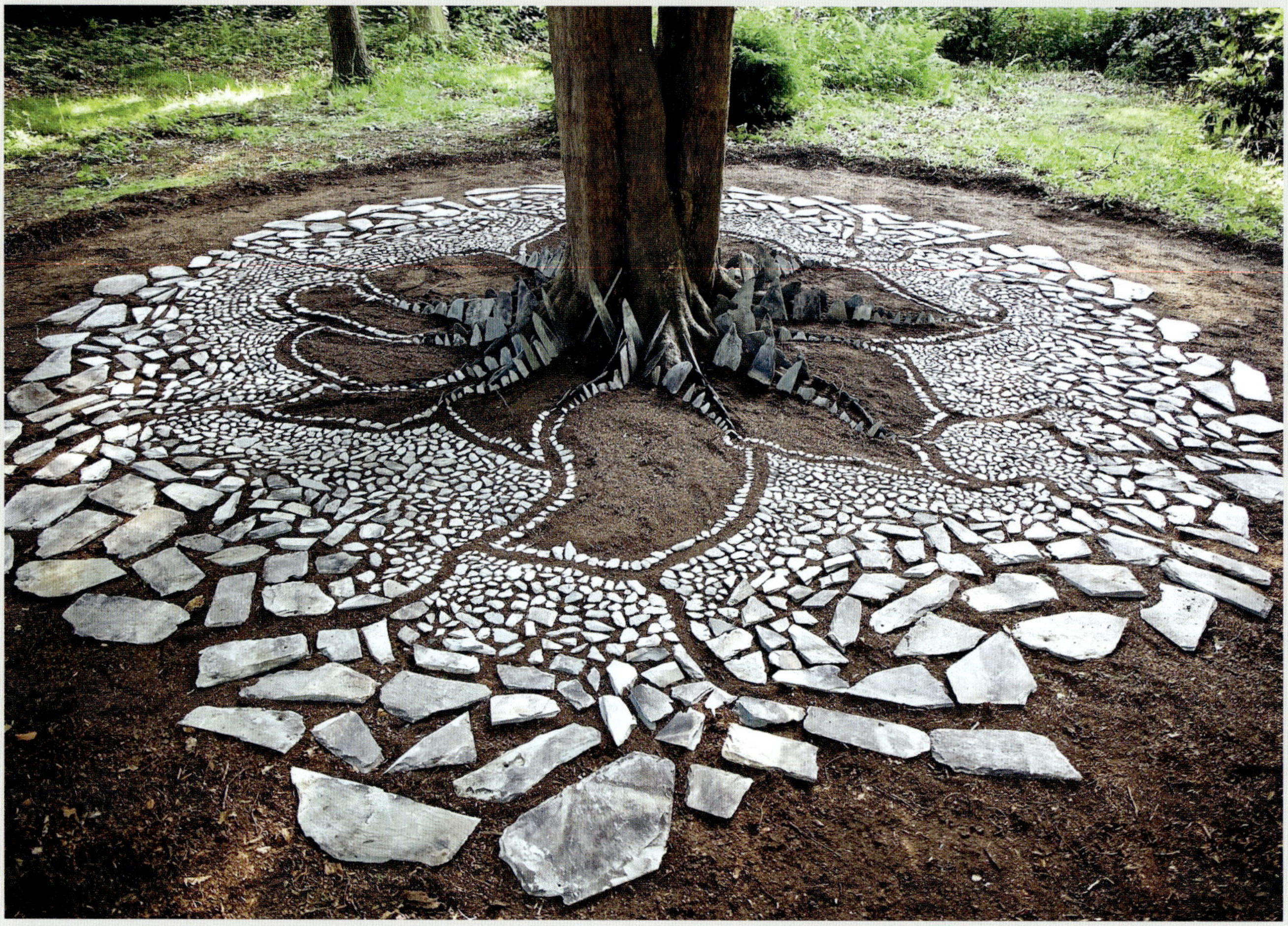

1. Created at Wentworth Woodhouse in Rotherham with Richard Shilling and Julia Brooklyn

This was the culmination of a week spent working with Richard and Julia in the gardens of Wentworth Woodhouse. We'd created a few things together during the week, and the opportunity arose to work with old slate roof tiles that were being replaced as part of regeneration work at the time. Richard and I revisited the work in 2021, when we were back at Wentworth for the We Wonder festival, reclaiming many of the tiles, now hidden under new growth, to create a new piece of work.

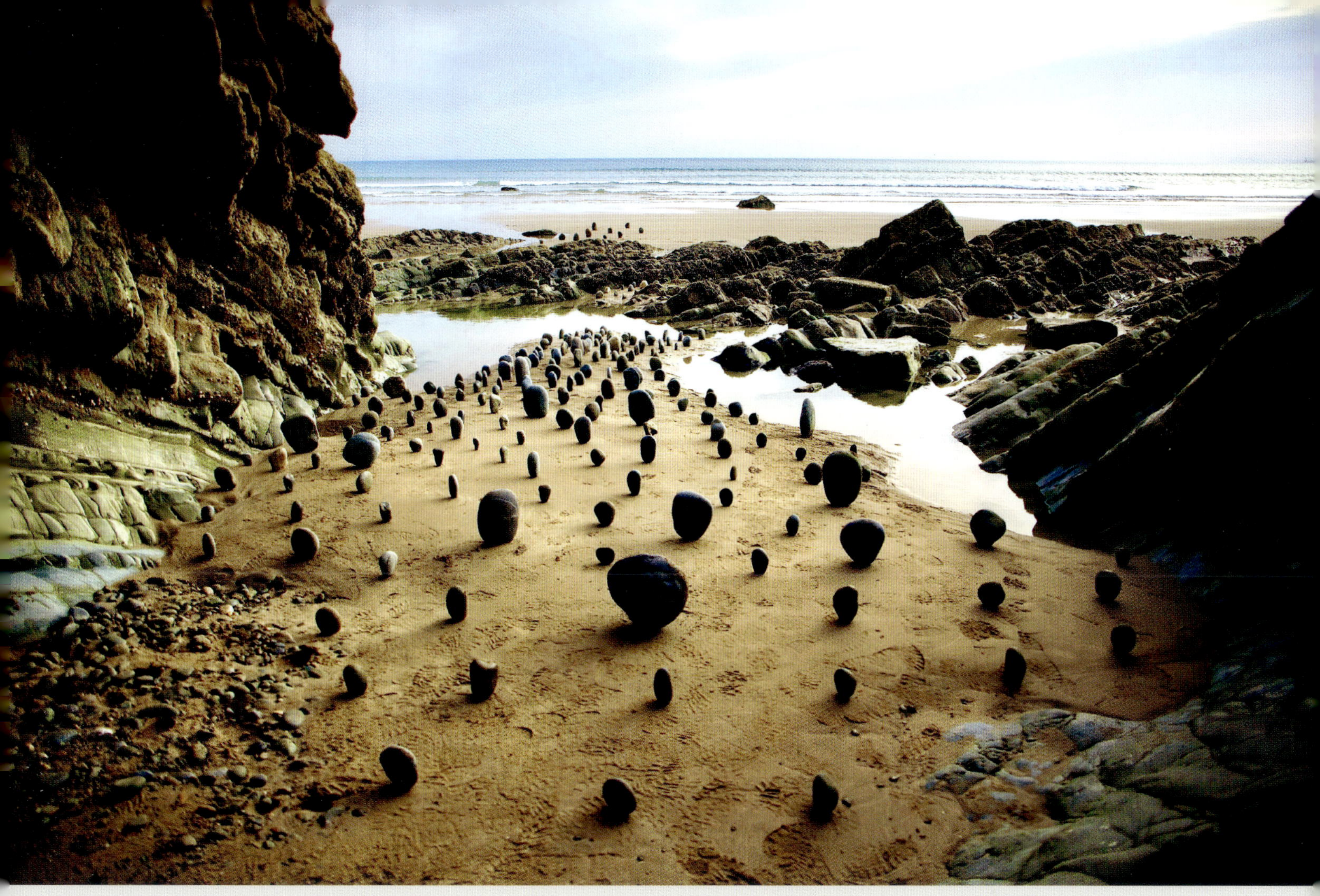

2. Created on Newgale Beach, Pembrokeshire, with Mark Antony Haden Ford

Mark and I were in Pembrokeshire, along with Richard Shilling and Jon Foreman, working on a piece for a big fashion brand client. During a bit of downtime in an otherwise hectic schedule, Mark and I headed off to explore the coastline. The collaborations I like are the ones where as soon as the idea is formed and a start has been made, there's no need to discuss anything, and this was one of those occasions. We both knew what outcome we were working toward, and there was no need for ongoing discussions about shape, form, scale, etc.

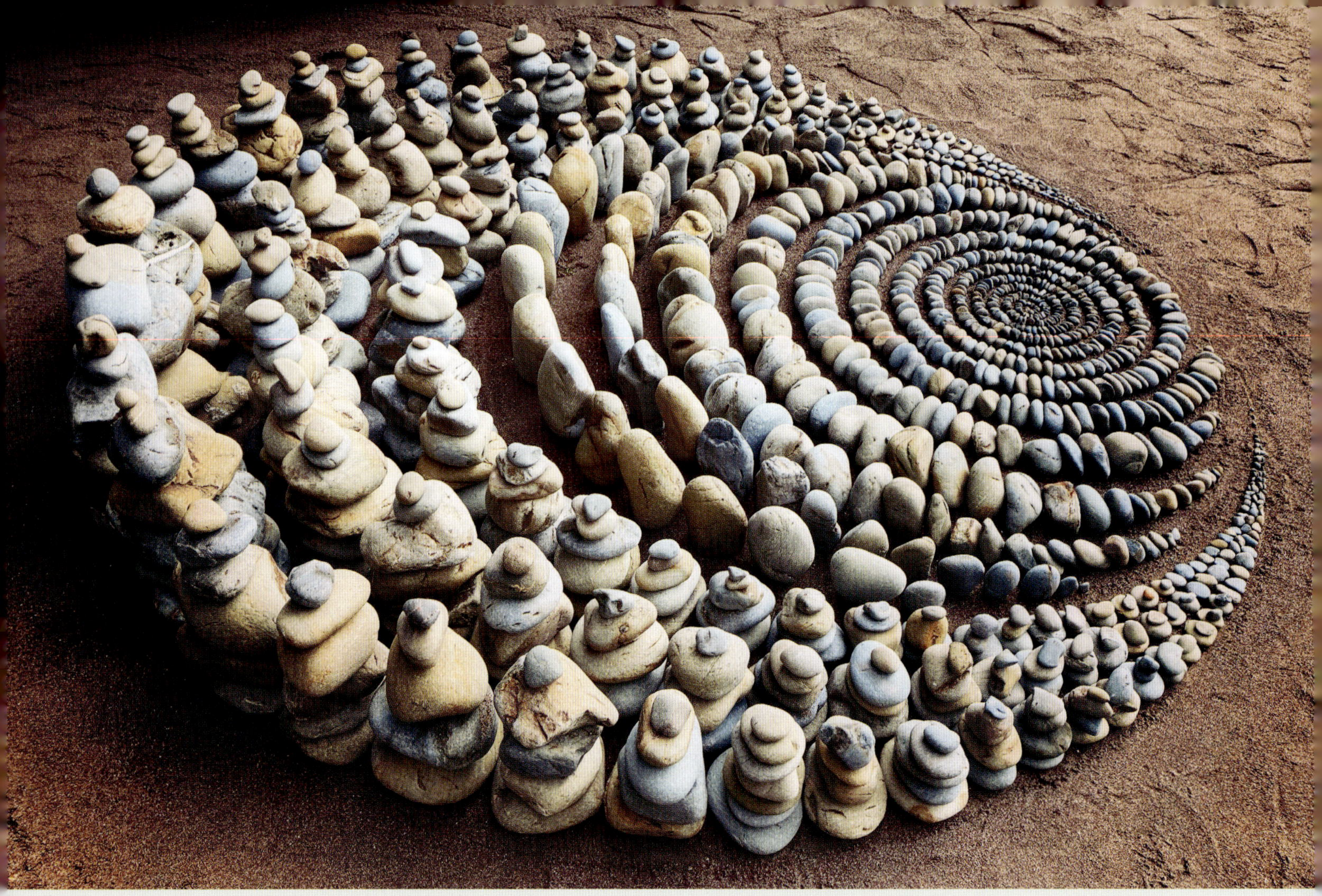

3. Created at Lindsway Bay, Pembrokeshire, with Jon Foreman

During the same work trip in South Wales, Jon had the opportunity to share one of his favorite beaches. He'd created many of his works here, and I could instantly see why. Tucked away in a quiet spot, and down a steep set of cliff steps, the beach is quiet, secluded, and wild. We went with the idea of individually working on two pieces, Jon on one of his familiar moons, and me working on the space within it, which as they met amalgamated to form one finished piece of work.

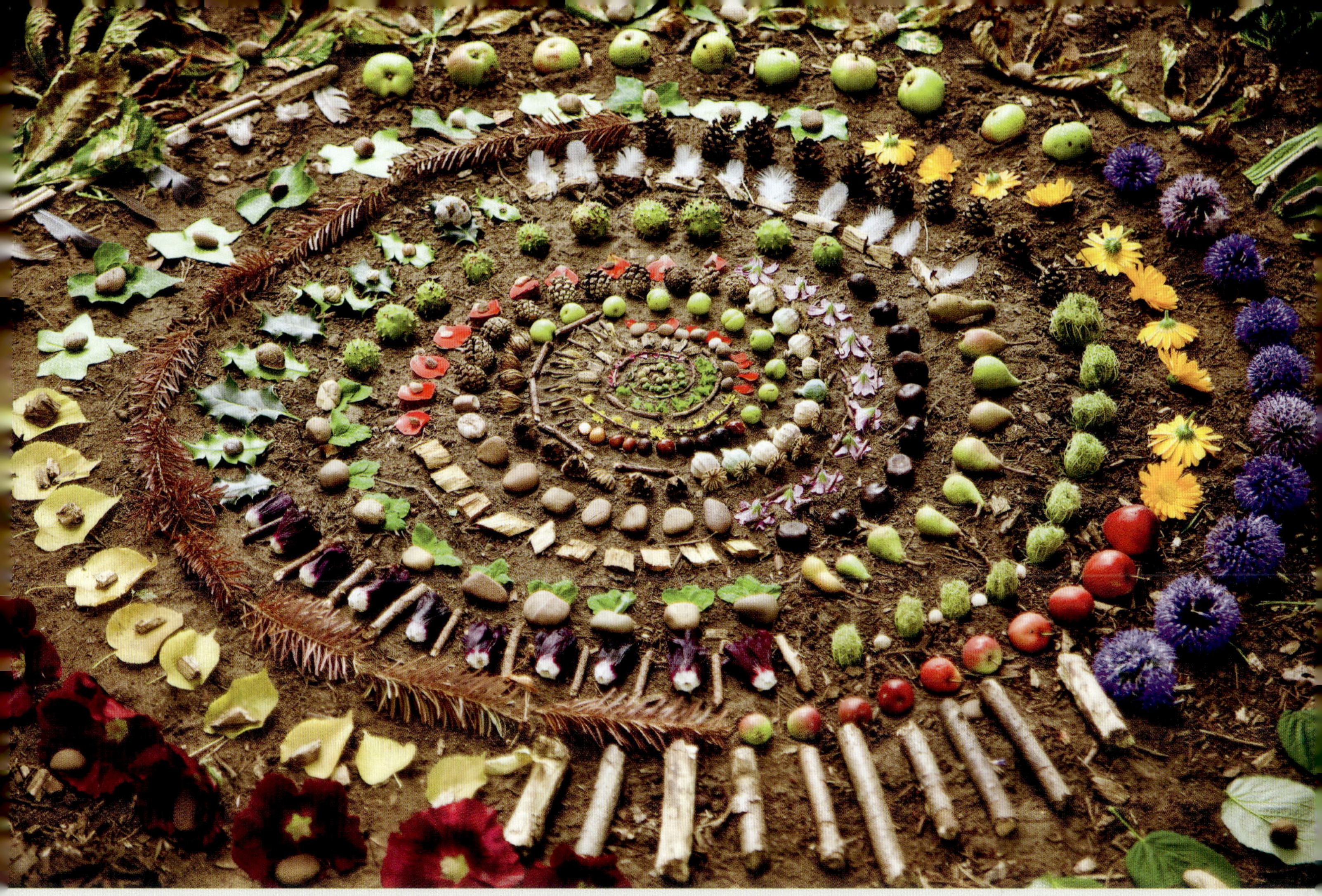

4. Created in Rob Carlyle's garden, Nottinghamshire, with Rob and his family and friends

Not all collaborations are with other artists; in this case it was a birthday present for Rob (nature lover and eco-house builder), and we gathered in his fantastic garden to celebrate his birthday. It's a haven for wildlife, and I got to see my first slow worm, and together we collected materials from the site and created this. The garden was an abundance of materials, but we quickly decided on the simple process of spiraling ten of each item we collected, starting with the smallest. The work was the catalyst for a wonderful day of conversation, laughter, and football songs!

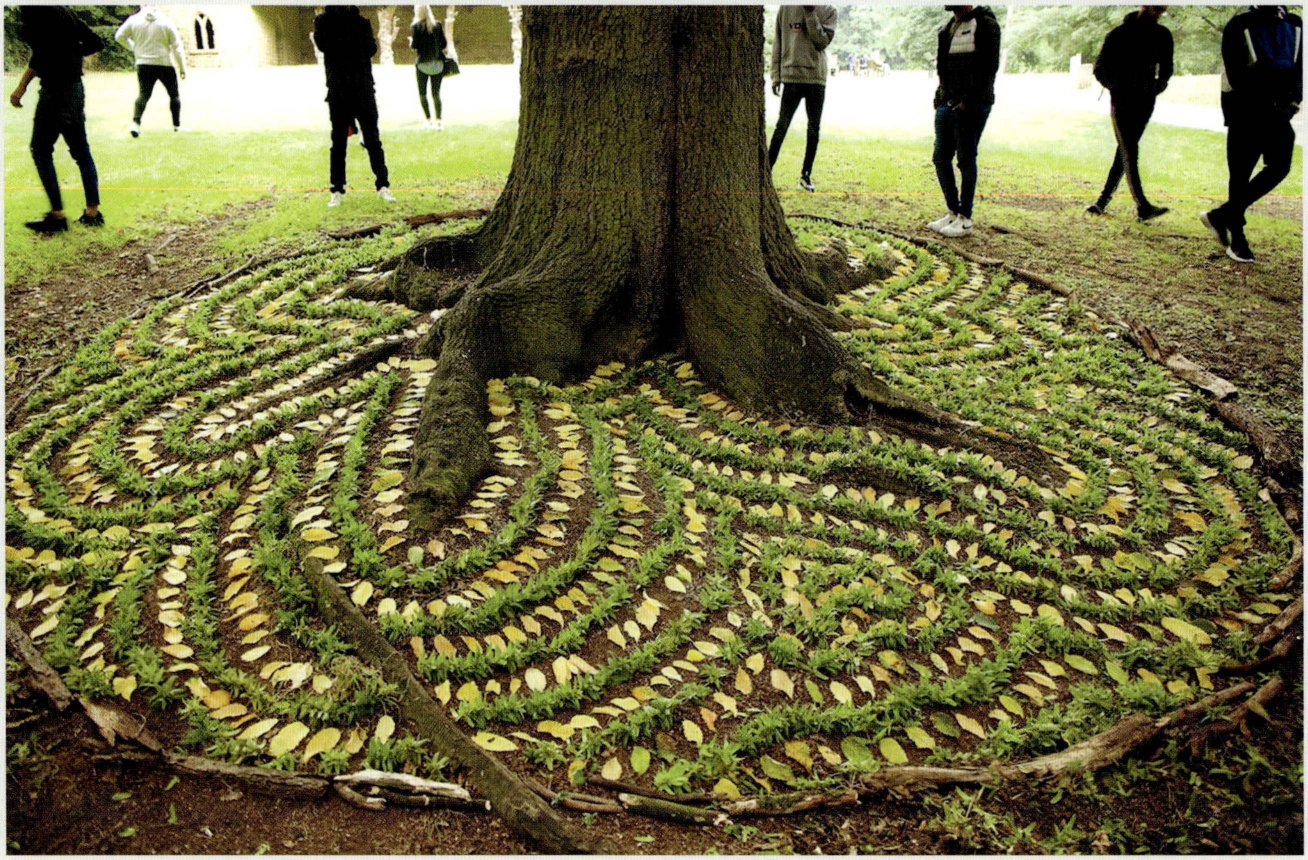

5. Created at Cannon Hall, Barnsley, South Yorkshire, with a group of young Syrian men, all of whom were new to the country

I loved this day; with very little spoken language between us, a connection was made, and we spent a morning transforming the ground around this oak tree, with the fallen debris from neighboring hornbeams. If you look, there are several little deviations to the design, such as the small, upside-down heart at the front right of the pattern. That was one of the young men, feeling confident enough, without asking for permission, changing the process to add his own touch. I remember first seeing him changing the pattern and feeling a bit overwhelmed by gratitude. That in a strange country, with very little verbal communication with me, we'd developed a connection and environment in which he felt safe enough to follow his own creative path and mix it up.

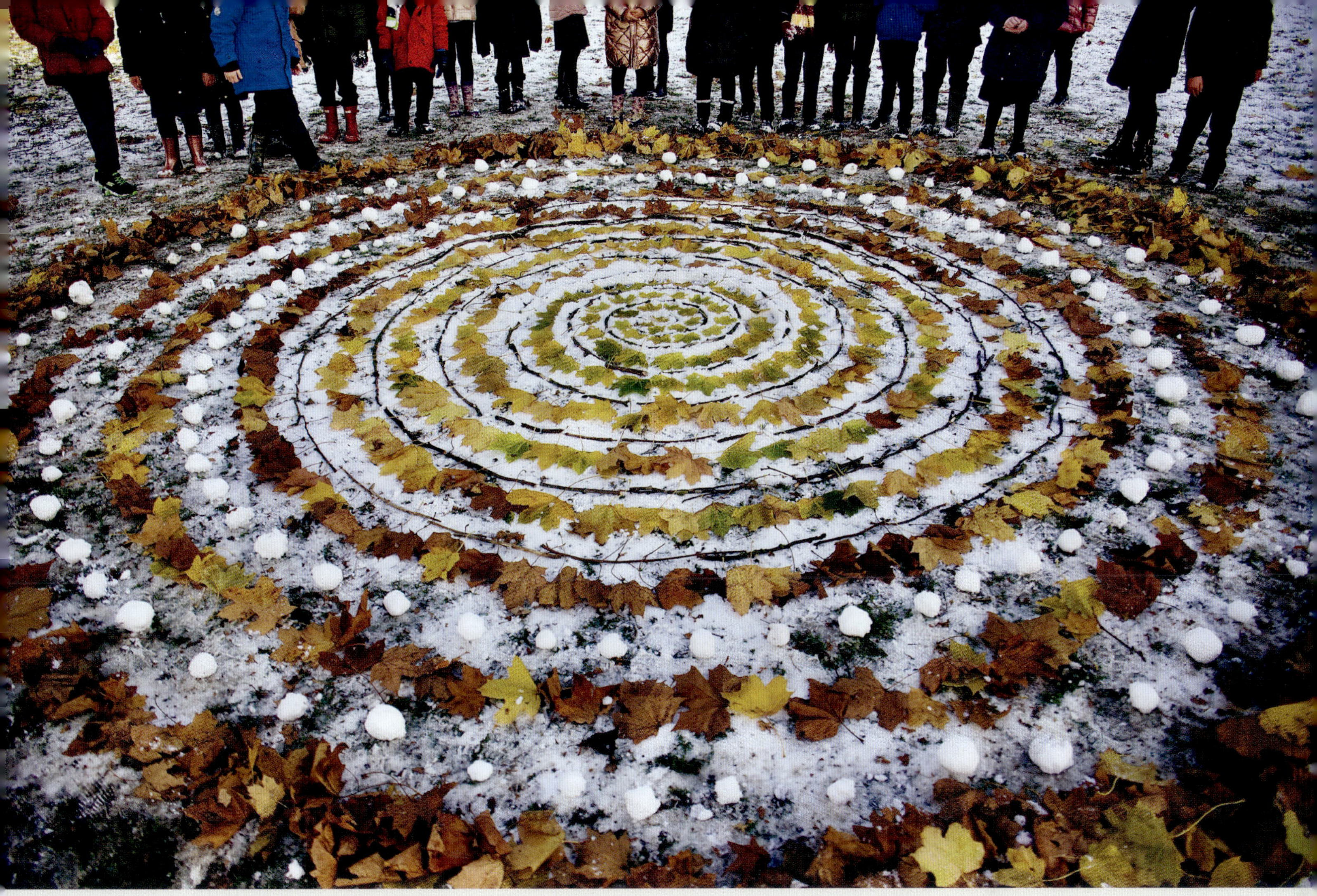

6. Created at Kiveton Park Infant School

I wanted to include a school collaboration. This was made with several classes throughout the day, in a school very close to where I live. The snow nearly canceled the day, but thankfully the school and the children were not put off. I'm so glad we carried on; the challenge presented by the cold weather was a worry at first, since the children were so young and the last thing I wanted was for it to stop being fun, but I needn't have worried. As the day wore on and the snow thawed, we were left with this at the end of the day.

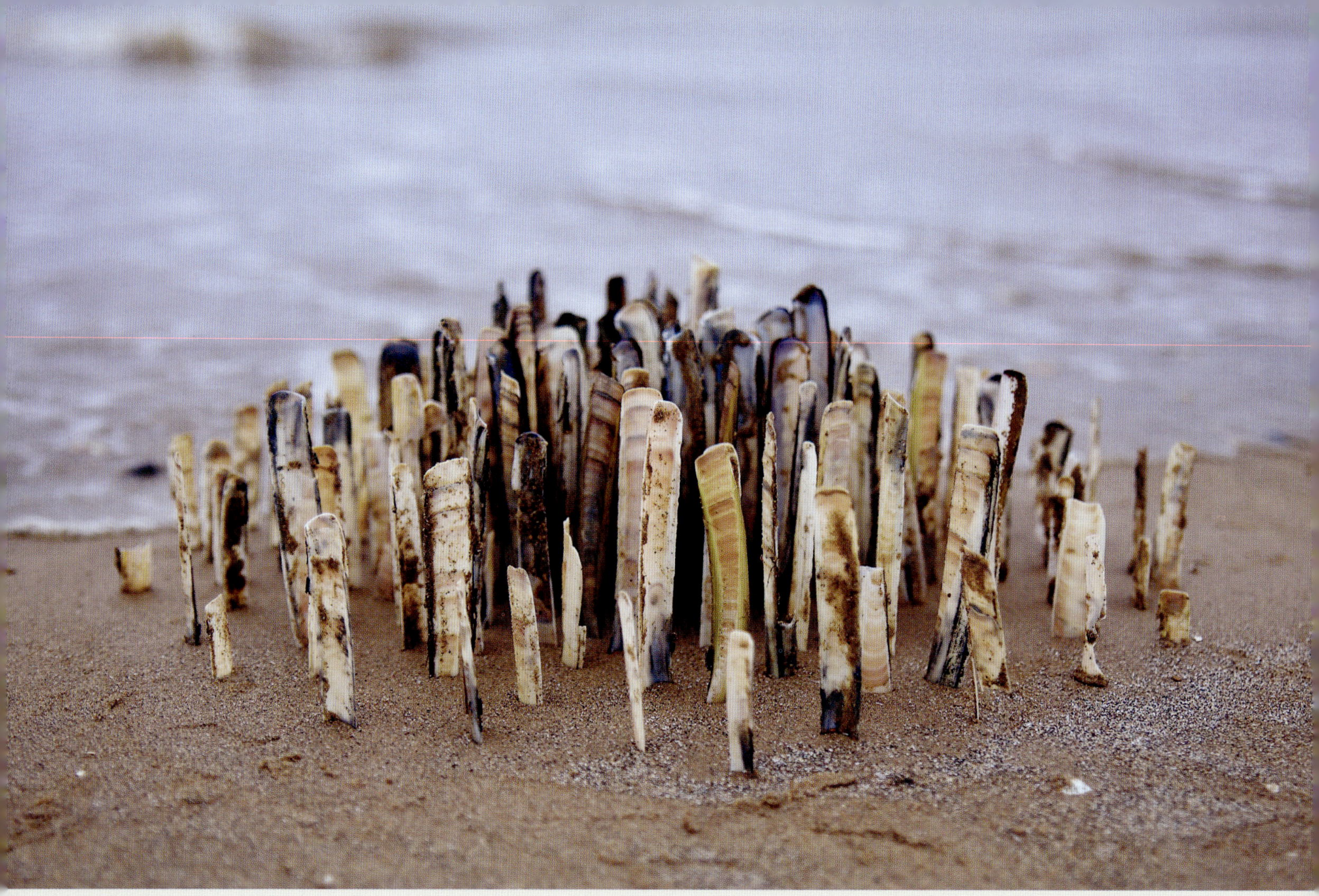

7. Created on Mablethorpe Beach with Tim Haywood

Tim and I work regularly together; I'm part of his Educational Health Care Plan and one of a team of personal tutors he now has. Tim, now seventeen, is living with mitochondrial disease, and as a result it meant that he missed out on most of the formal education most people his age had access to. That said, he's sharp, funny, and way cleverer than me. For example, during the COVID-19 lockdown I taught him to play chess online. I've played on and off most of my life, but after a few months, I'm lucky if I win a game.

We made this on Mablethorpe Beach on the Lincolnshire Coast after a trip to see the gray seal colony at Donna Nook.

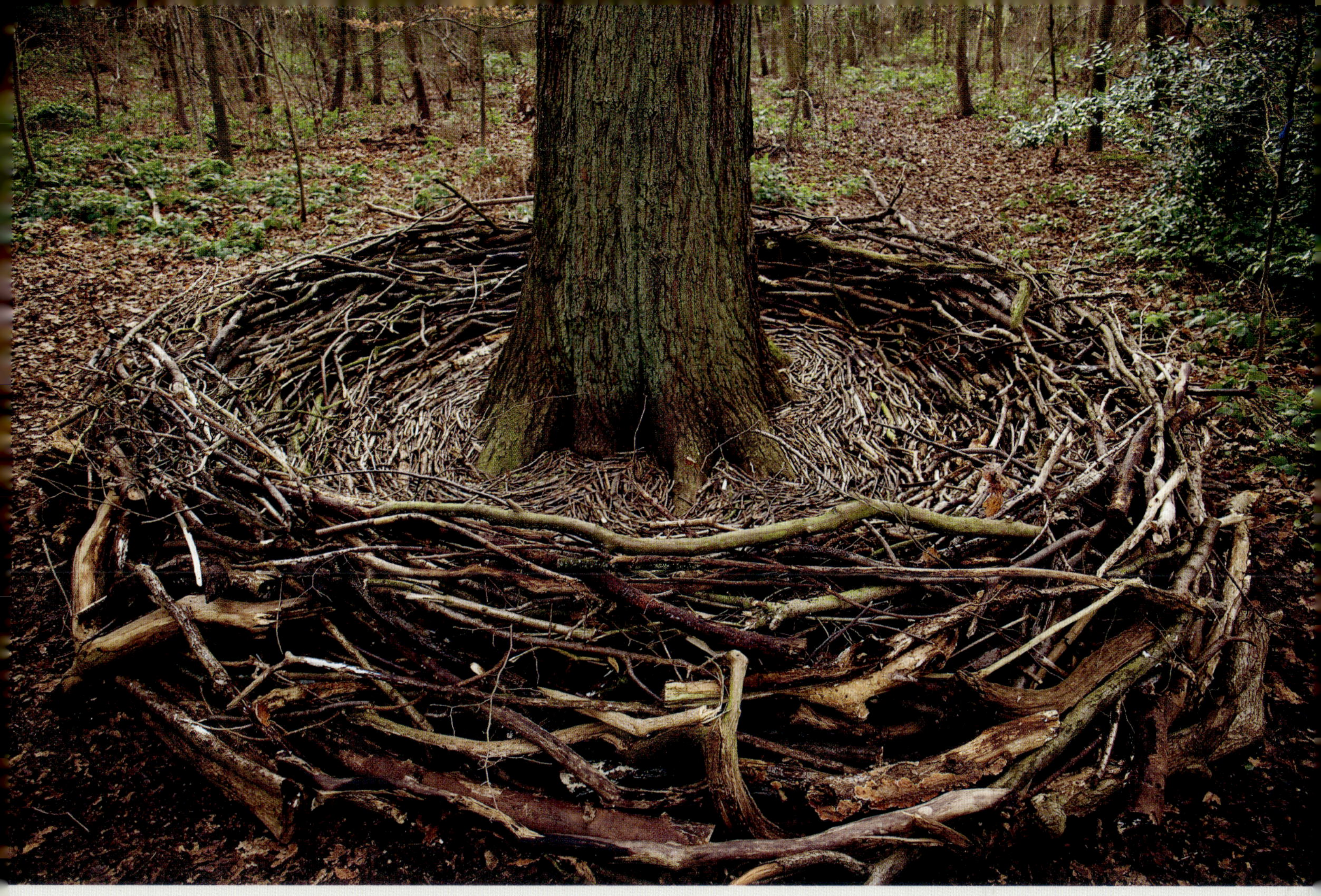

8. Nest, created at Monkwood Primary with ten classes over the course of a day

At the time of writing, this was the last school session I'd done, and I'm including it purely because it was such an inspirational day. I love it when everyone buys into an idea, and the combined efforts of everyone culminate into something so special. At the end of the day, I hang around and watch the children excitedly show their grown-ups what they've done with such pride. I go home very happy and enriched.

Invitation to Play 4 *(Natural Mandalas)*

Here we go for the last time, although please don't make it your last time! The final little prompt for you to try is a natural mandala. If the term "mandala" is new to you, a simple Google search of natural mandala will provide you with plenty of inspiration. But to try to explain, a mandala is, for me, a geometric circular pattern using a range of different materials to explore shape, texture, colors, etc. I never set out to make mandalas, but often the materials I find in a location dictate what emerges, and a mandala just seems to evolve naturally. My friend Ana Castilho, or "Mandal.ana.s" on social media, would be the perfect place for more inspiration.

For your mandala, I would urge that you try not to approach the task with an outcome in mind; don't predesign or draw out a plan. Let the materials, location, and weather be your guide.

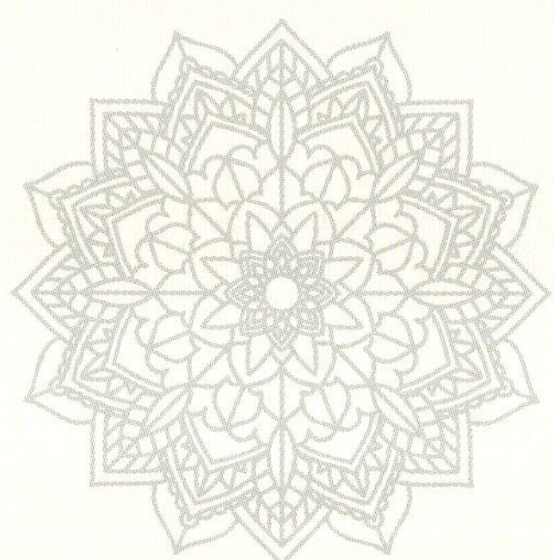

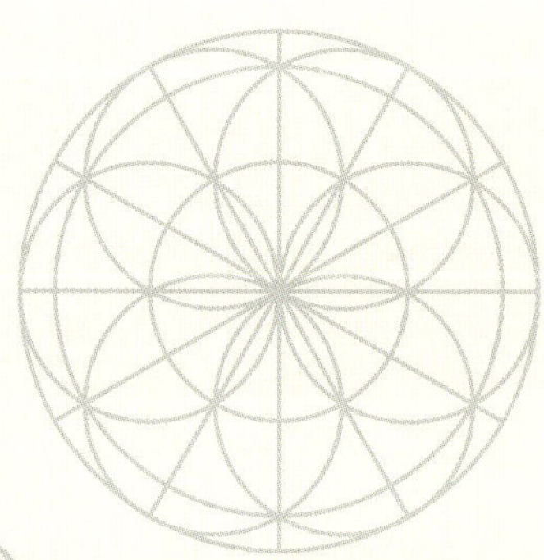

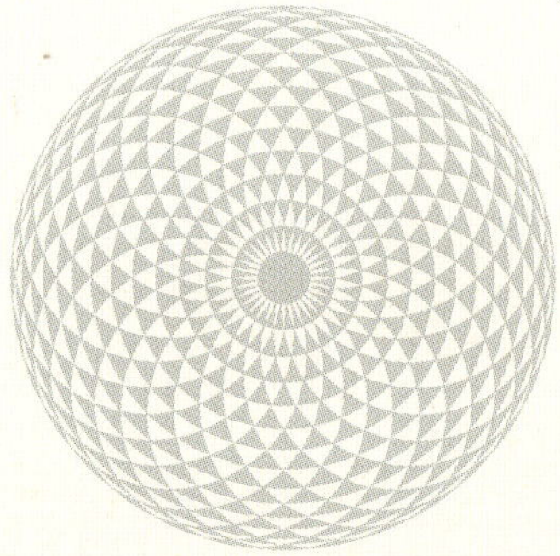

You know the score by now.

- Step 1—enjoy your walk and surroundings (of course).
- Step 2—as you walk around, look for an interesting mix of materials, textures, colors, shapes, etc.
- Step 3—tidy up the space and remove loose materials from the surface of your chosen space (you don't need to dig stuff out or pull out living plants; just work around them).
- Step 4—the most important part of a mandala is the start. That will dictate what happens next, which in turn will inform the next layer to the work. It's this approach of responding to the previous layer that begins to build up the overall picture that the eye will see.
- Step 5—intuition. Carry on this process until you get the feeling that the piece is finished and visually it fits within its environment. Adding another layer won't benefit the viewer experience. This is something that you will get better at with practice, but trust your judgment; it will probably be right.

Mandala tips

A few things that you may find useful:

- Consider the season. Fall will give you much-easier access to an abundance of different colors and shapes, with all the different wonderful leaves littering the floor at that time.
- If materials are harder to come by, you could carry a bag to collect different items as you walk, meaning when you settle on a place to work, you will already have a selection of materials to get you started.
- While a mandala may appear more intricate, more complicated even, I personally want the process to remain simple, and I think it is. I thought this might be a nice moment to go through the making of a piece of work in more detail and, I hope, demonstrate what I mean. So I headed out to Anston Stones Wood to create a winter mandala.

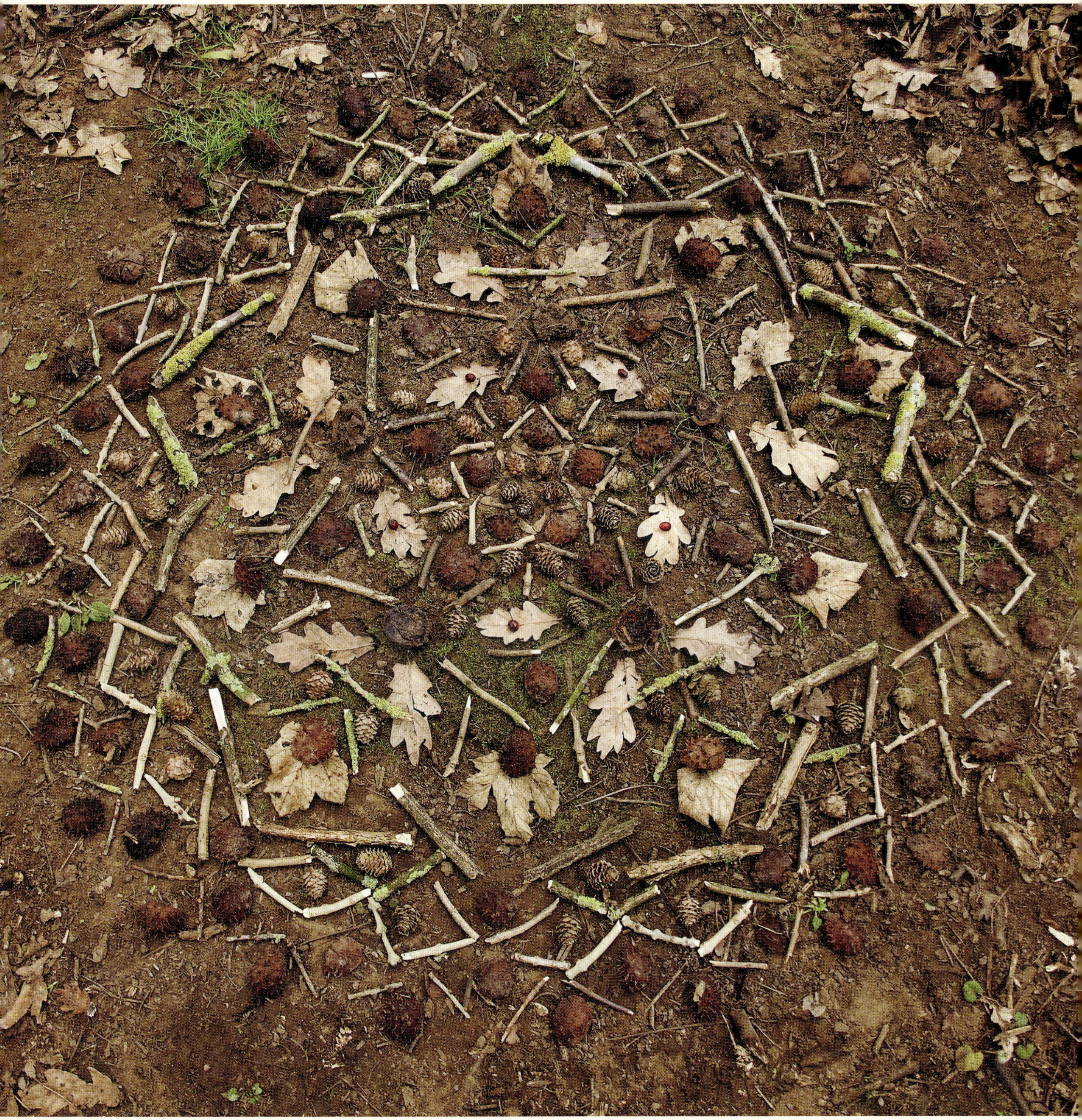

Note: The images that accompany this invitation to play follow the steps in the text.

1. So, my winter mandala started with these five small cones. I've already mentioned that the start is the most important part of how the artwork will play out, and the negative space between the cones is what will inform the next step. The cones were collected during my walk; I found several fallen branches with the cones still attached at the side of the path, so I picked up a few as I walked.

2. I didn't have to move to find these old sycamore keys; they were within arm's reach of where I began the piece. The keys are placed to accentuate space dictated by the cones, and this is key to a mandala. Try to think of each additional material added as a new layer, and as the layers build up, you want to fill the spaces that the last layer created.

3. These horse chestnut shells were nearby, and the remnants of a previous work I'd made; in fact, they'd featured in at least two previous works before this reincarnation—look out for one of them in this book! Note that the five initial cones are dictating everything else, and we are using multiples of five, so ten sycamore keys and now five horse chestnut shells.

4. Ash twigs are used to frame the horse chestnut shells, again accentuating shape, making it easy for the eye to read it.

5. Back to the cones I'd picked up during my walk, but this time slightly larger ones. Also the spaces we are trying to fill are getting larger too, so this time I've included two cones in each space.

6. Another layer of twigs, just to further dissect space and create a story for the eye. At this point it's worth just pointing out the different textures, which all add to the story. The twigs create line and help the eye make sense of the pattern that is beginning to build.

1

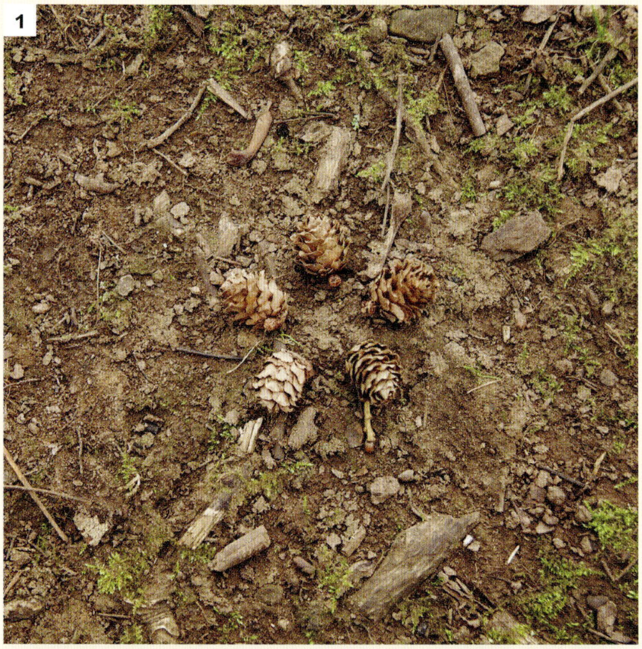

2

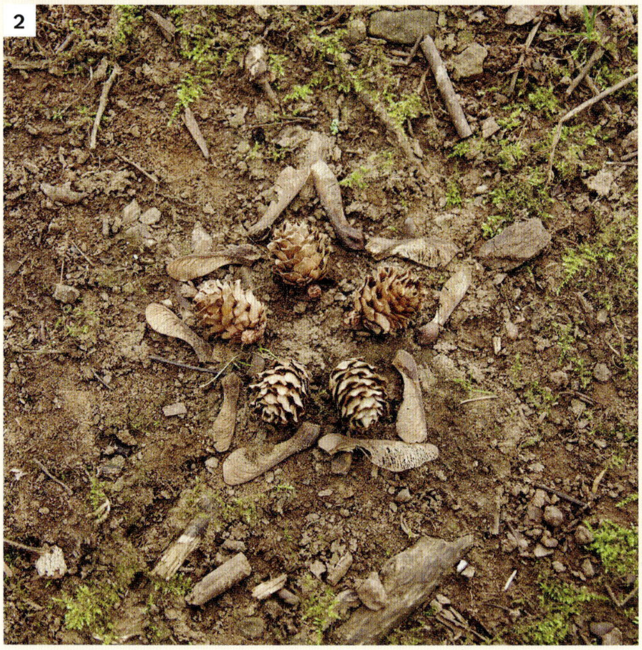

3

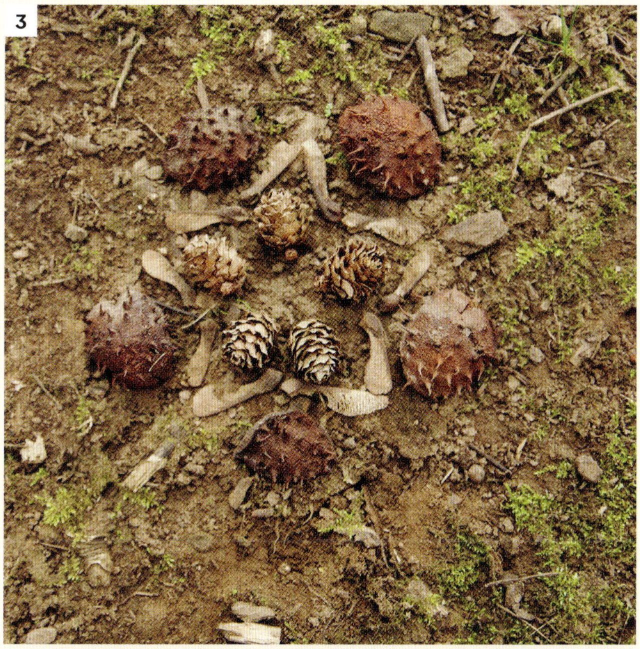

5

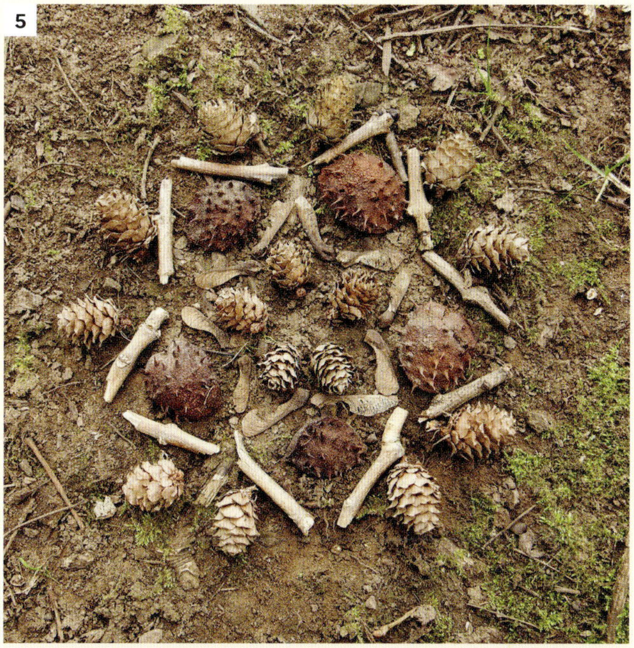

4

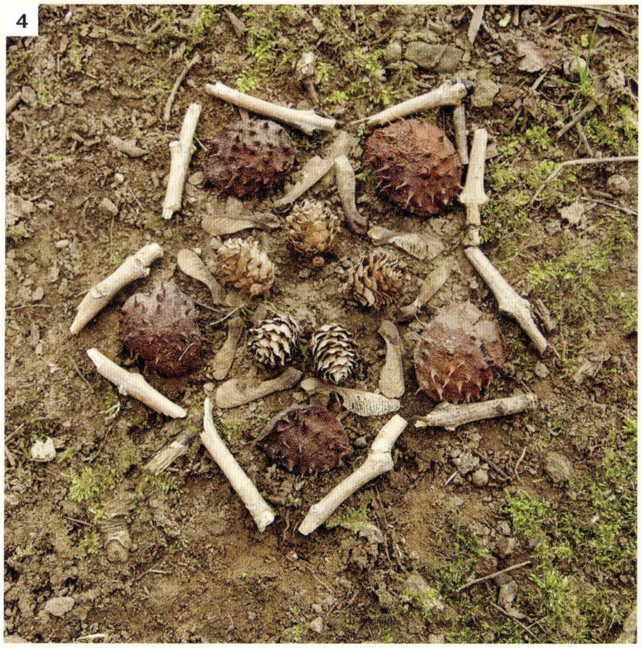

6

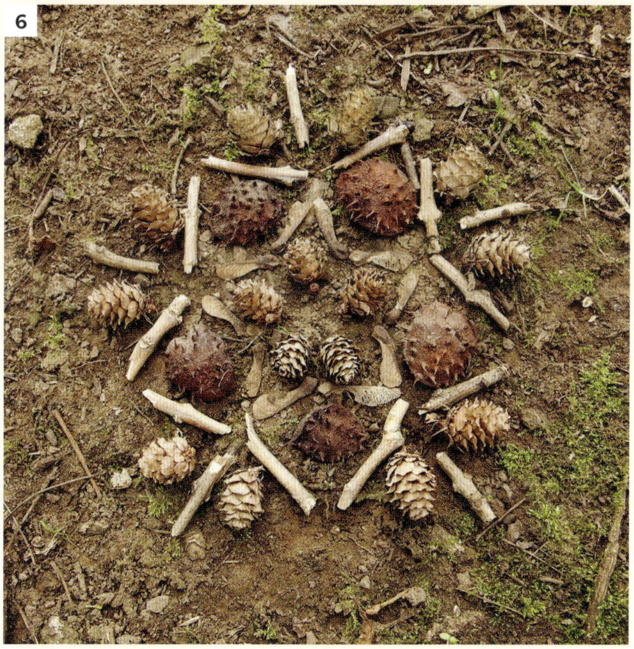

7

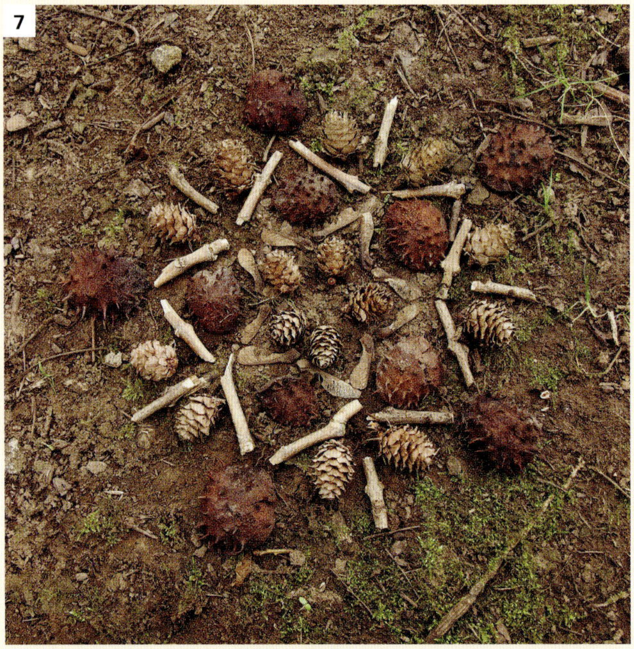

8

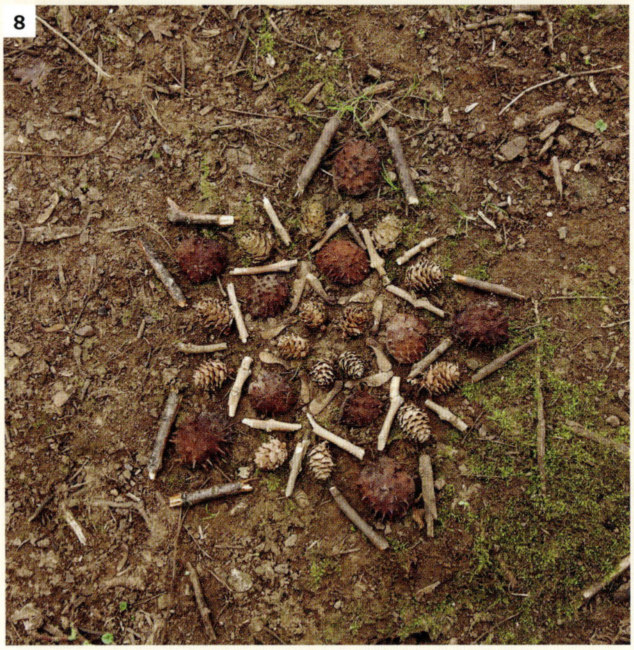

9

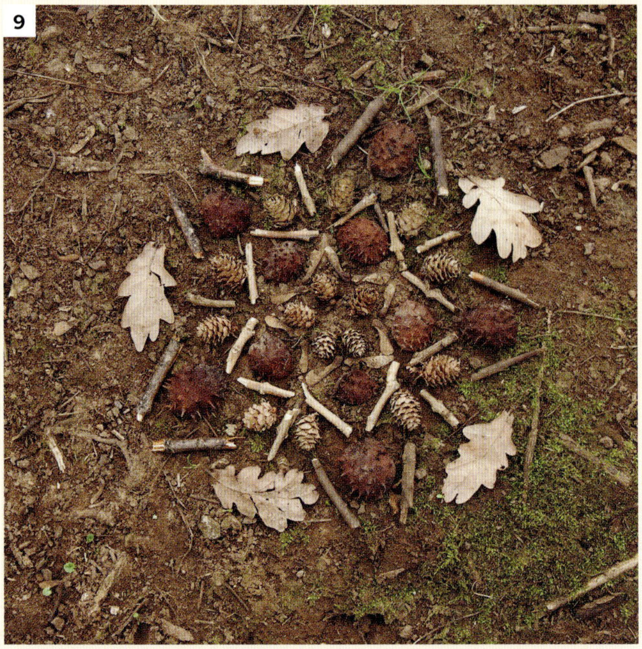

10

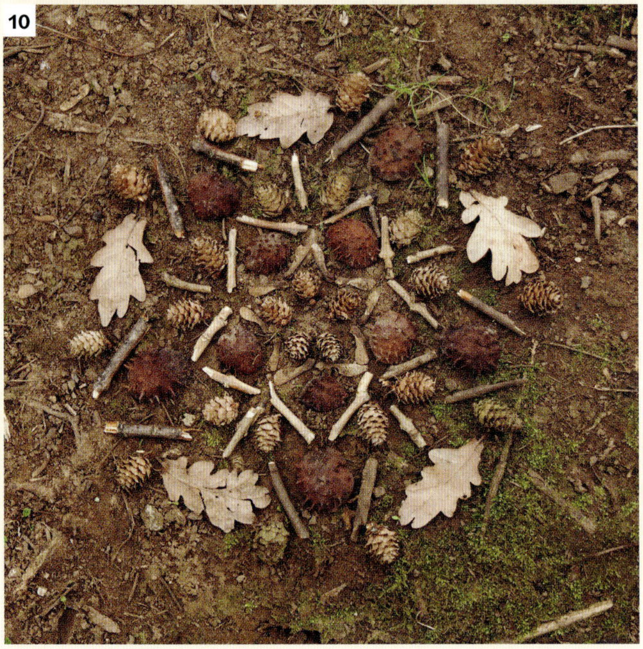

7. A horse chestnut layer now, I think, creates balance between the textures. Just to be clear, though, I wasn't thinking this at the time; the process of making was much more intuitive.

8. More twigs, slightly thicker and darker in color. I hope by now you can see the repetitions.

9. These old oak leaves seemed appropriate now; the spaces we are creating are getting larger, and so is the artwork. Increasing scale as we get bigger helps with the visual story.

10. The next layer again uses the cones to fill the empty space.

11
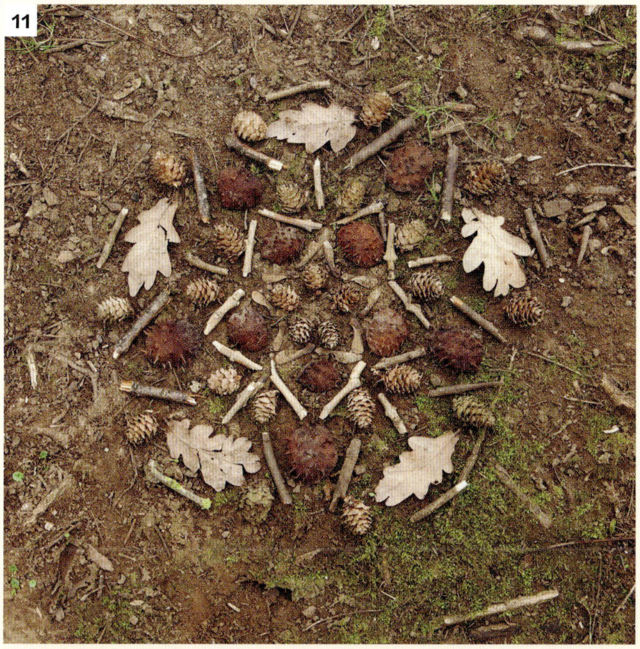

13
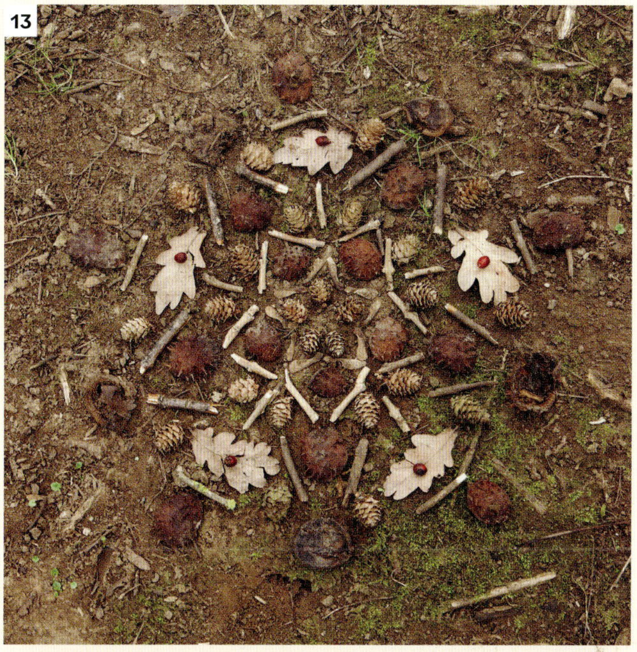

12
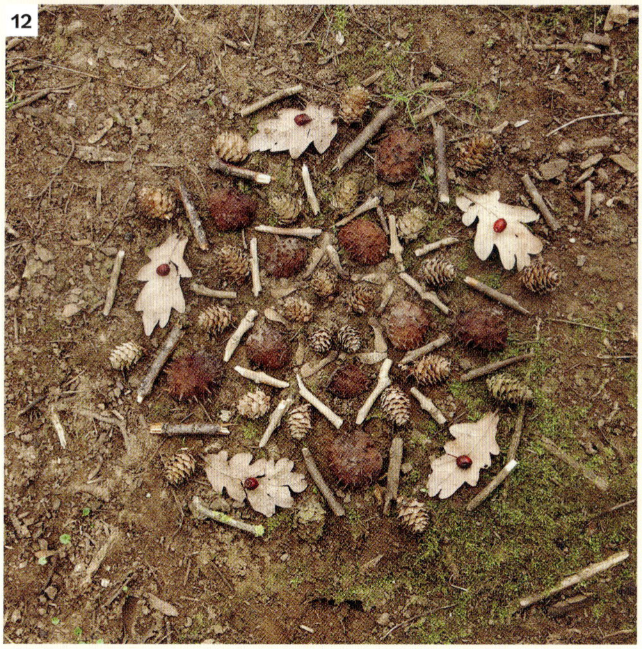

14
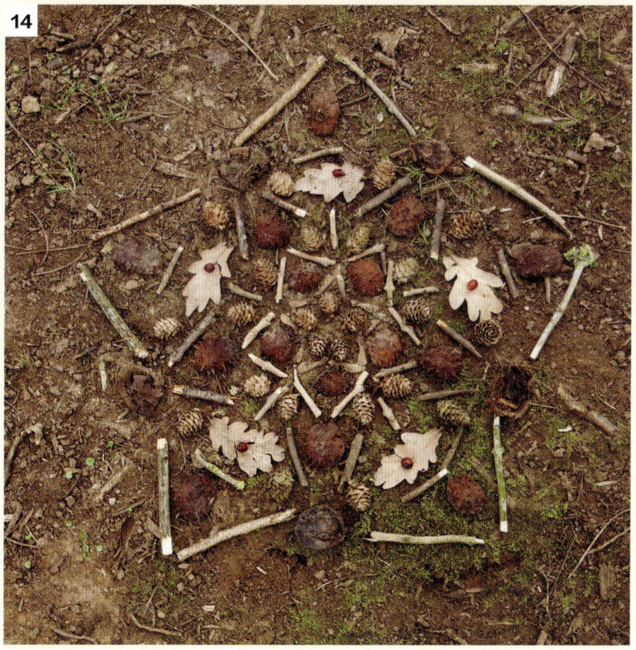

11. More twigs to define space and shape.

12. The little hawthorn berries on the leaves add, I hope, an extra layer of detail but also crucially add a little bit of weight to stop the leaves from being disturbed by the wind.

13. and 14. Familiar layers, repeating the same process that has built up the scale of the work.

15

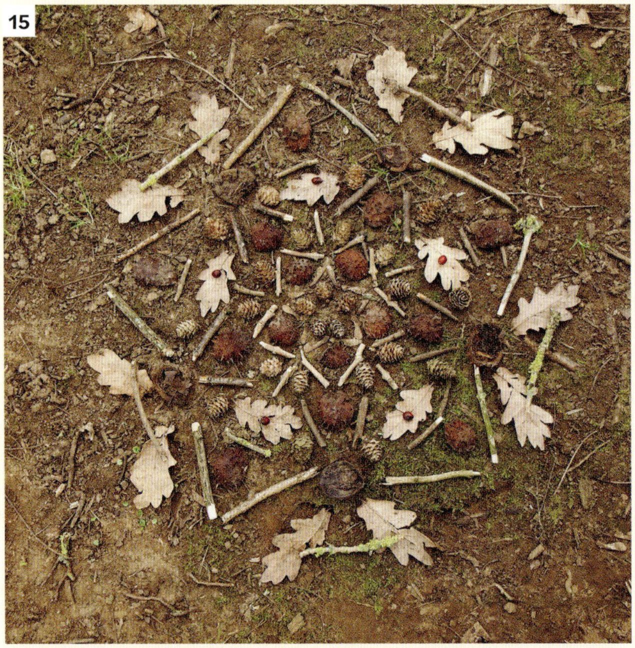

17

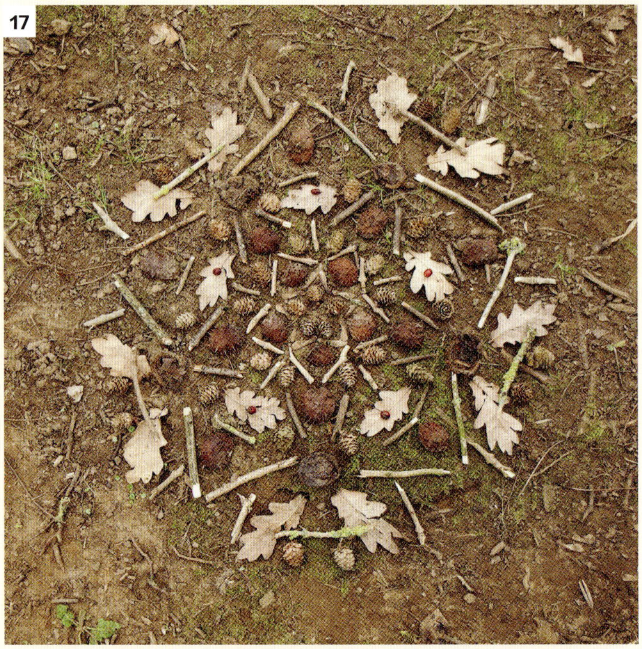

16

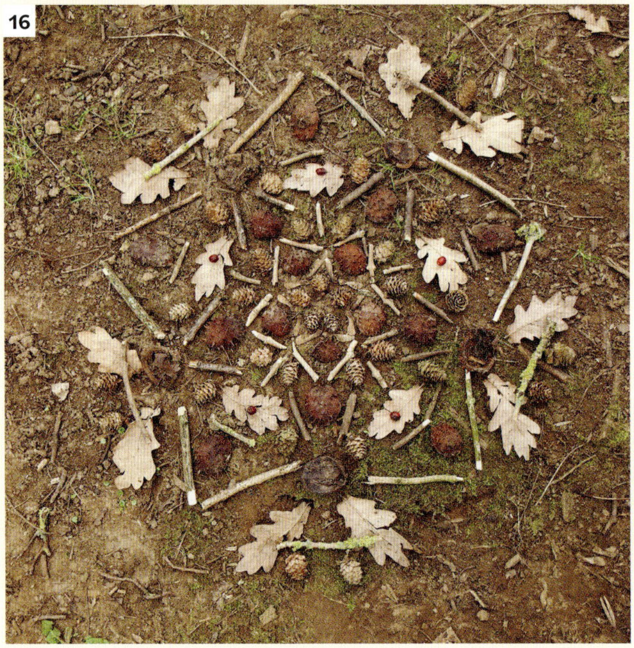

18

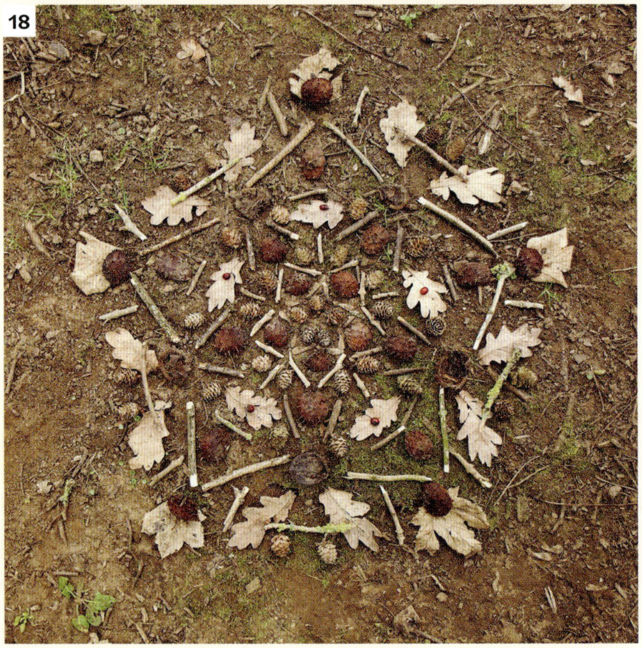

15. Creating a new visual pattern using the oak leaves; look at the correlation with the previous leaves. Again, this wasn't a conscious decision, but one of the lovely things about making work like this is the natural patterns and relationships that appear through the process.

16. and 17. Uses the familiar materials to continue the journey.

18. For this layer, I've introduced old sycamore leaves. I like the relationship with the sycamore keys I used early in the piece. What I wasn't so keen on was the shape at this stage; the pentagon shape was a bit jarring, so I wanted to try to work that out of the piece.

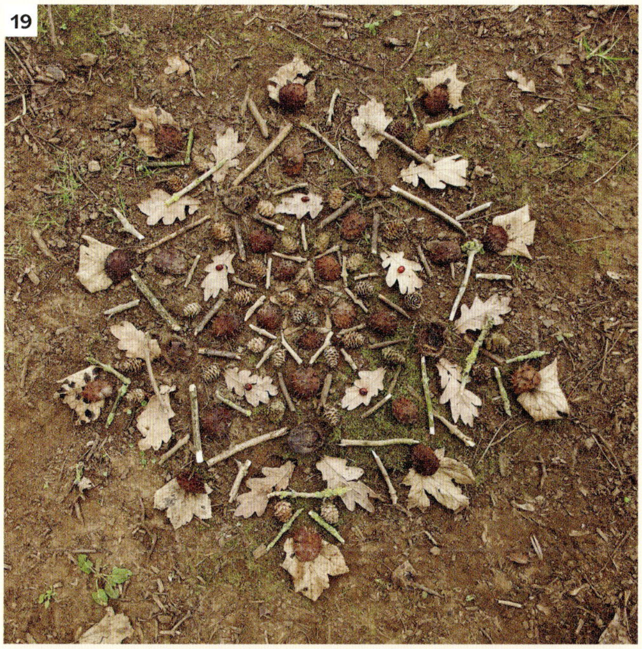

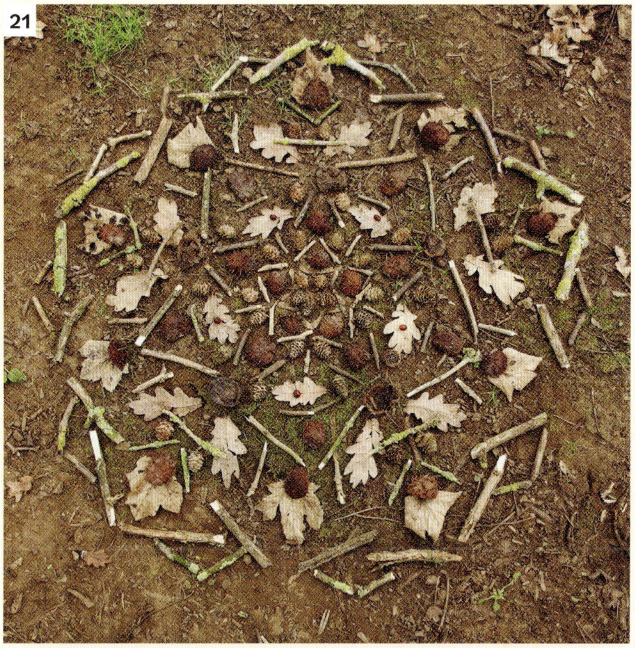

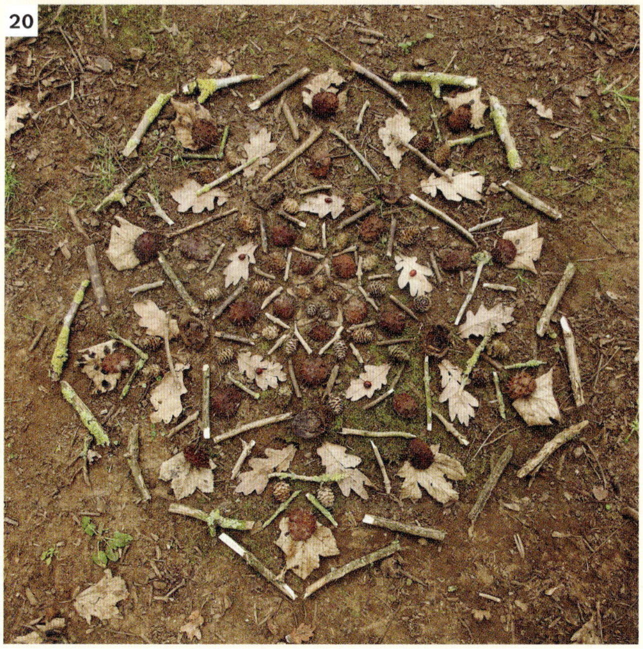

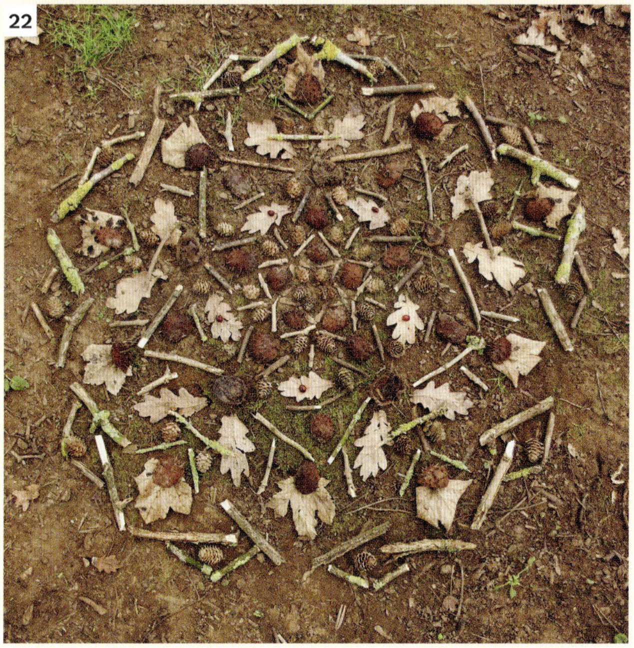

19. The obvious way to do this, I thought, was to extend the new sycamore leaf layer.

20.–25. Following the now-familiar process and familiar materials, the next few layers are both building the structure of the piece and, I also realized, working toward the conclusion of the final artwork. However, I didn't want to end with such a strong outline created by the twigs.

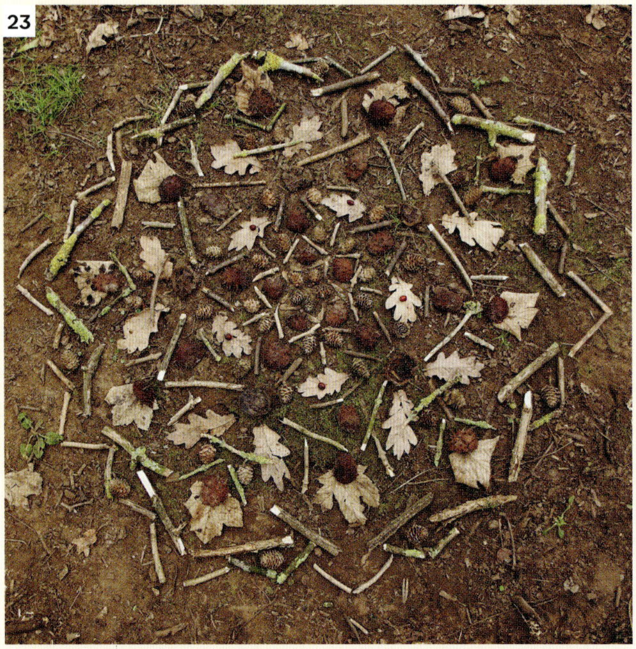
23

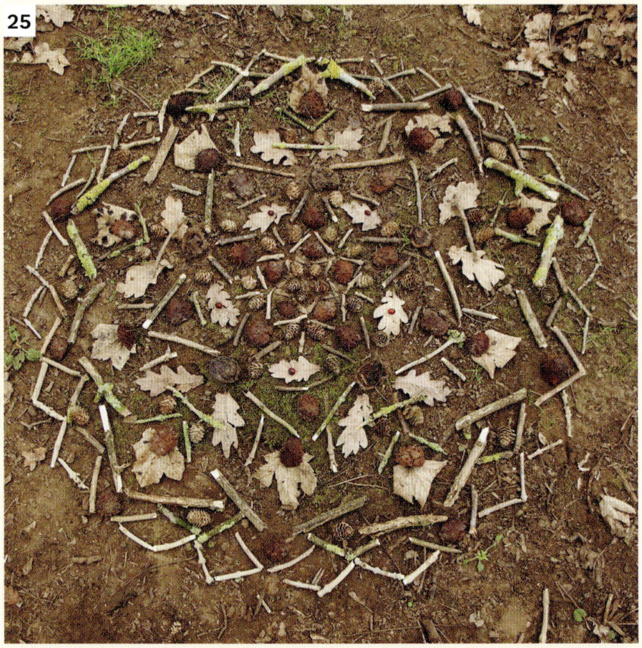
25

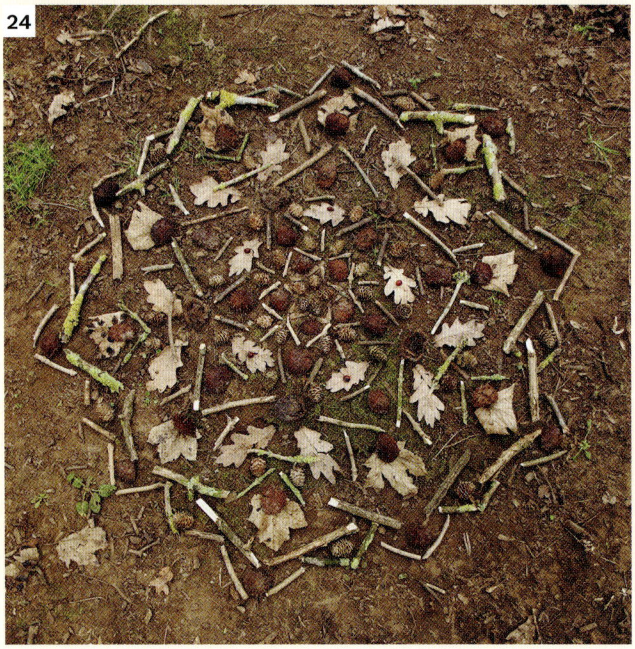
24

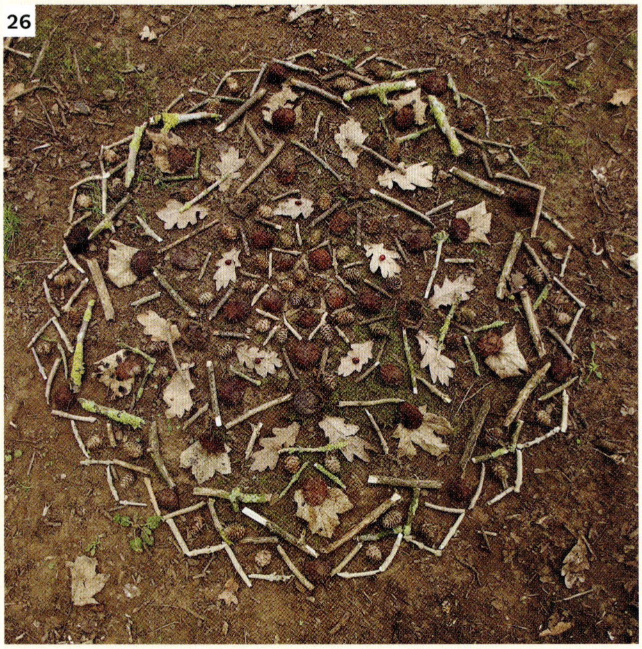
26

26. and 27. I used the horse chestnuts to try to disseminate the work and take the edge off that strong line, to make it softer.

27

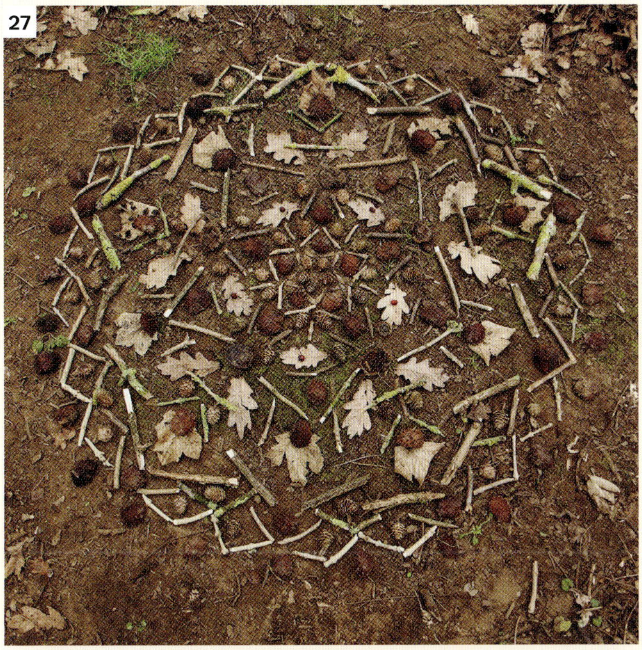

28

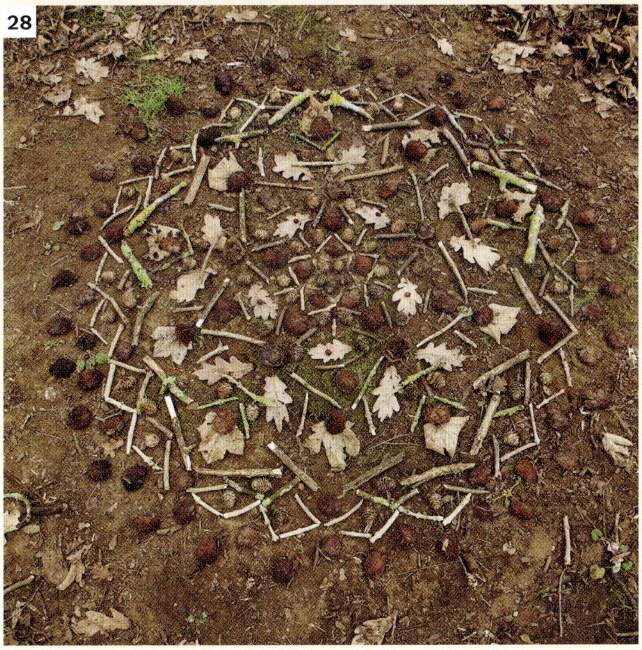

28. The final image uses thinner twigs to add definition to that final stage.

And that's it; the work is finished. I found it quite difficult to try to put the process into words; I hope it doesn't come across as me having a headful of elements to think about while making, because hand on heart, it was a far more organic process than that. Altering the pentagon shape that was evolving and didn't feel right was, I think, the only element that I consciously considered during the making process.

I do hope it was useful, though, in helping you get out there and create your own mandalas.

This is my last little prompt for you, but there's so much more for you to explore. I hope that by now you have the confidence in your relationship with the natural world to find your own new adventures, but here's a couple of additional things you could try:

1. **The 100-Leaf challenge**—I started this challenge on Twitter a few years ago now. It's exactly what it sounds like. Collect 100 leaves—they can be the same or different; it's all up to you—and use them to create a piece of work. It's a lovely simple challenge and lovely to do with groups or schools. I was blown away by just how it took off on Twitter. Search the hashtag #100leaveschallenge and scroll through some of the fantastic pieces, maybe even adding your own.

2. **X10**—I've been having loads of fun with this recently. On a walk, collect ten of a range of things: leaves of different types, the same-length sticks, pine cones, acorns, maple keys; anything you come across. Once you have a healthy stock of natural materials, use them to make your piece.

3. **Collaborating**—Invite a friend or family members to join you. See how the dynamics change when working with others.

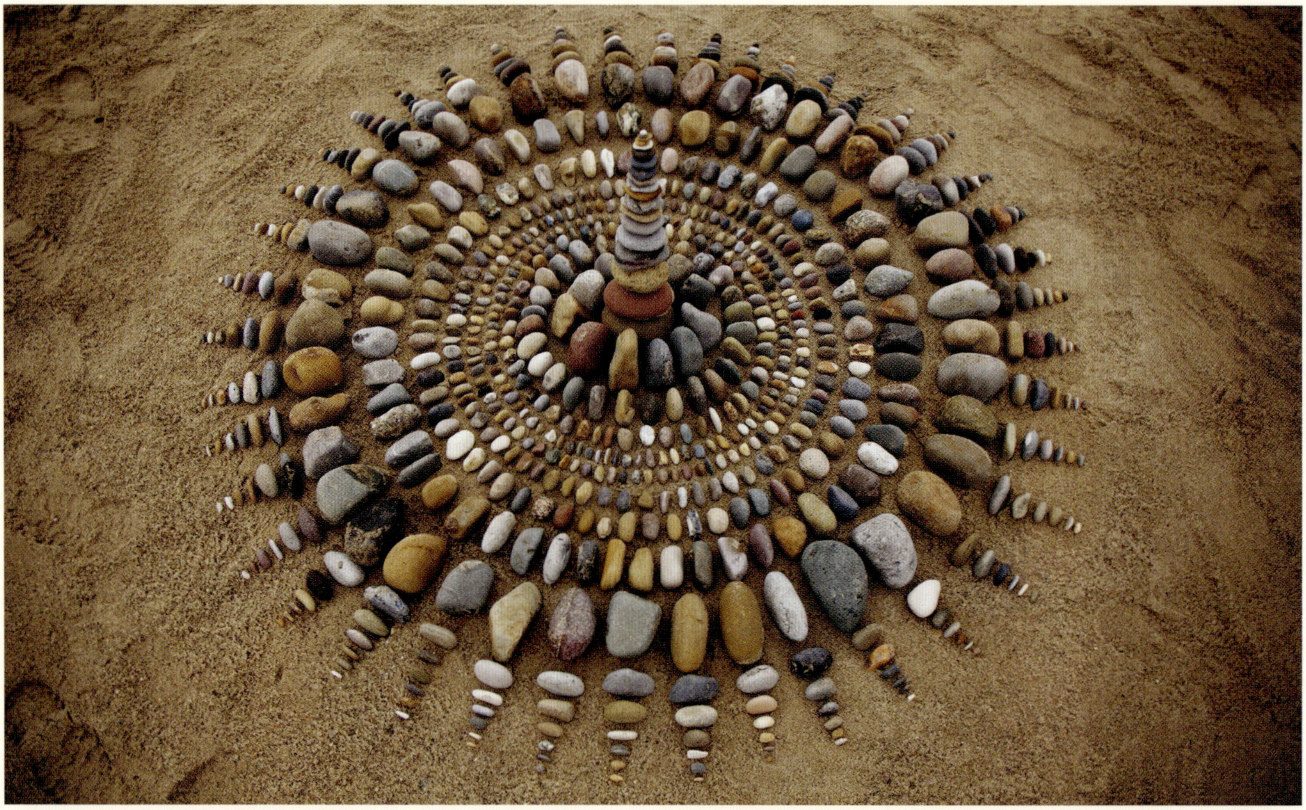

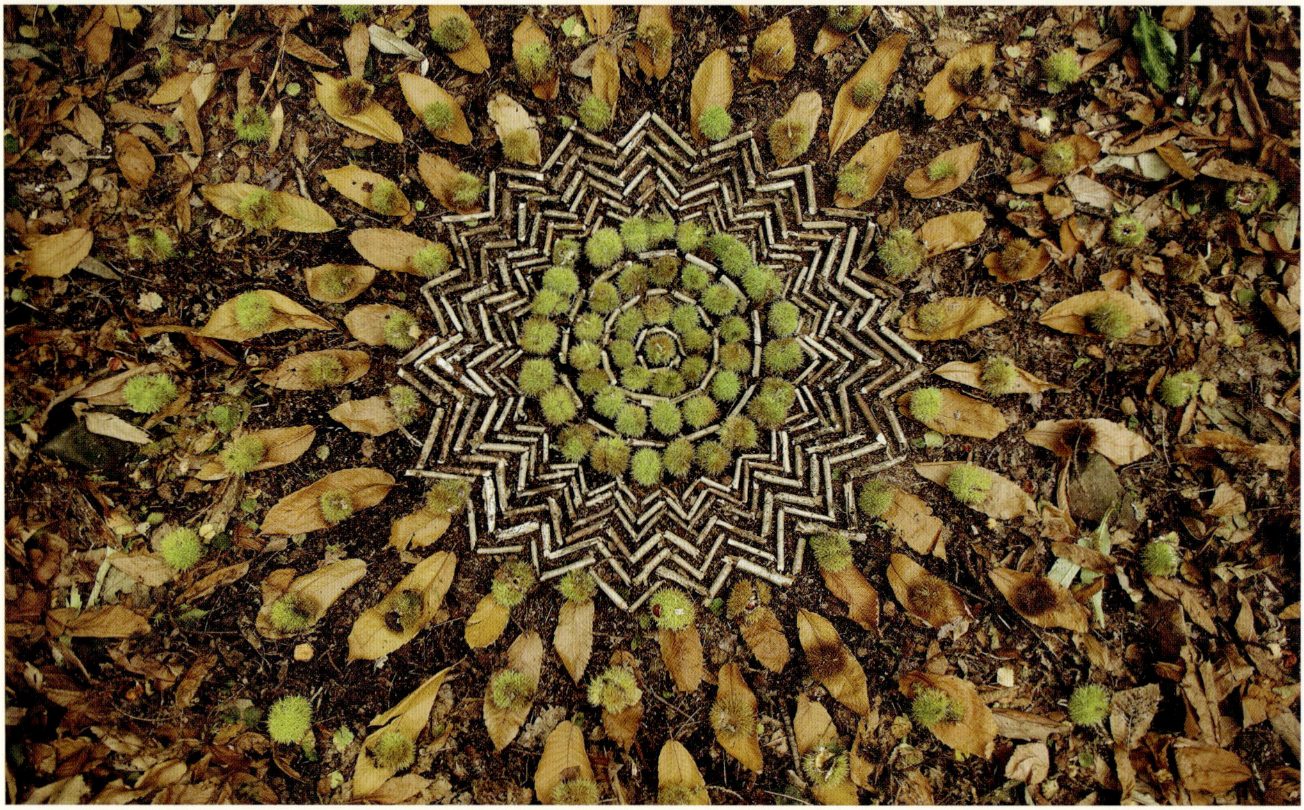

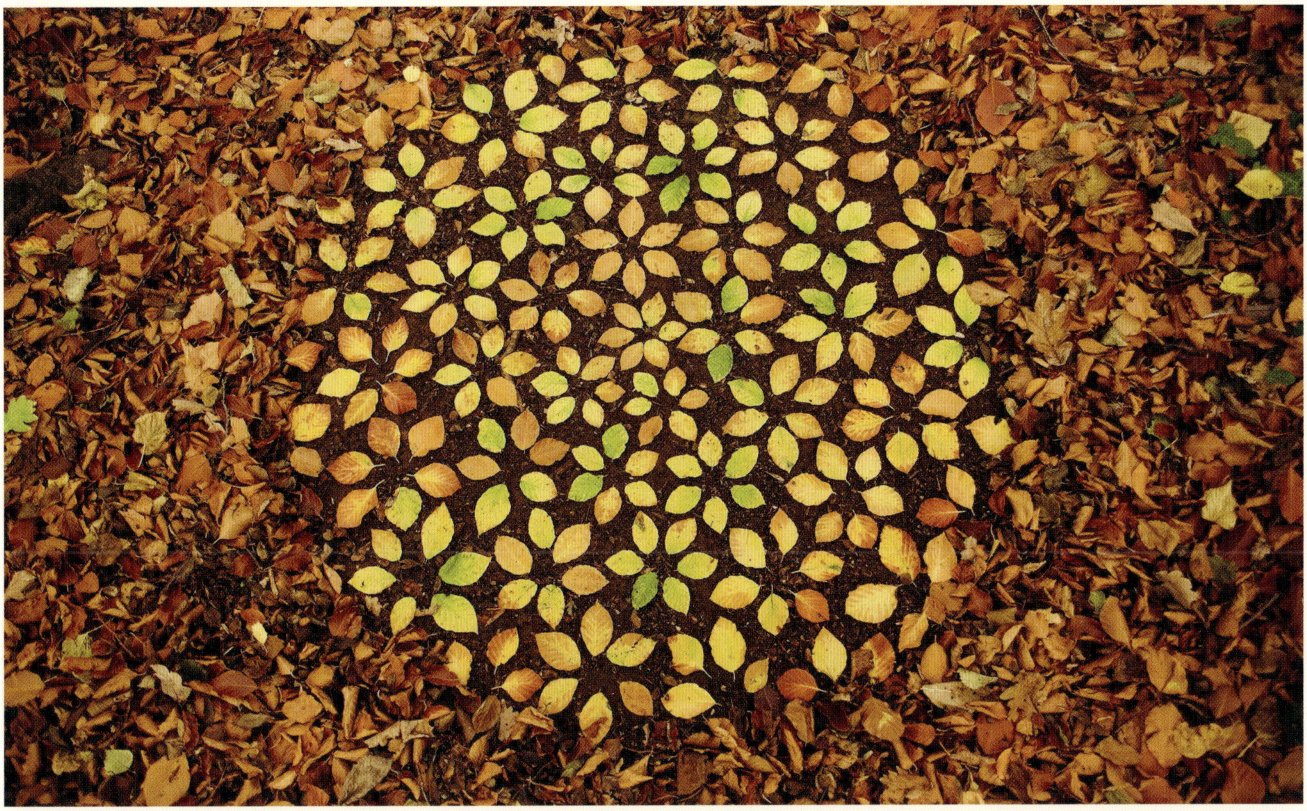

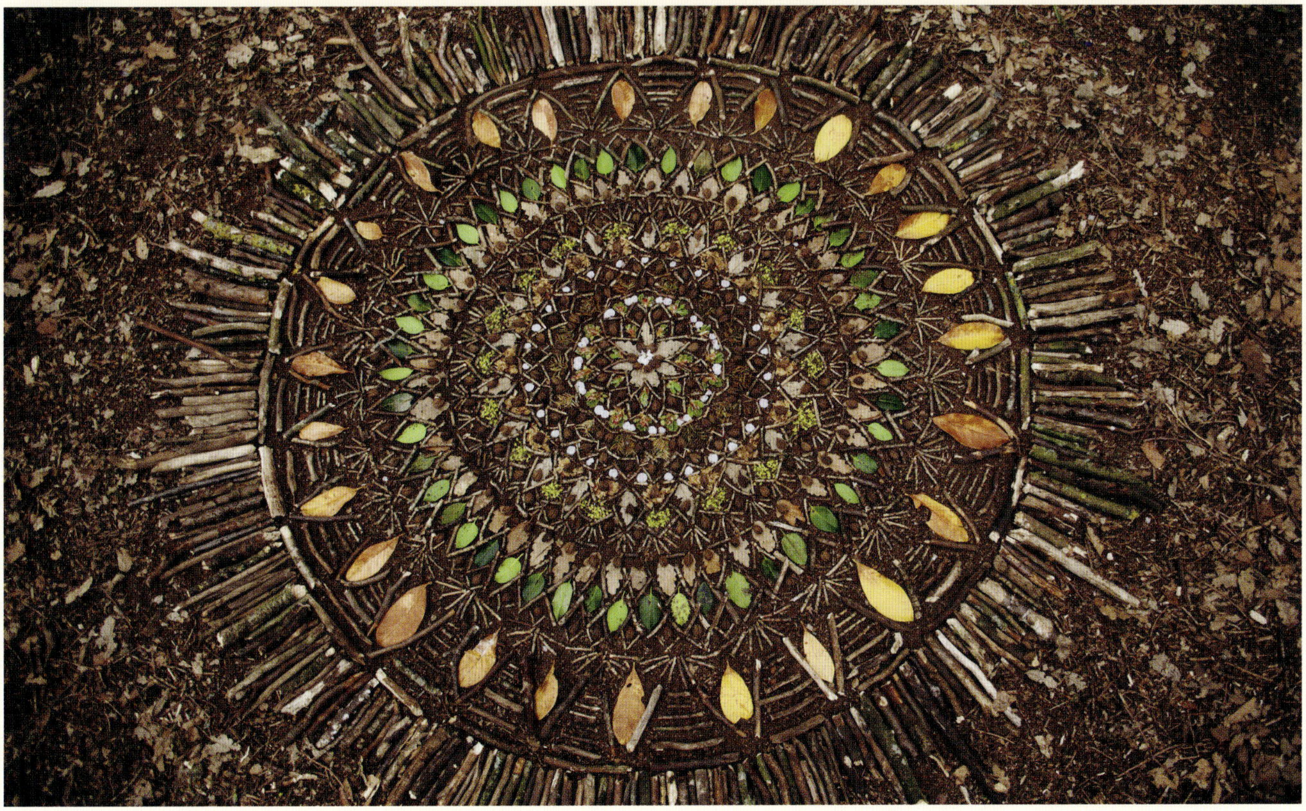

A Year at Weleda

In 2020, I was invited to spend a year working in a 13-acre biodynamic herb garden. "The Field" is the UK home of Weleda, makers of global natural, organic skin care and medicinal products. Based in Ilkeston, Derbyshire, what makes Weleda unique is the control they keep over the products they produce. By growing and harvesting all the sustainable ingredients themselves, they have a unique set of principles. Founded in the 1920s by Dr Rudolf Steiner, the philosopher and social reformer who many will know from the growth of Steiner-influenced schools, Weleda is now represented in fifty countries in five continents, upholding their core principles.

Weleda is a special community and company with great values, and the biodynamic approach to their product range is truly fascinating. In a nutshell, biodynamic gardening and food production is defined by the Biodynamic Association as "a holistic, ecological, and ethical approach." In practice, what I saw and learned was fascinating, but I wouldn't do justice trying to put down in words their company ethos and the ins and outs of their working practices, so I won't even try. But if you want to find out more, do check them out. Suffice to say, their approach to working land, respecting every living thing that they share space with, is totally in tune with my own working approach.

Back to Derbyshire

I was invited to create work over the course of a year, capturing the change of seasons and a year in the life cycle of the working environment. Part of the 100 years of Weleda celebrations in 2021, it was a fantastic opportunity for me to immerse myself within a very different environment and, for the year, be a small part in the land's story. It felt like being slipped into the holistic working cycle of Weleda for a brief period, resulting in my own response to this very special plot of land.

The most significant difference I found was being able to work with the knowledge that I would be undisturbed. I could immerse, respond, and create without one ear listening out for approaching dogs. I didn't have Foxy with me, so I chatted more to the wildlife around me—the robin ever curious, the kestrels nesting in a nearby ash, the fox whose eyes I met through a thicket of trees. I spent the year looking for the resident grass snakes and was finally rewarded when not actually looking for them, stumbling across one on a path through the meadow. One lunchtime I sat and shared my lunch with a blackbird, who became so friendly she spent the next hour hopping into and continually rearranging the work I was trying to make; it mattered not, the friendship far more precious.

Weleda is a place where everything—plants, wildlife, and we humans—works harmoniously together, sharing space, equal billing. I came to see it as an oasis of how, if we put our minds to it, humans could have a much more positive relationship with, and impact on, the planet and the flora and fauna we share it with. Within this context, I felt very at home at the Field, part of the environment, at one with all the living things around me.

These are my observations, month by month, season by season, during the year I spent there.

***Below:** My first work at Weleda, on a wet March day, when the smell of damp rotting deadwood filled the air.*

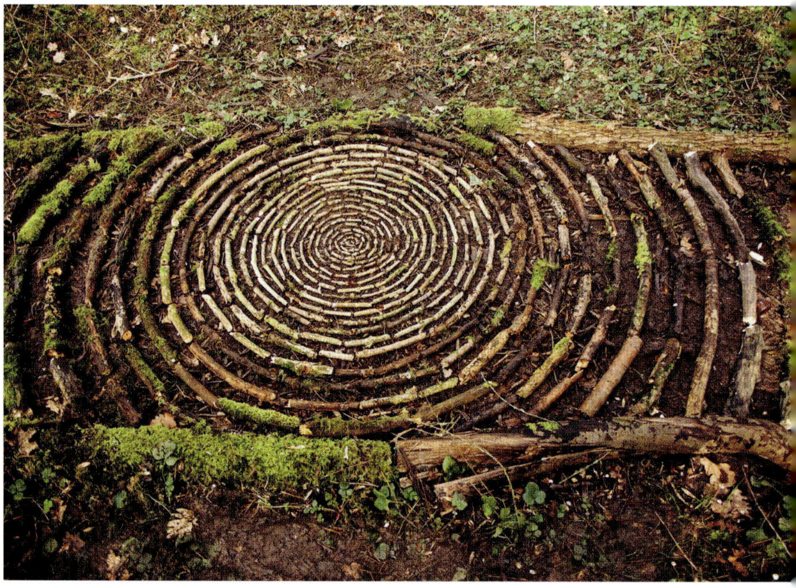

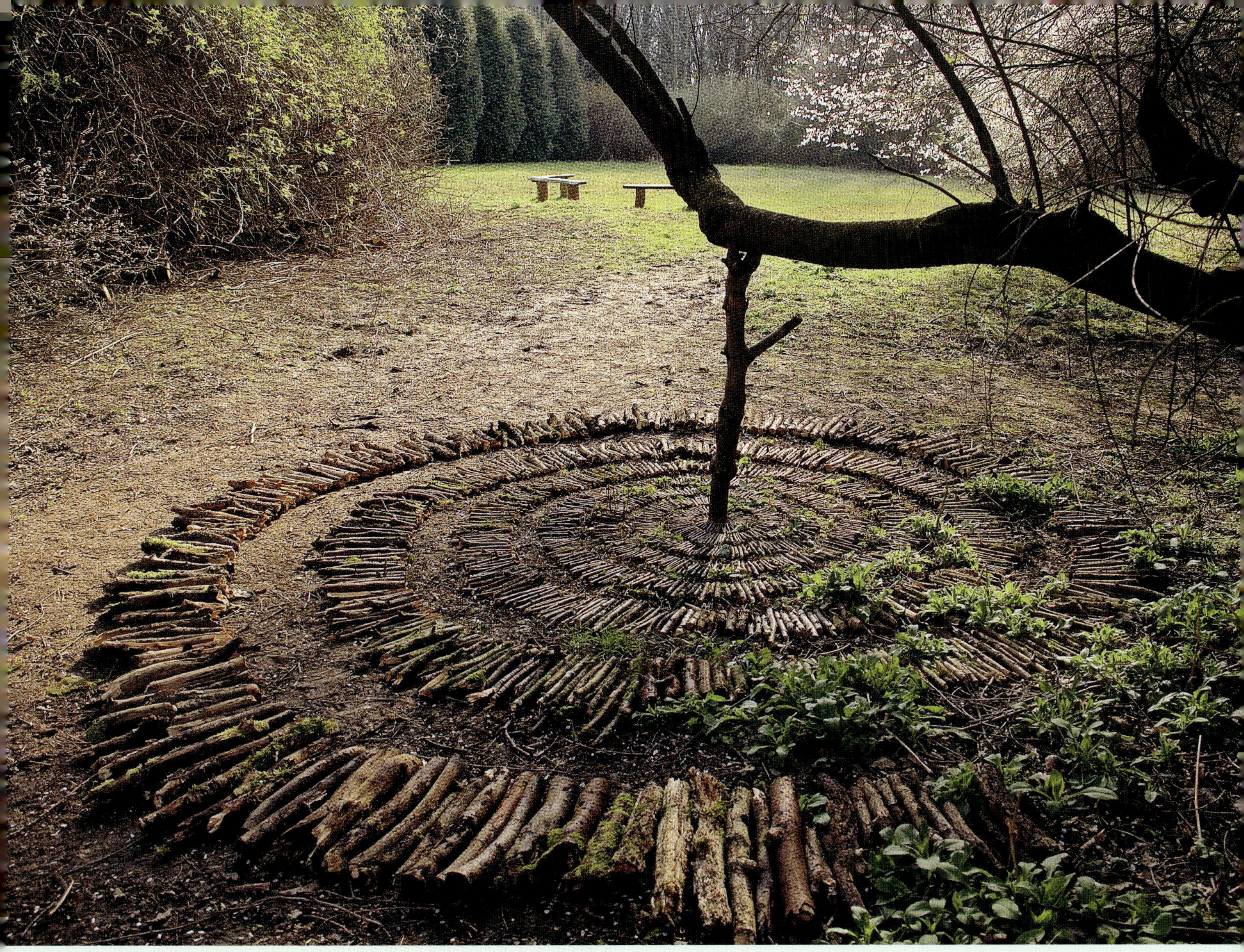

Spring

March

Change
Hope
Help
Support

I began my year as spring was knocking on the door, yet to take hold but definitely there, silently waiting for the right moment. Unfamiliar landscapes waiting to be discovered, with woodland still dank, the ground wet beneath me, the branches still bare, decomposition in full swing. Work on the land going on around me was necessary, with the promise of reward to come further in the year. With the robin as company and dirt under nail, I made friends with the trees. The laurel provided, branches supported, and I walked increasingly familiar paths, waiting for the land to wake.

***Above:** I loved this log supporting the branch; it seemed very symbolic of the Weleda ethos.*

Below: *Low-water twigs next to the pond. I'm drawn to the reflection of the blue sky and cloud.*

Right top: *Laurel and twigs on a standing log. The depth of field between the work and ground created an interesting illusion here.*

Right bottom: *More laurel play. Even in early spring there's color to be found.*

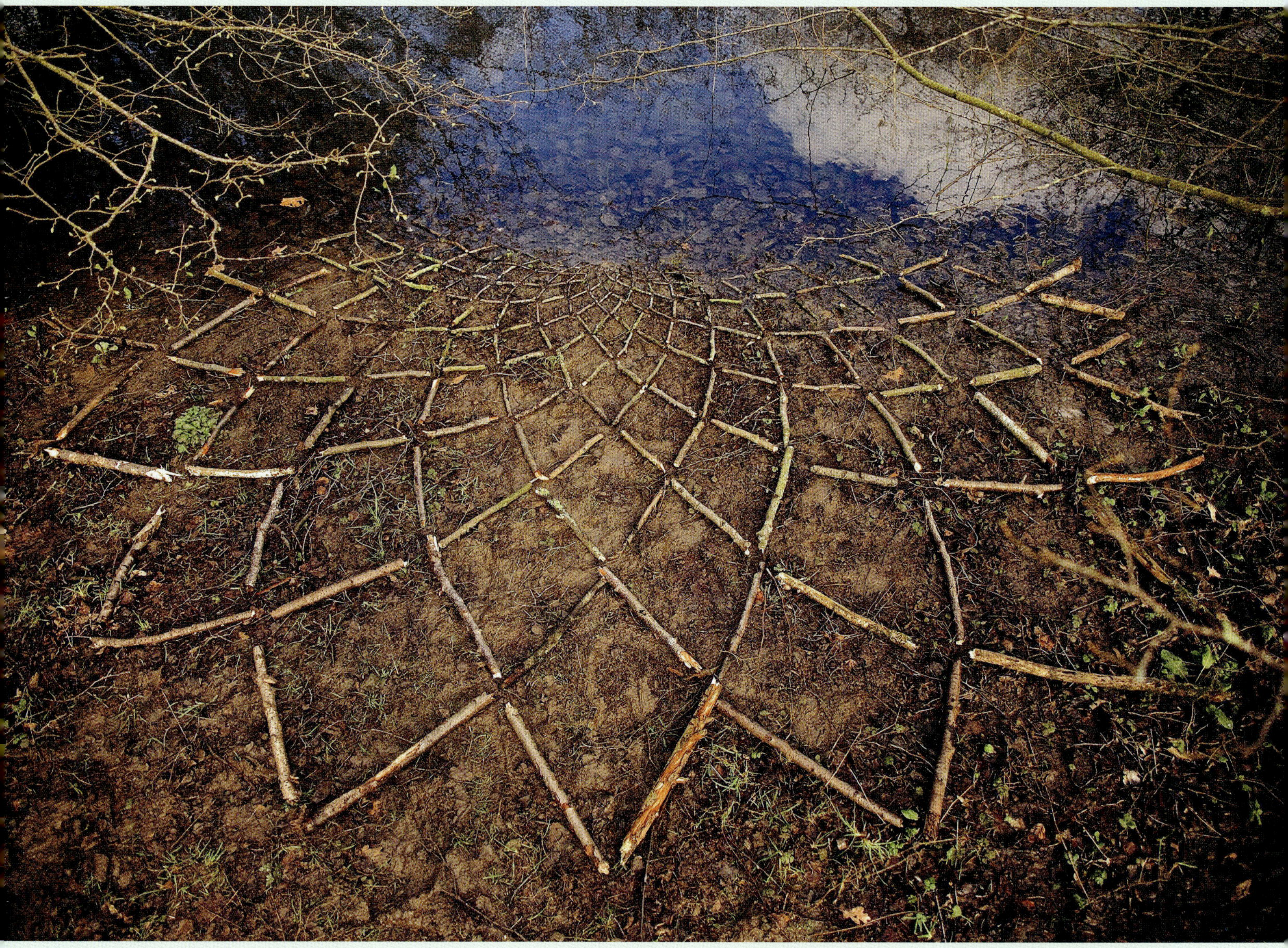

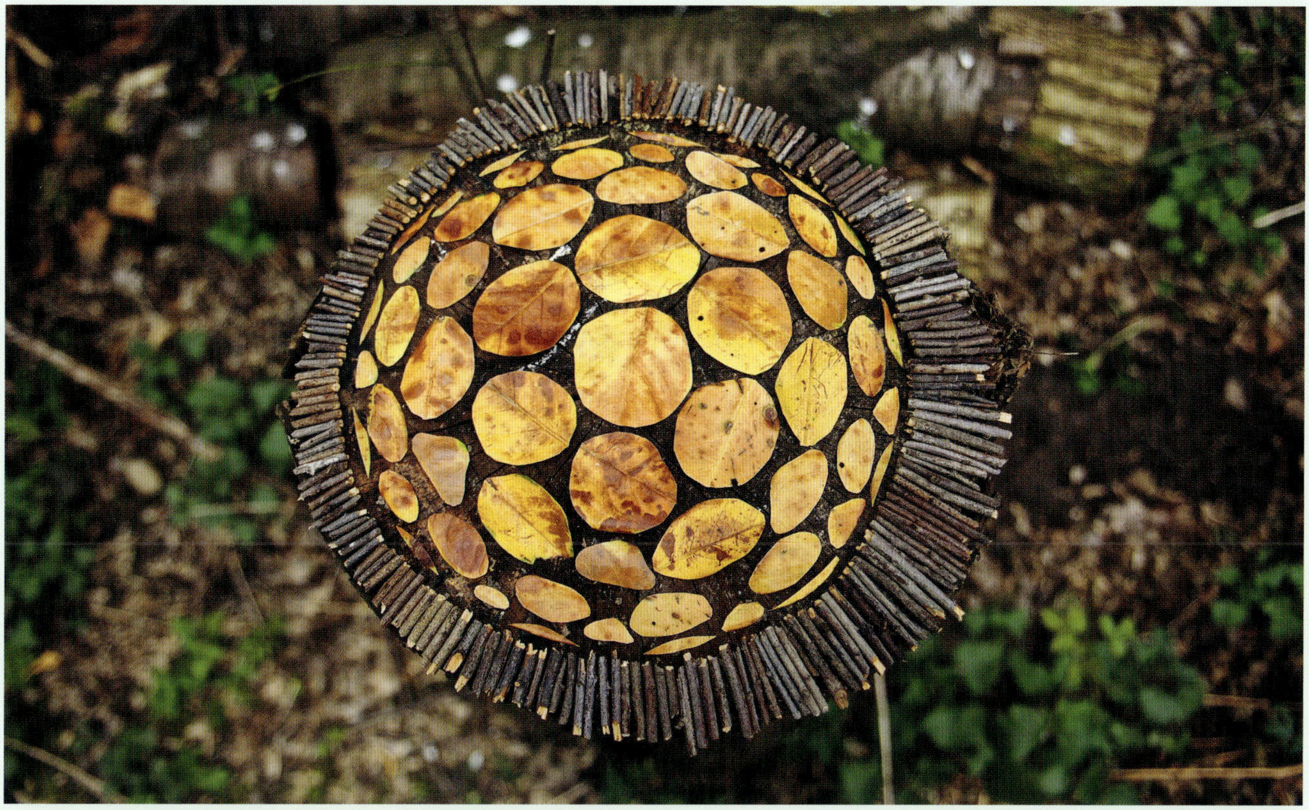

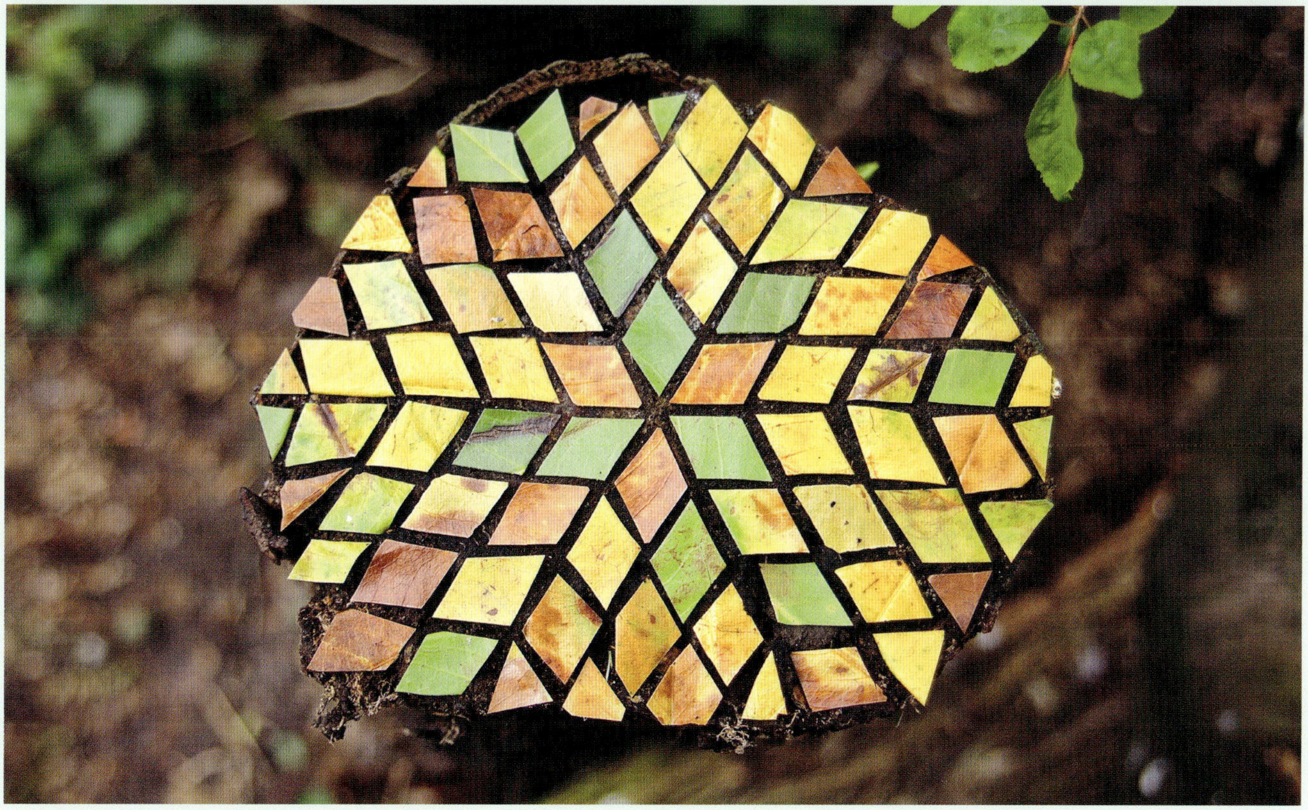

April

Growth
Flourish
Busy
Emerge

Change came quick; a new week, a new palette, a new picture. The first crop was harvested, geum root with leaves as a gift, and creatively I grew with the land. Cherry plum blossom burst on branches; a new light crept through the trees. The weeks pass, a transformed landscape, the greens have purpose, working the land intensifies, cropped chamomile, and a gift for a tree.

***Right:** Working with Weleda's waste product after it returns from the production line to be composted.*

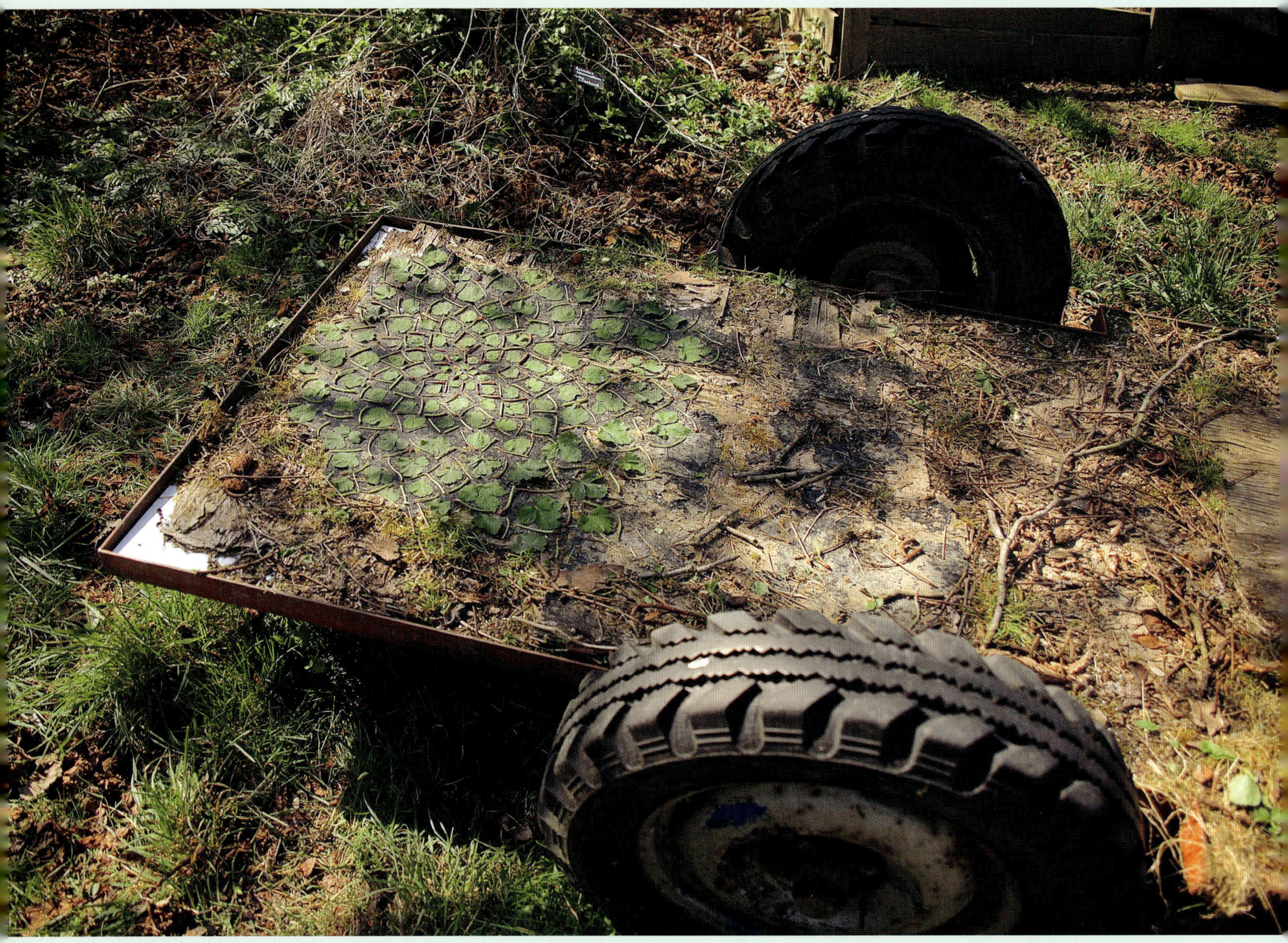

***Above:** Utilizing an old trailer to create with harvested geum leaves.*

***Right:** My work at Weleda was often about responding to the locations that called to me that day. I'd passed this tree base on many occasions and not seen the opportunity.*

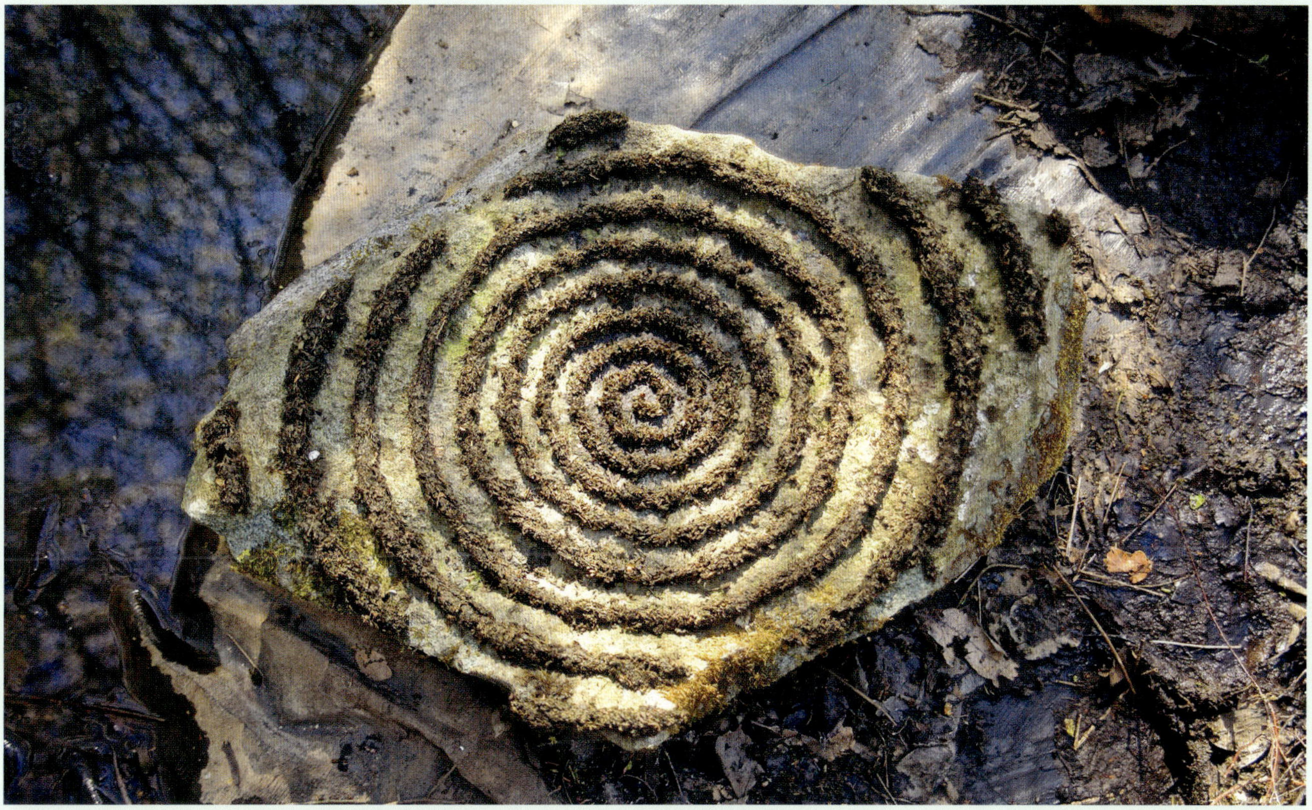

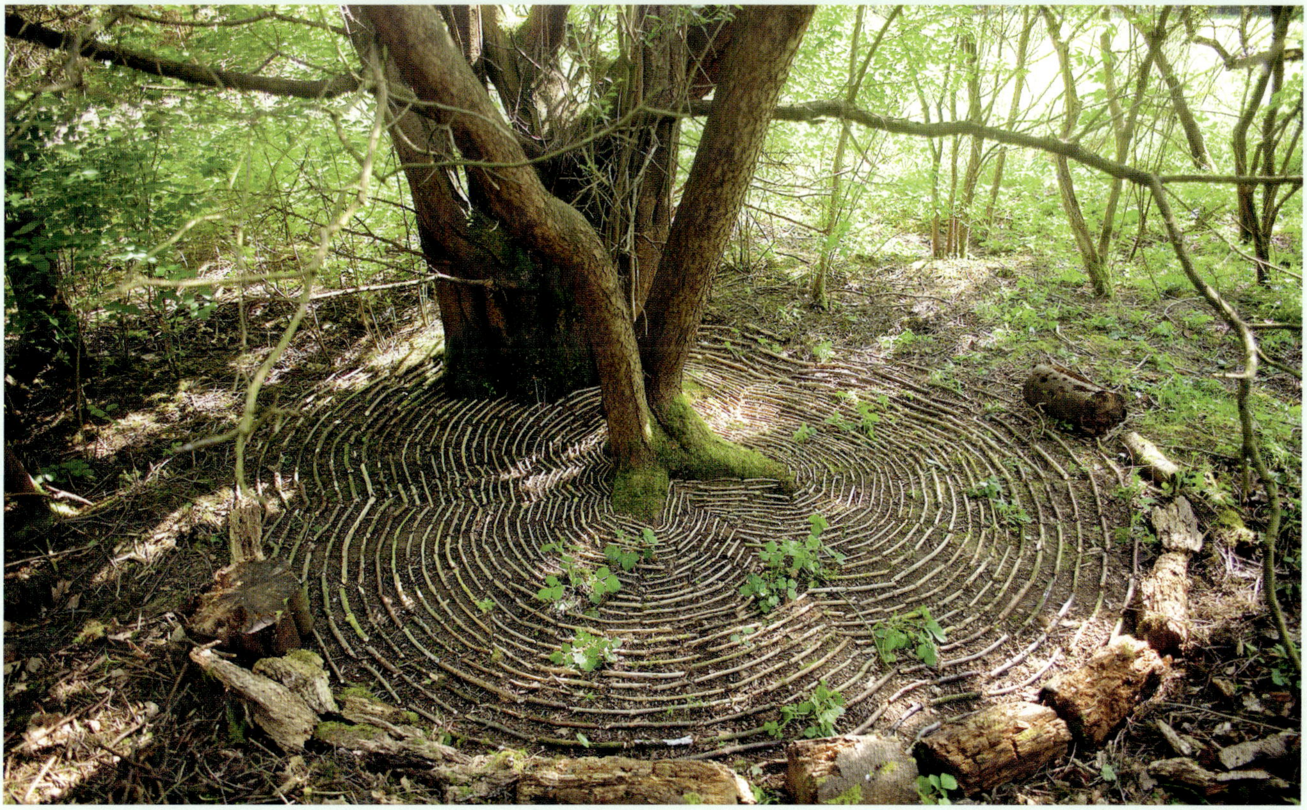

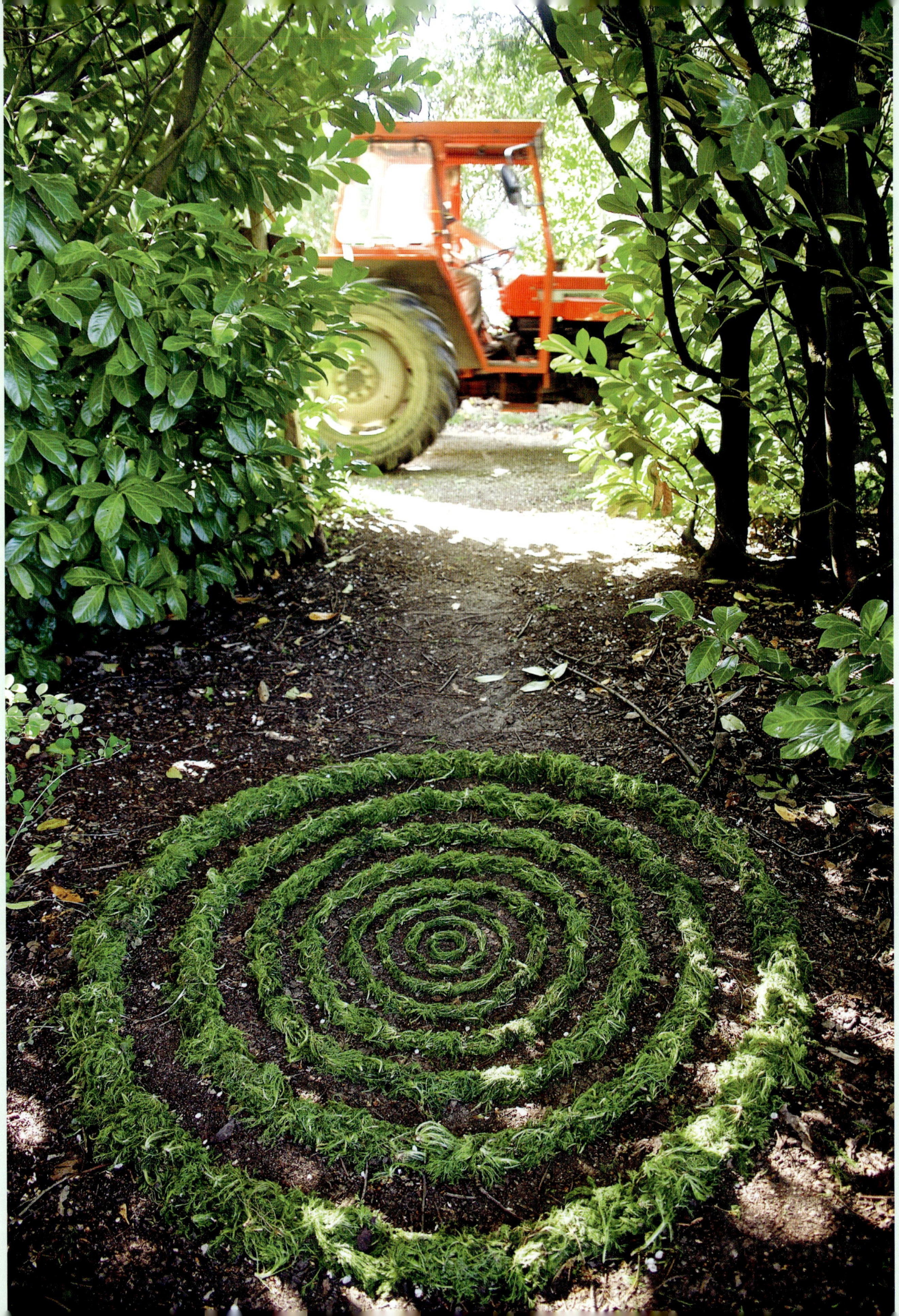

May

Life
Lush
Early
Fall

The sun shines and I'm searching for shade. The Field grows quickly; young leaves from the silver birch join catkins on the floor. We keep watch for the kestrels nesting in the ash, a familiar call as the green woodpecker busies somewhere in the distance. The fox takes advantage of our safe, welcoming space.

Below: *Finding respite in the shade. I remember being caught out by the heat and seeking shade to stop me from burning. Not a great reflection of a beautiful May afternoon.*

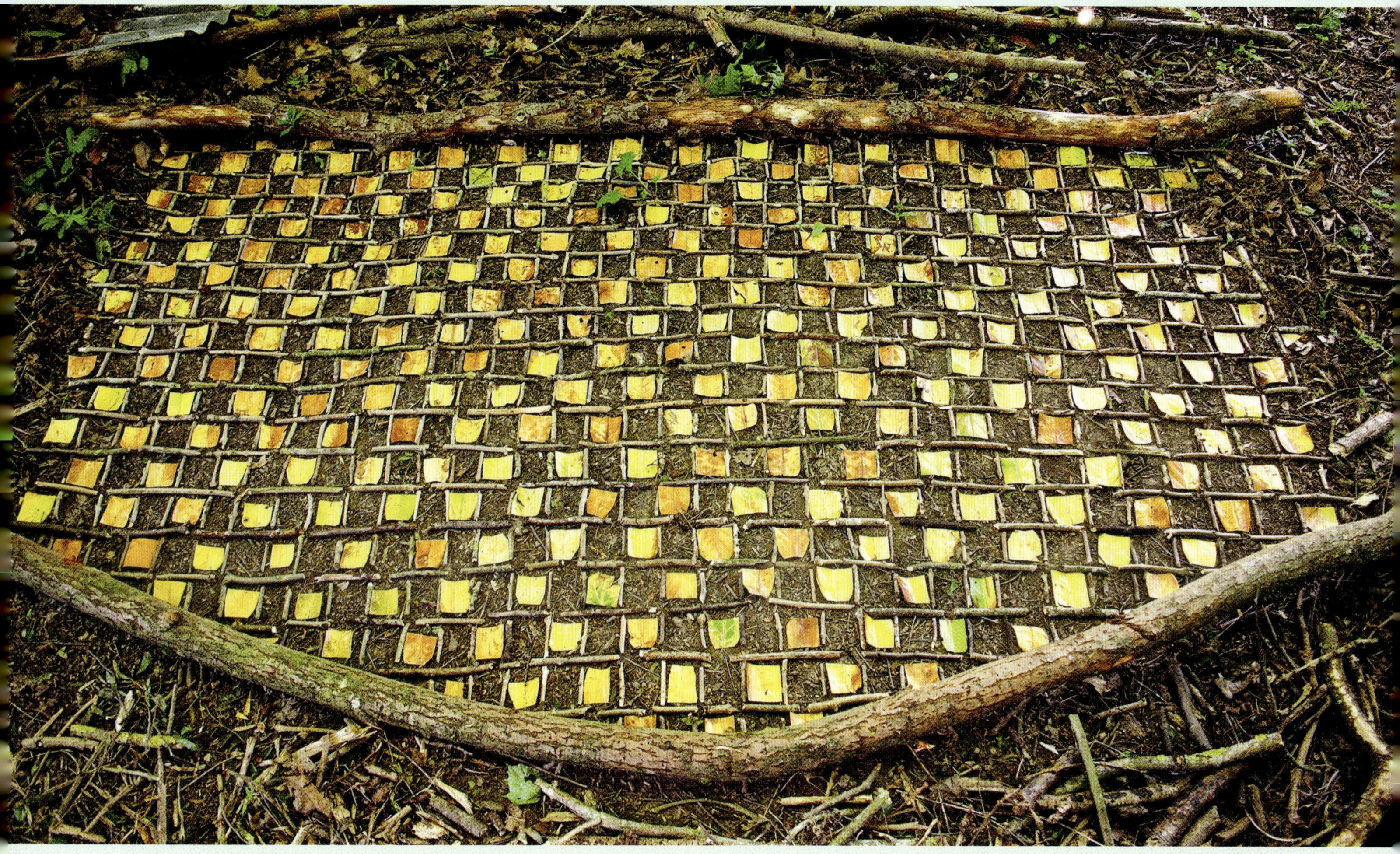

Left: *Fitting in around the working environment. I loved how I was very quickly accepted as part of the working life of the Field. This is harvested chamomile.*

Summer

June

Crop
Harvest
Color
Create

Thriving, alive, hope in full swing! Smiles on faces as work at the Field begins to reap reward. There's genuine excitement for the calendula harvest; I'm given buckets of flower heads to say thank you to the crop.

Below: *Calendula crop. Returning harvested flower heads to the calendula beds.*

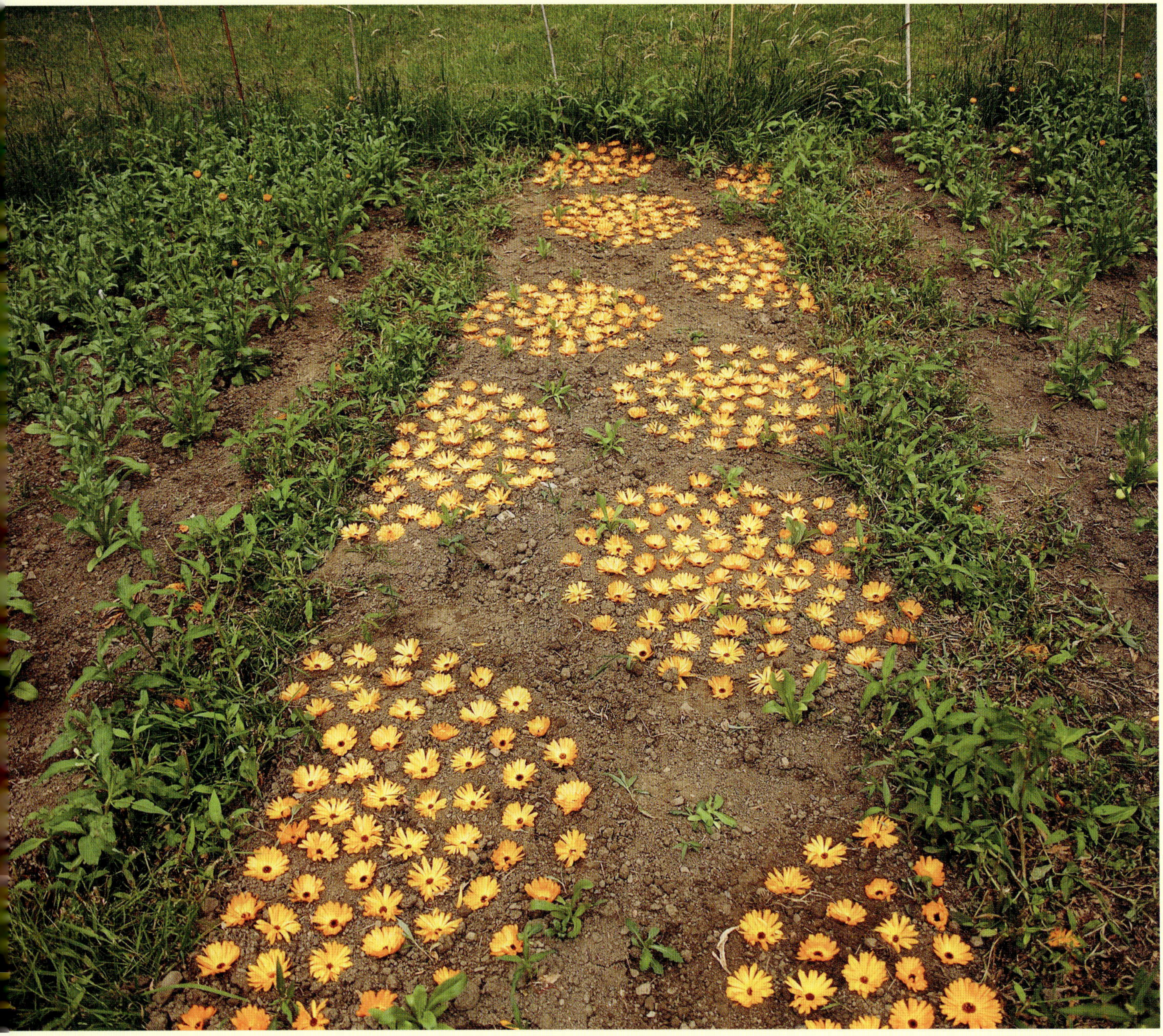

Below: *A summer nest. I enjoyed creating these little works on the paths for staff to stumble upon.*

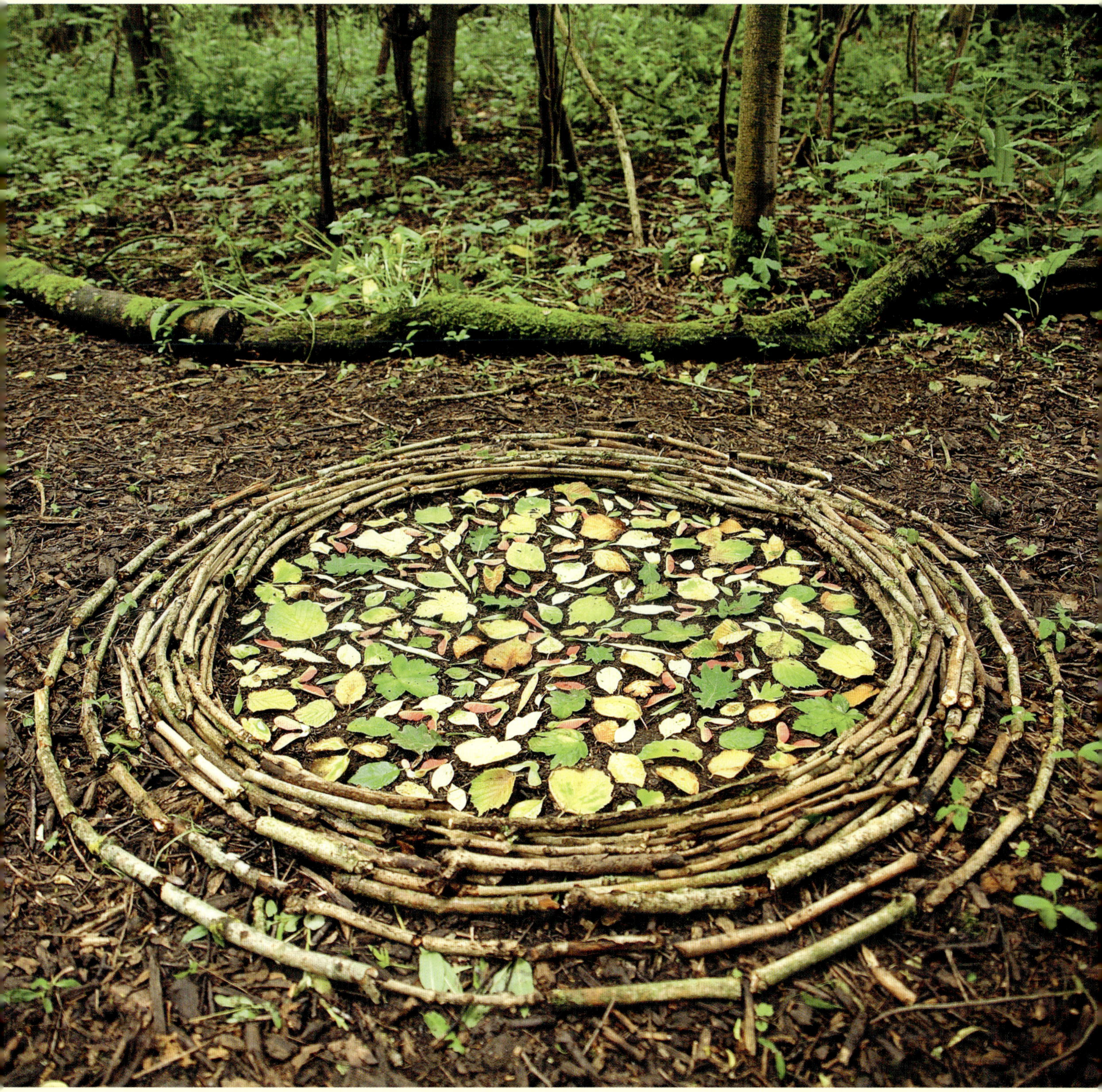

July

Follow
Pick
Shift
Subtle

A subtle change in the air, a hint of the future, with treasures to be found under horse chestnut. Unwanted leaves begin to litter the floor. An invite to pick thistle was met with reluctance; a pep talk was needed to remind me of the land's role within the Weleda family. Alive with insects, the hives in full swing, hands stirring, picking, churning, this was the Field with all cogs turning.

Right: *Mixed leaves. As the year drew on, the materials continued to change, allowing me to celebrate the diverse species at Weleda.*

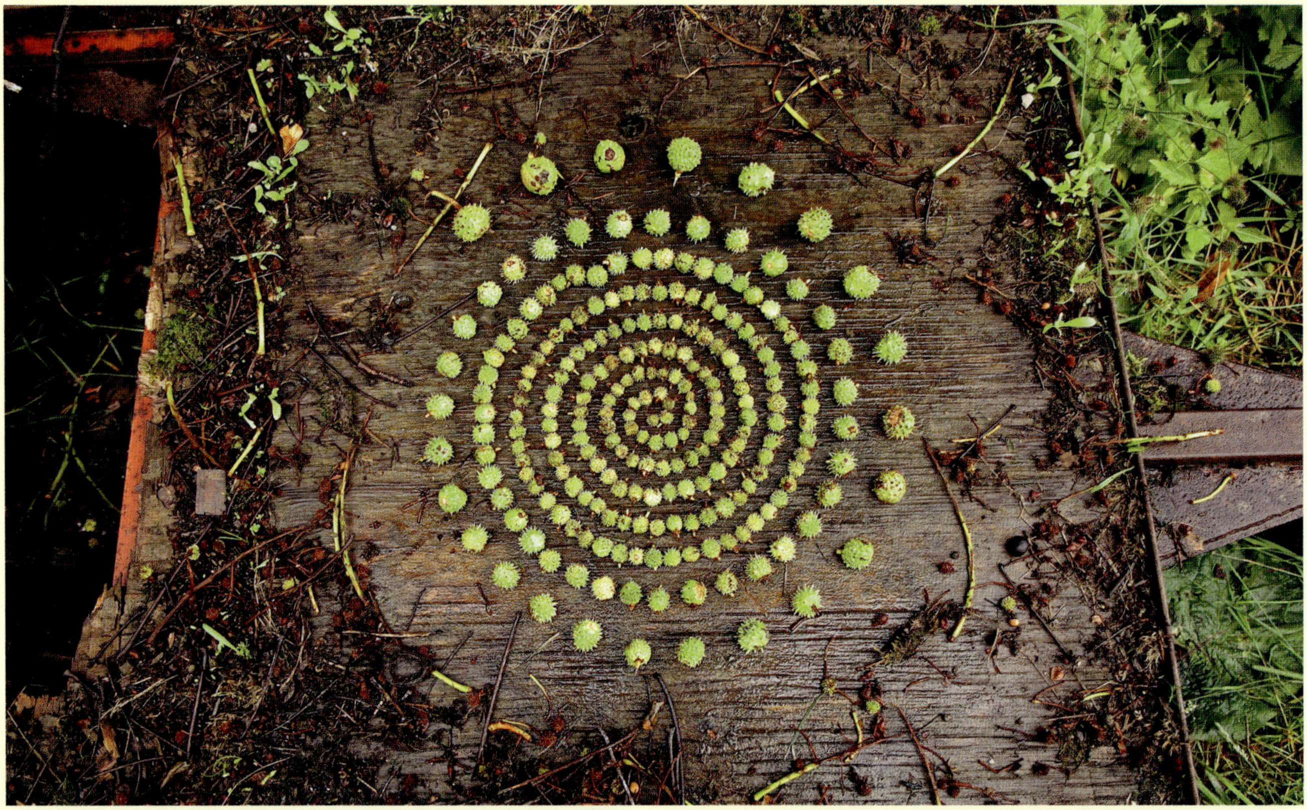

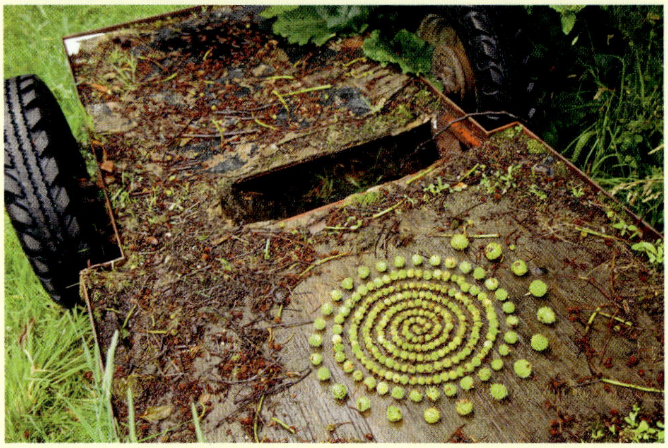

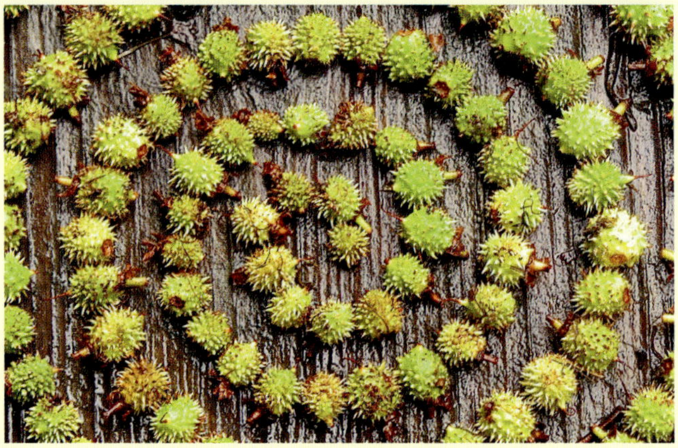

Above: *Early fall horse chestnuts on the old trailer again, a nice background for these little green gems.*

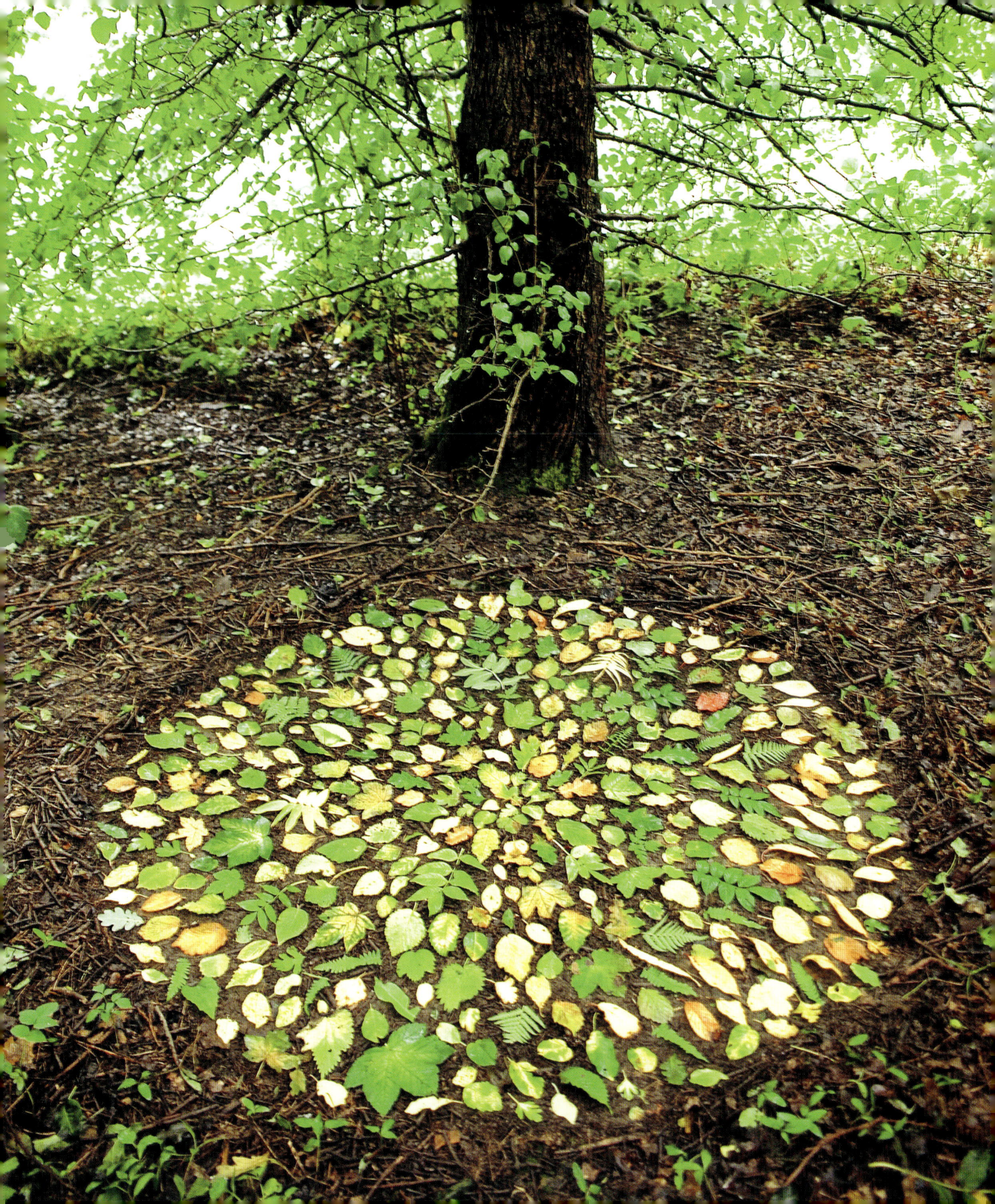

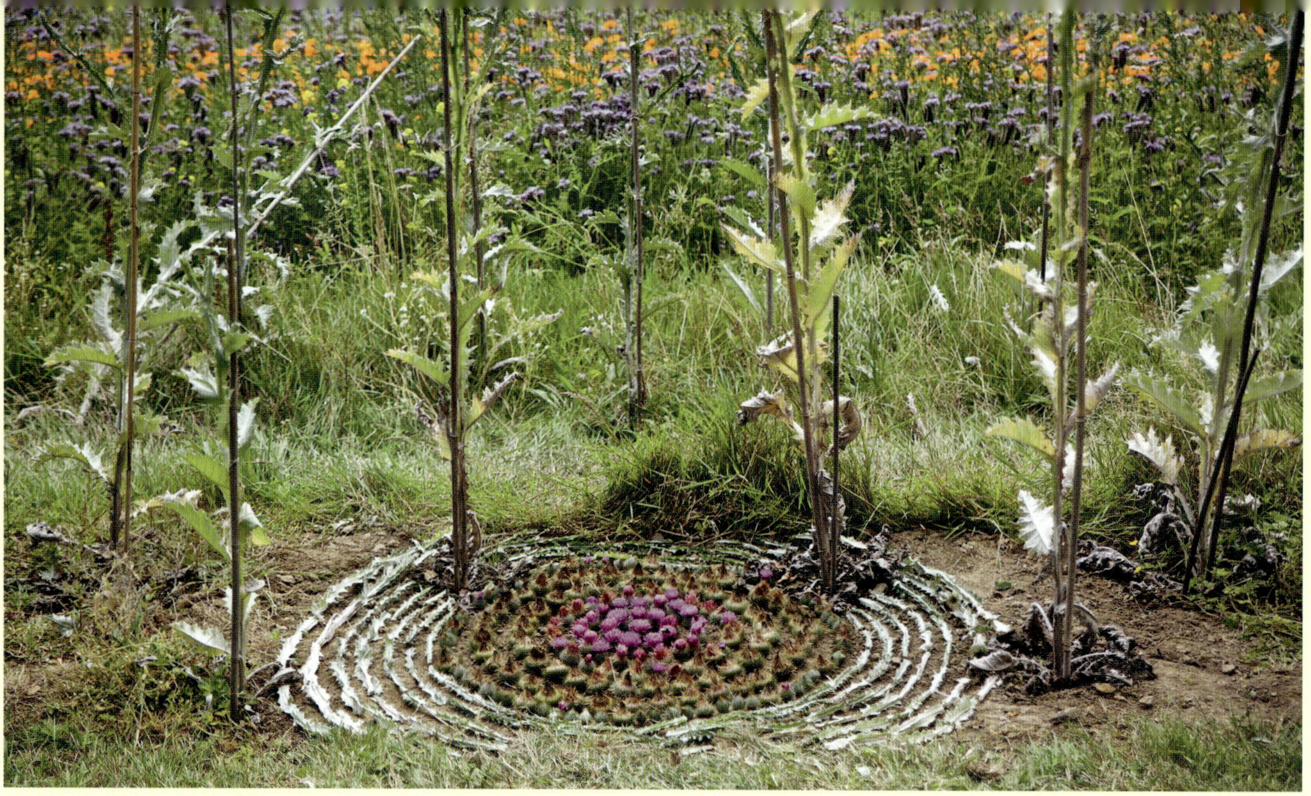

Above: *After the thistle harvest. I was invited to pick the remaining thistle heads, and after being gently reminded that this was a crop and the beds would be cleared soon, I allowed myself to do so. As a nonpicker of living materials, it was a strange experience.*

Below: *Some very early signs of the autumnal color to come, in this Weleda mandala.*

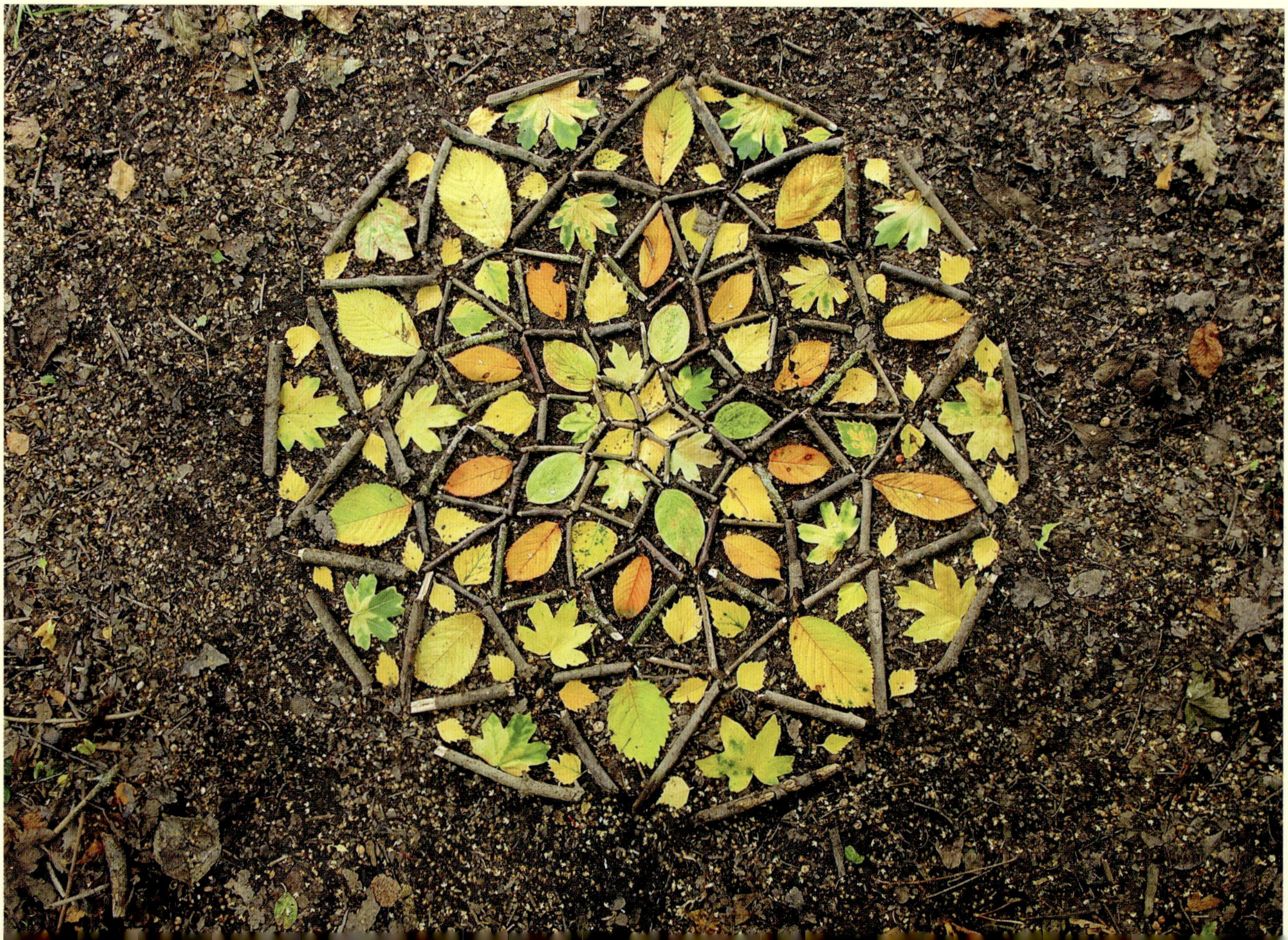

August

Dropping
Seeing
Sorting
Watching

Summer fading means invitations to play; under the oak with the hive, leaves tried to blow away. Silver birch by the pond, green with duckweed. Attentions begin to wander to the winter to come, when the land returns to sleep and its caretakers begin again.

***Below:** Silver birch leaf arrangement. I was often drawn back to the pond at different stages throughout the year.*

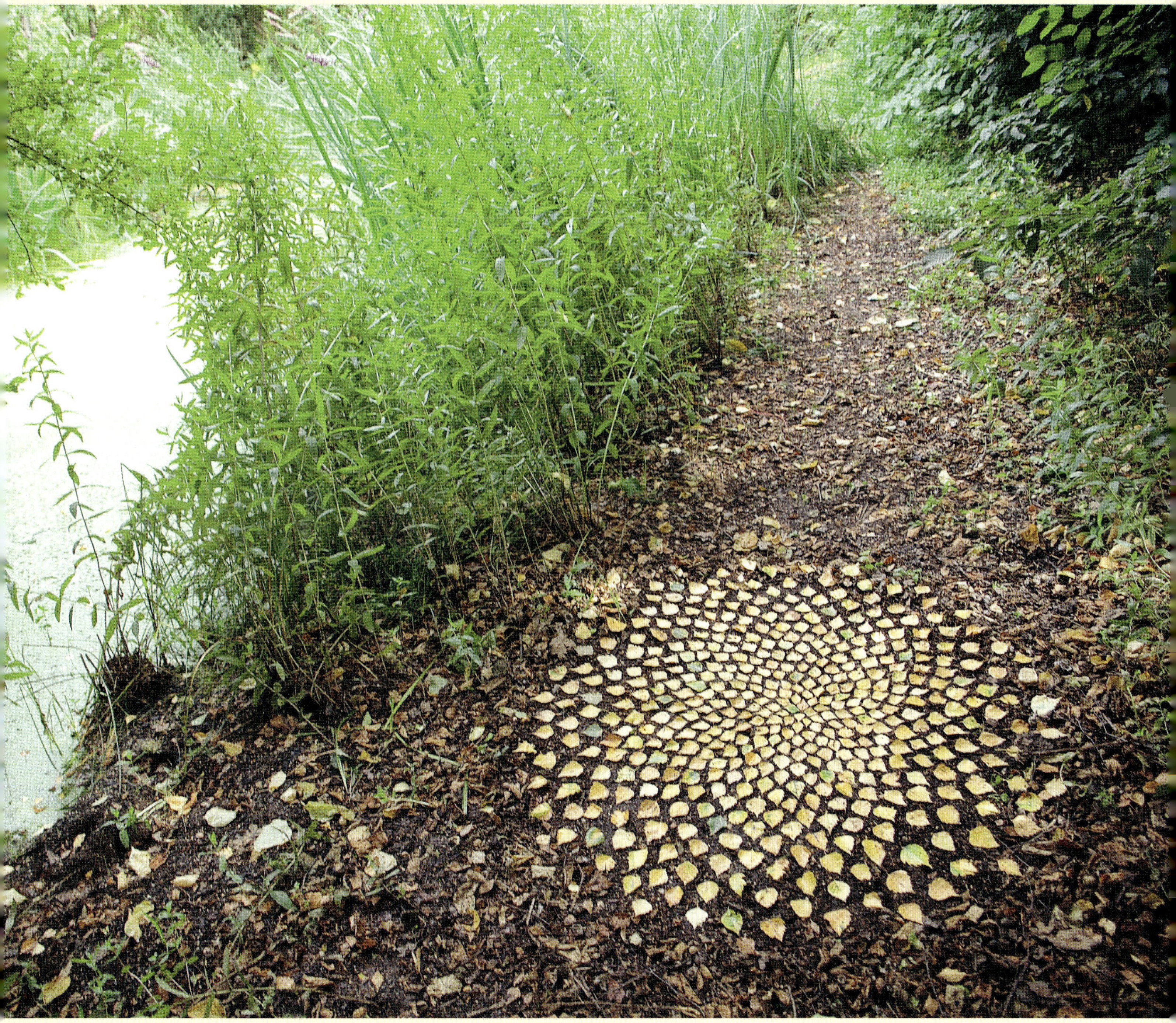

Below: *Under Weleda oak. Look carefully at the oak leaves that continue under the twig spiral.*

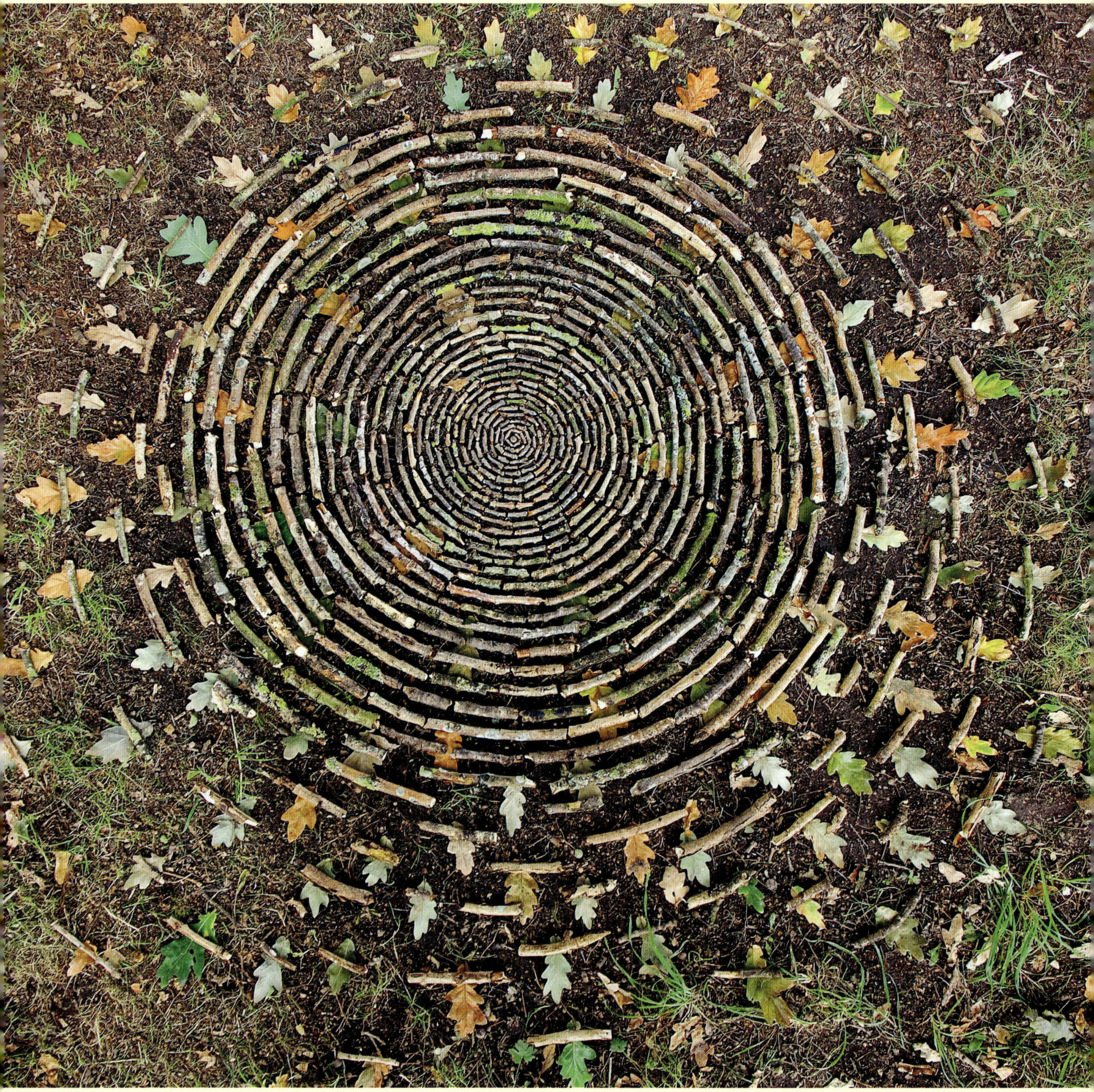

Fall

September

Shape
Color
Layer
Construct

Oak on a path, hawthorn hidden in the bramble. A process of layering sumac, oak, field maple, and birch, experimenting with new. While elsewhere the old and decay begin to catch my attention.

Below: *Hawthorn gifts. I like finding these little pockets of space to fill. This was directly under the hawthorn, so the work feels very at home here.*

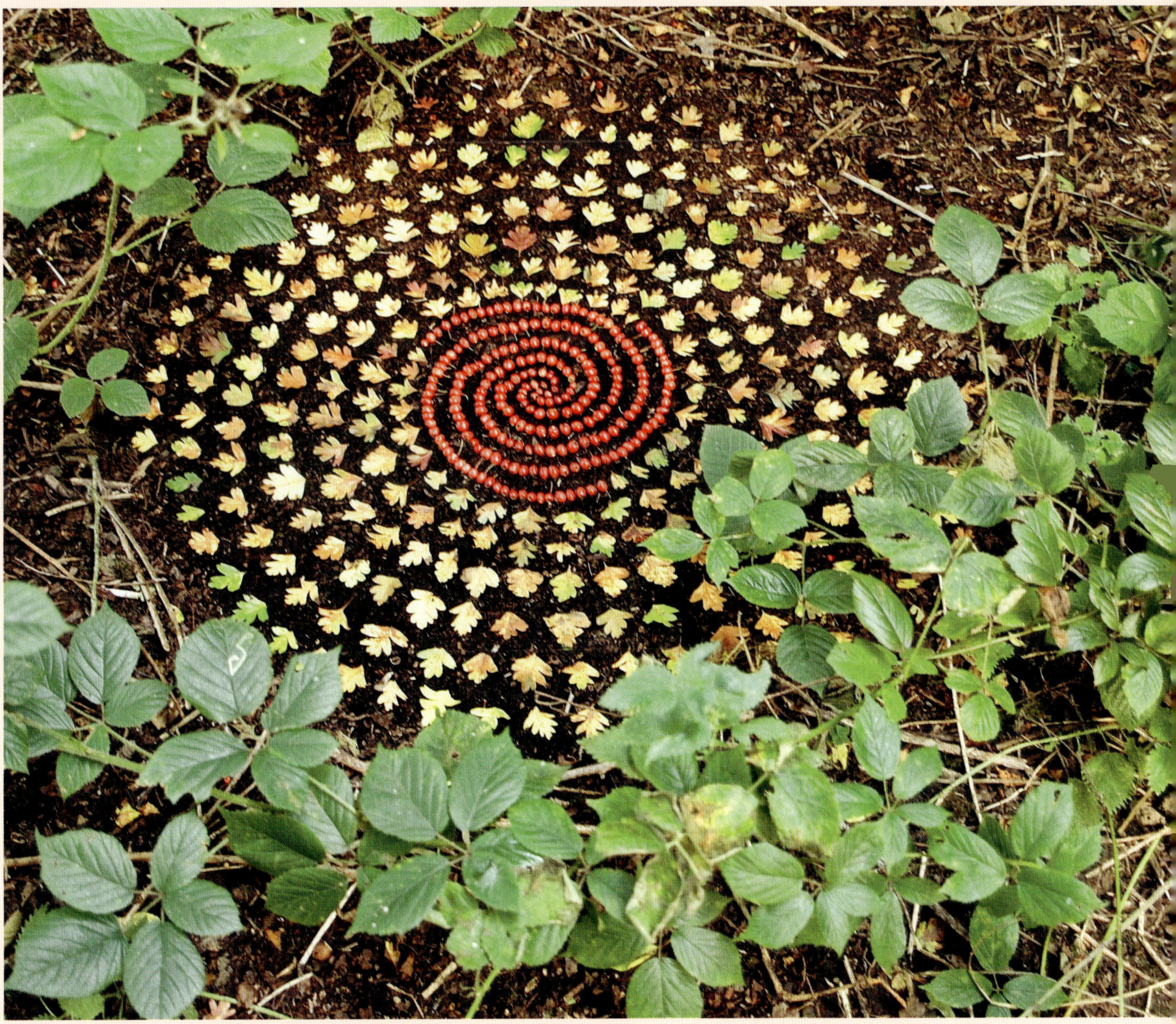

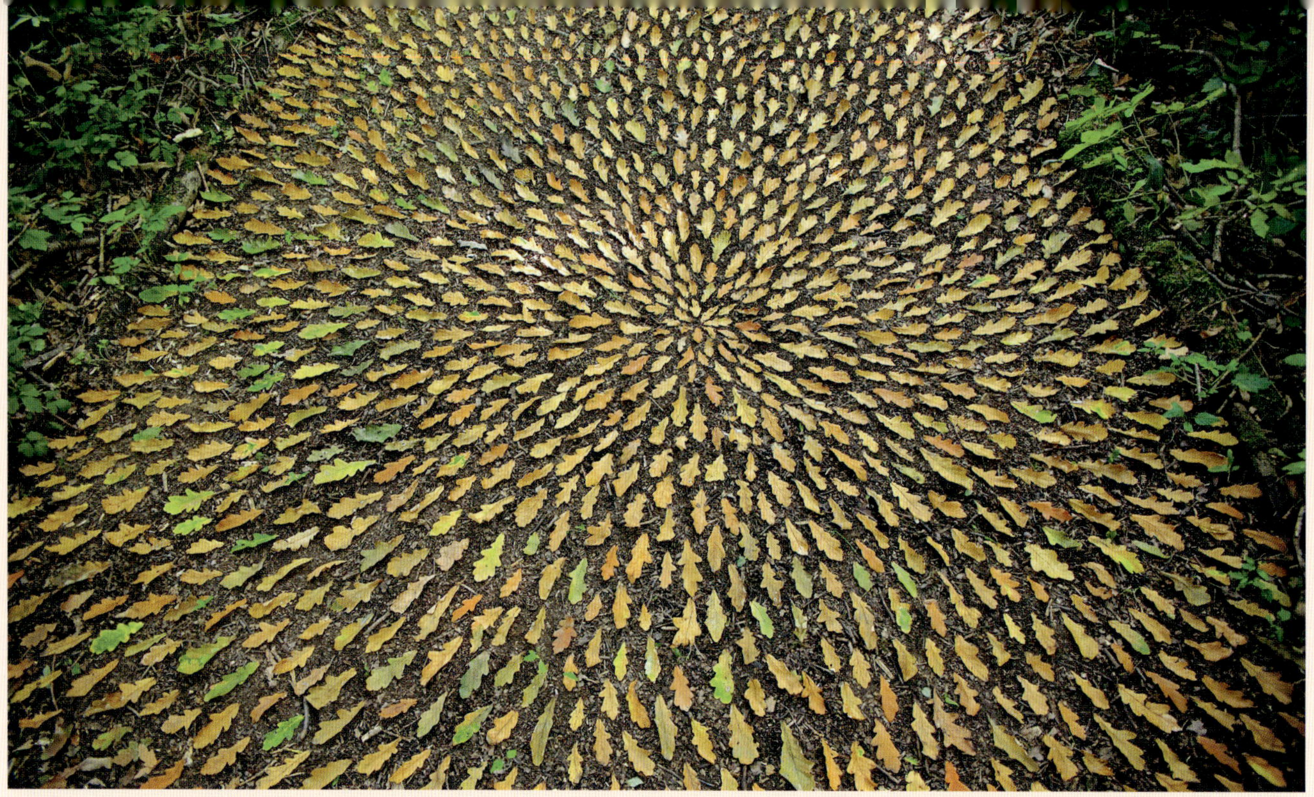

Above: Oak on path. I often tell people that the weather is a partner in all the work I make. It's very rare to have the conditions to spend this long placing leaves.

Below: Layered leaves. Silver birch on field maple, on oak, on sumac. Trying something new, I really liked this structured layering approach and was quite taken by the results.

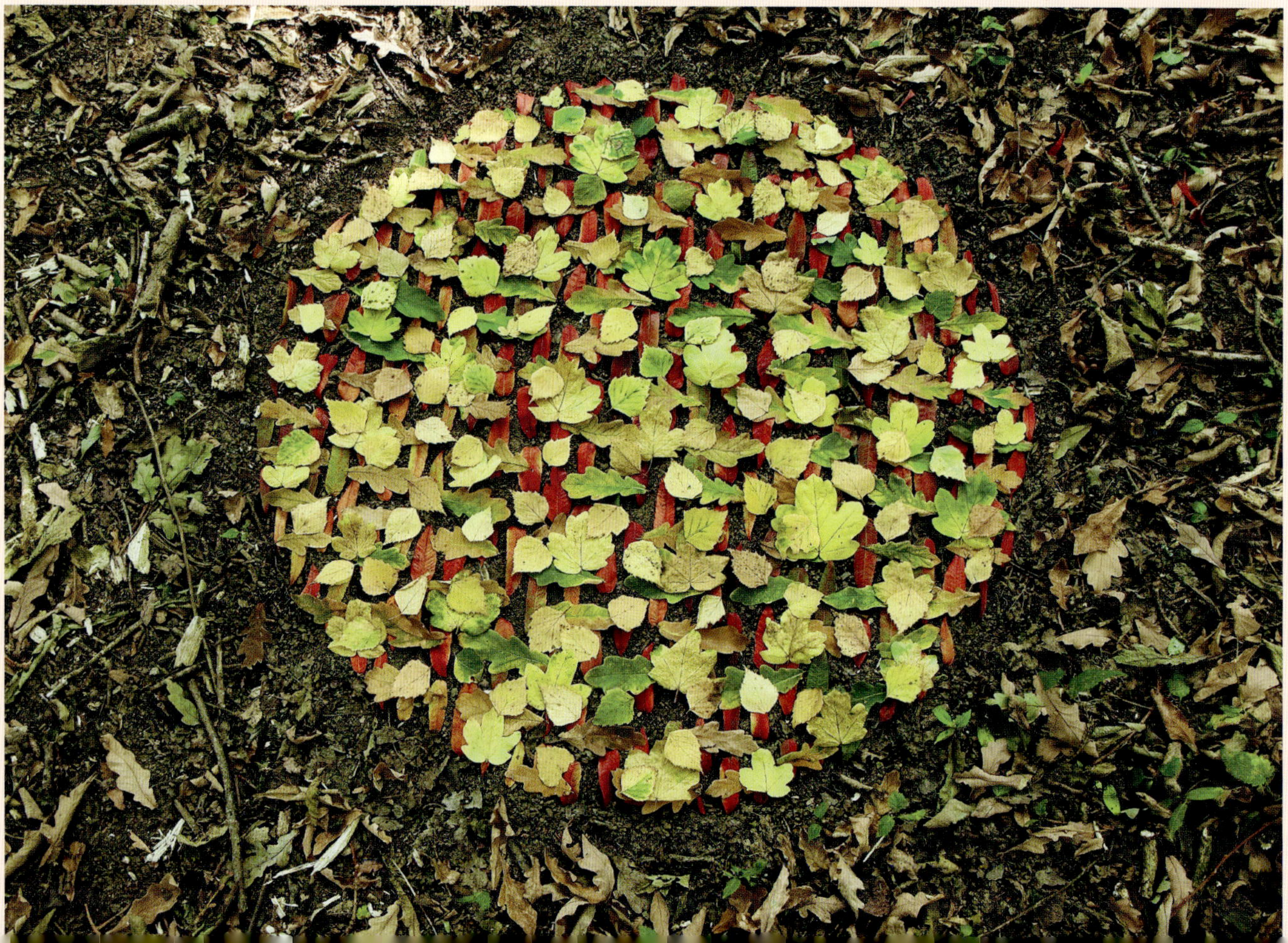

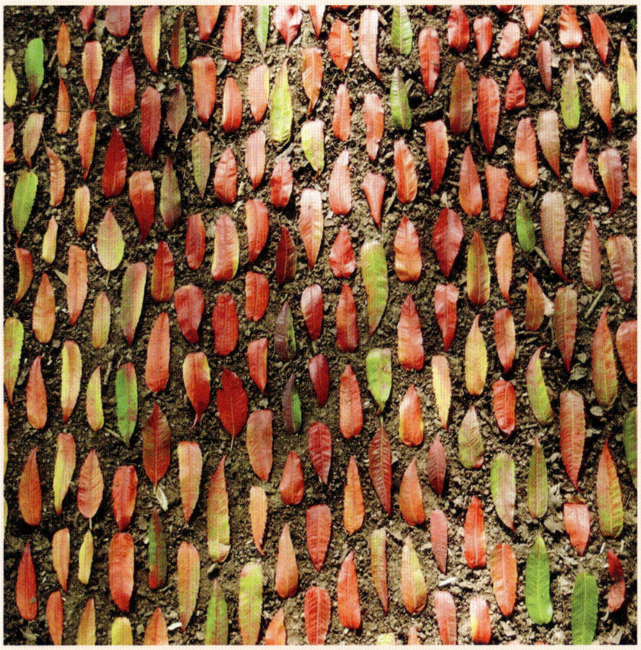

Above: *The beginning. This was the first step to the previous layered piece, lovely sumac leaves.*

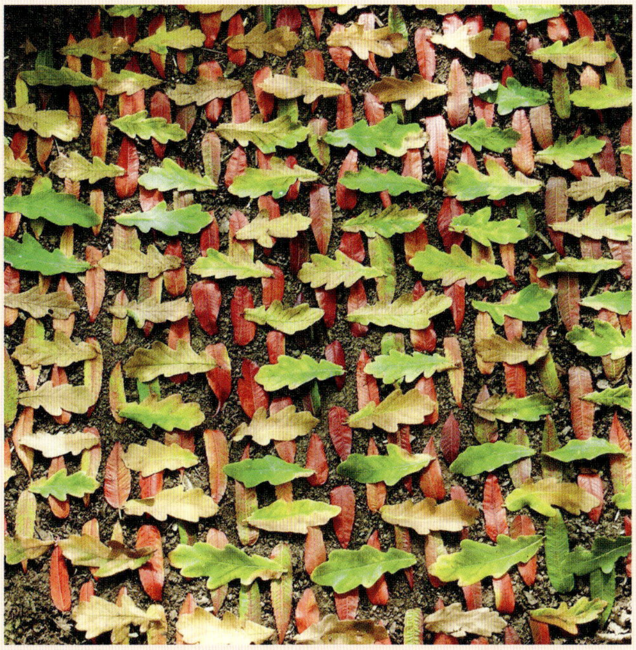

Above: *Making the layers, oak on sumac. Midway through the layering process, I think each layer worked well in its own right.*

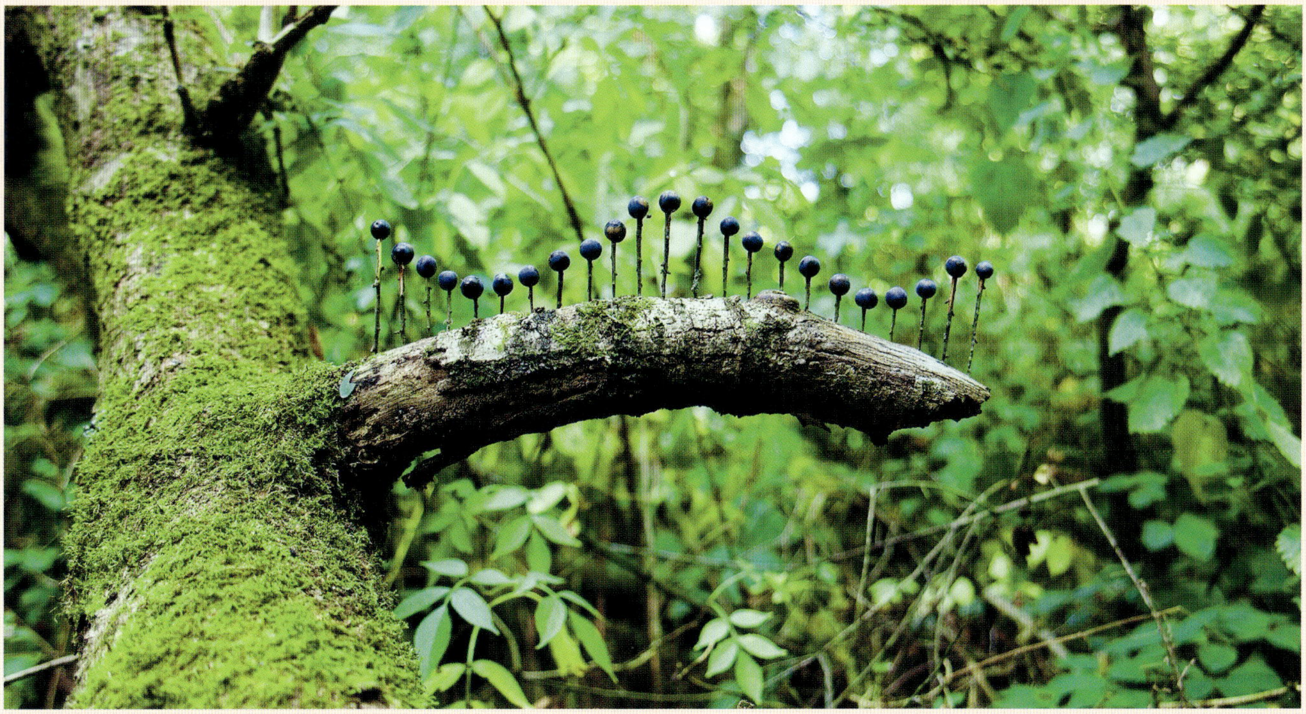

Above: *Blackthorn fruit (sloes) and thorns on deadwood outcrop. In fall, as well as the obvious color I also begin to notice the decay again.*

October

Work
Hands
Hurry
Alter

Back in the woods, damp returns to the air, blackthorn on log, hazel on path; I'm lost in fall. The wings of a resting migrant hawker teach me a thing or two about beauty.

Right: *Fall mandala. Using the different colors, shapes, and textures to create pattern is something everyone can try.*

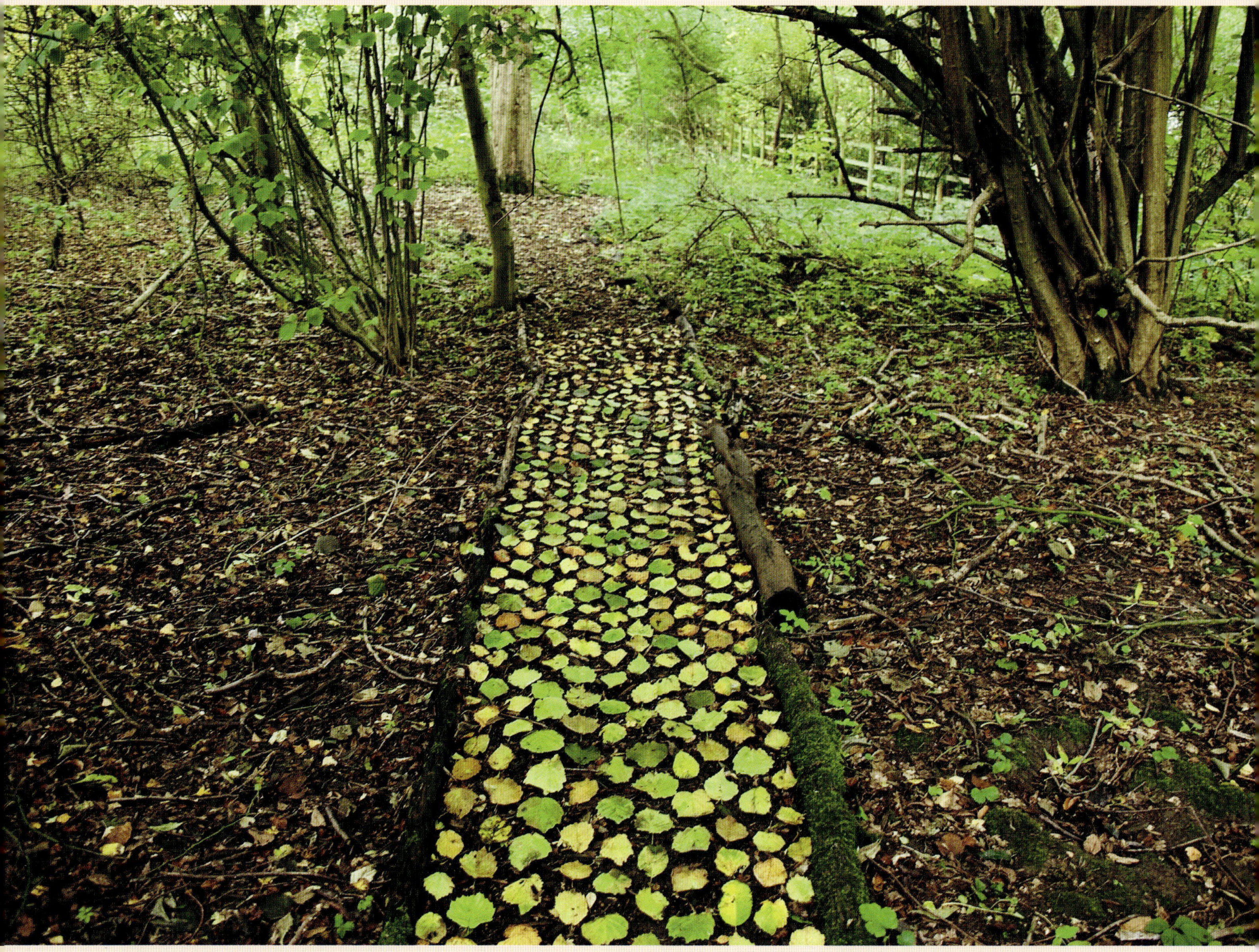

Above: *Hazel on path. I was finding inspiration everywhere by now.*

Far right: *A migrant hawker dragonfly. Stumbling across this stopped me in my tracks. I looked at it for ages, marveling at the delicate wing structure.*

Right: *Sloes on log. I really enjoyed the experience and challenge of making this piece, although we did have a few words at times.*

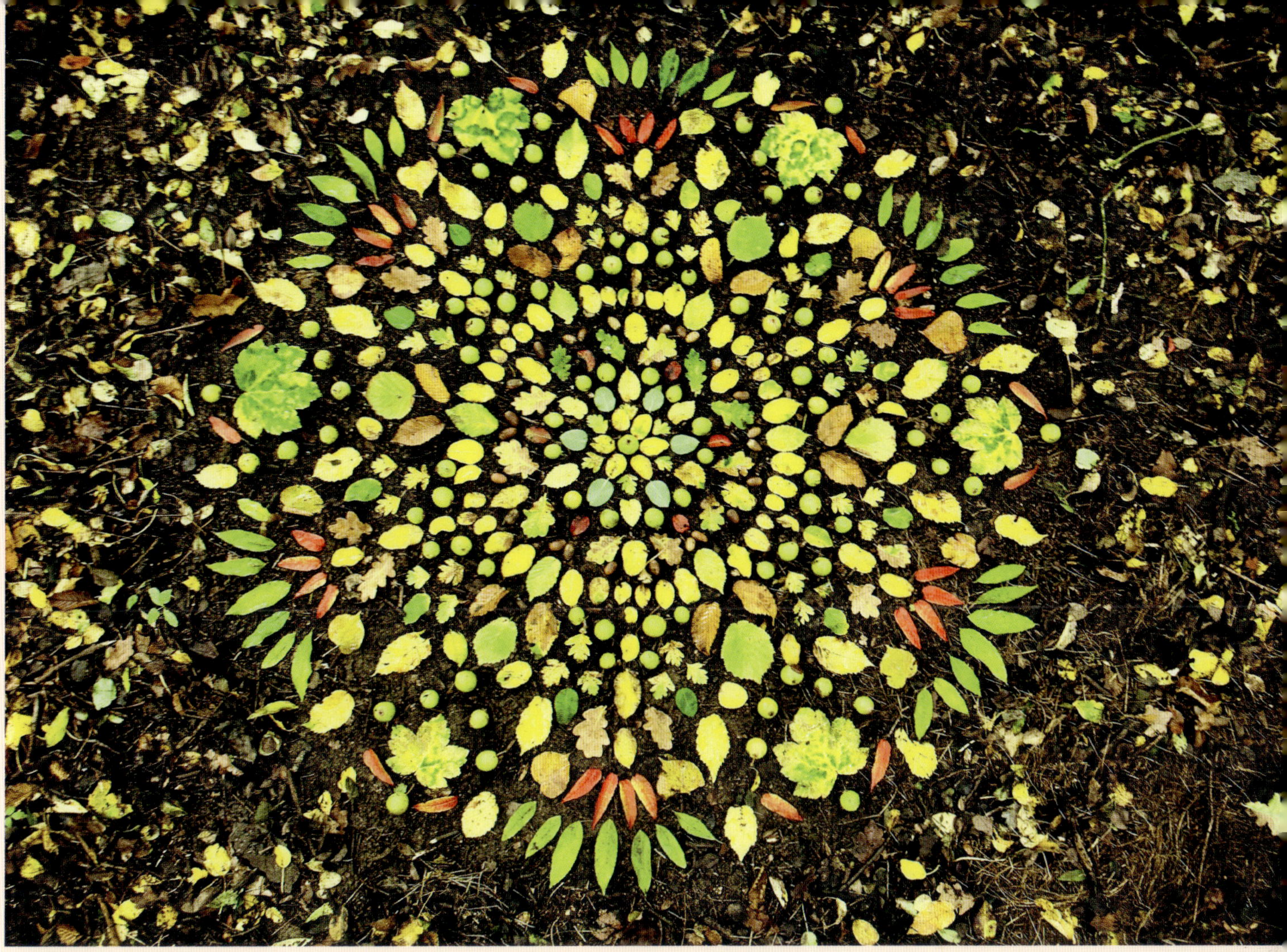

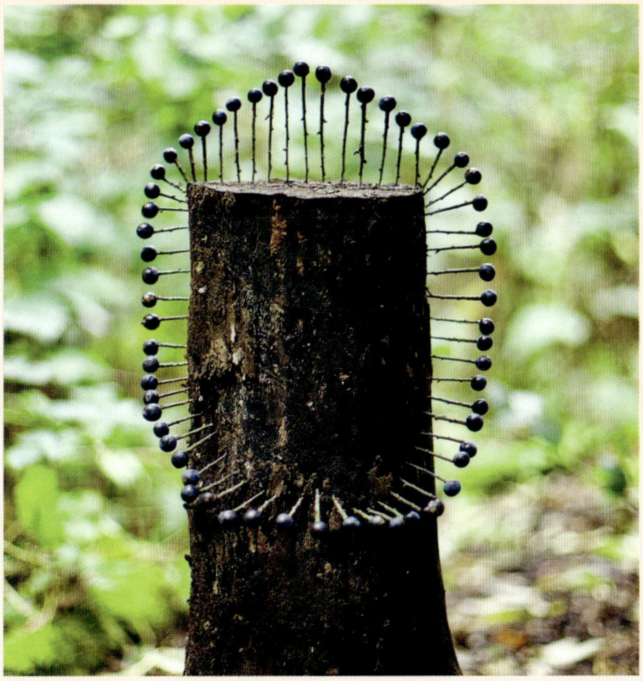

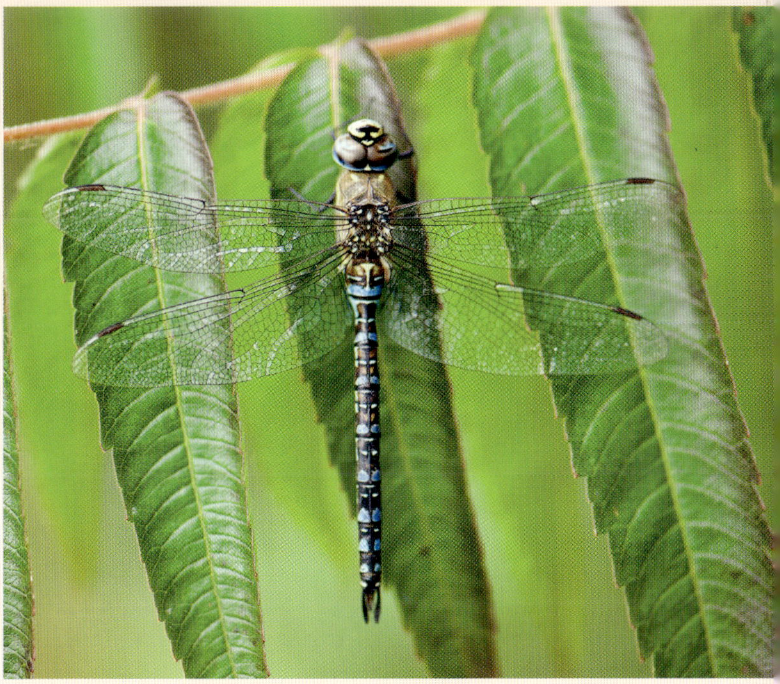

November

Splendor
Gifts
Transform
Celebrate

Good weather returns and I take a step back, a last flash of color, new friend sumac star of the show. Showcasing place, I'm engrossed and I'm happy and at one with the Field's daily flow.

Right: *Sumac spiral with Ally Pally (shelter made by gardener Alistair) in the background. I wanted to capture some of the Field's uniqueness within the work.*

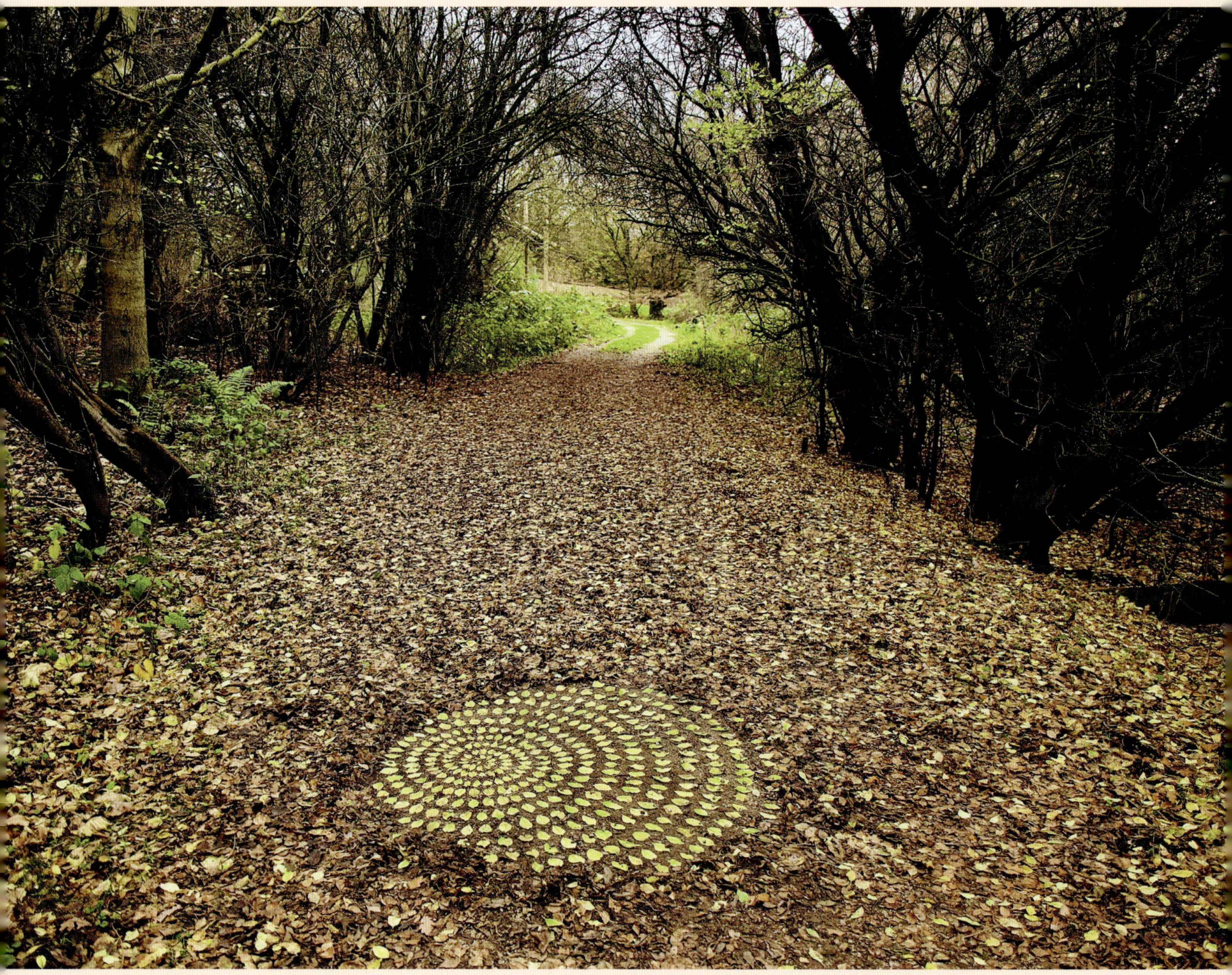

Above: *Spiral on path. I often make work that has the look of being uncovered, revealing only part of the work.*

Right: *Twig spiral by the pond. The Field often inspired me either to experiment or, like here, to follow familiar paths.*

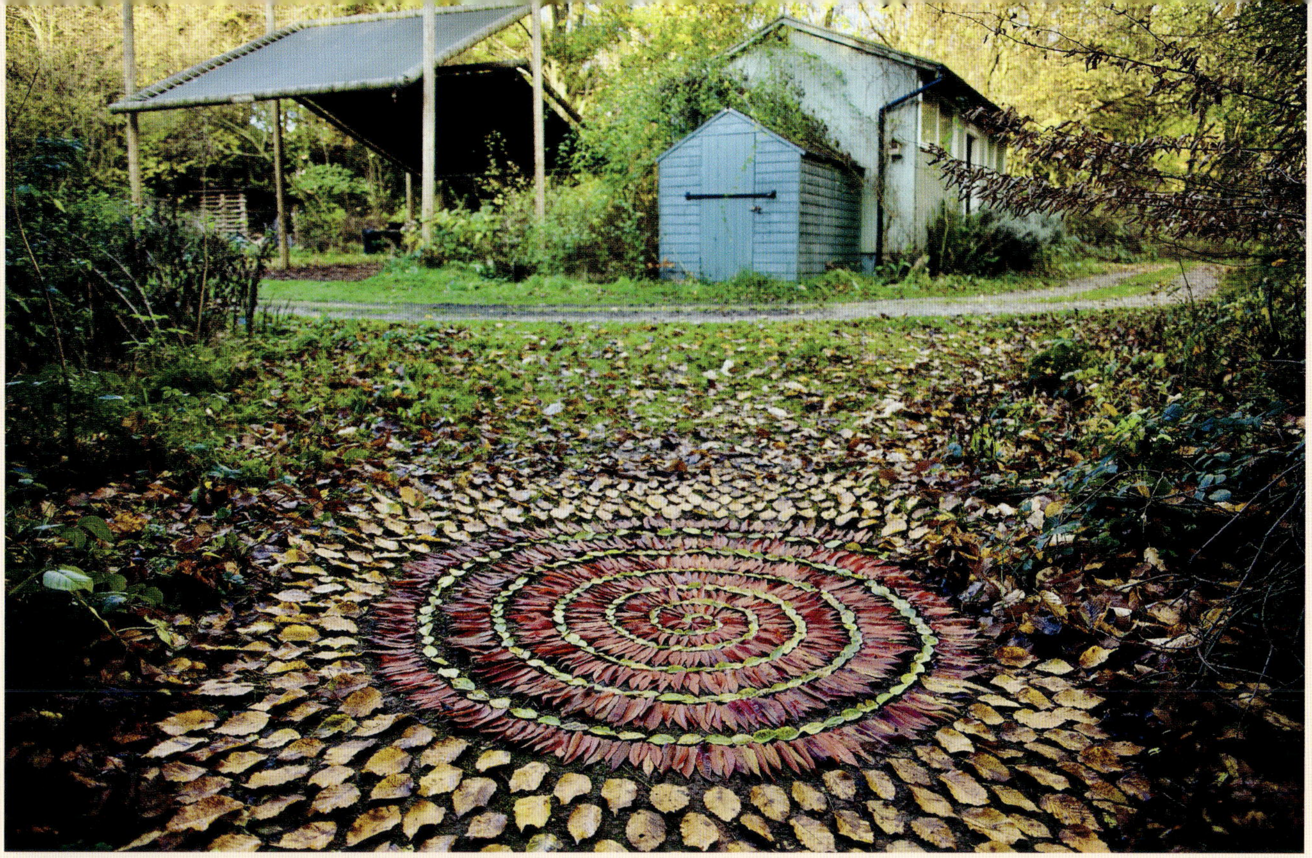

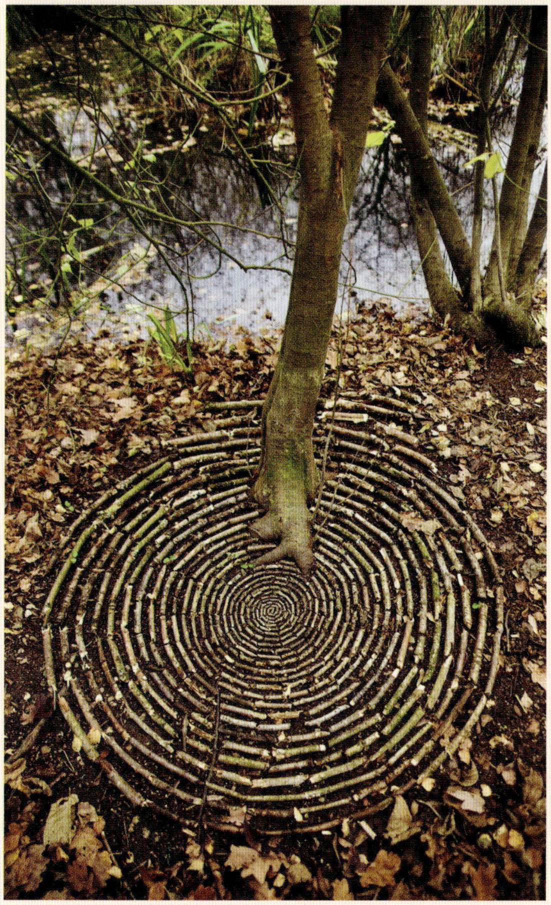

Below: *Another favorite leaf, the field maple. I love the depth that both the size and the darkness of the background give.*

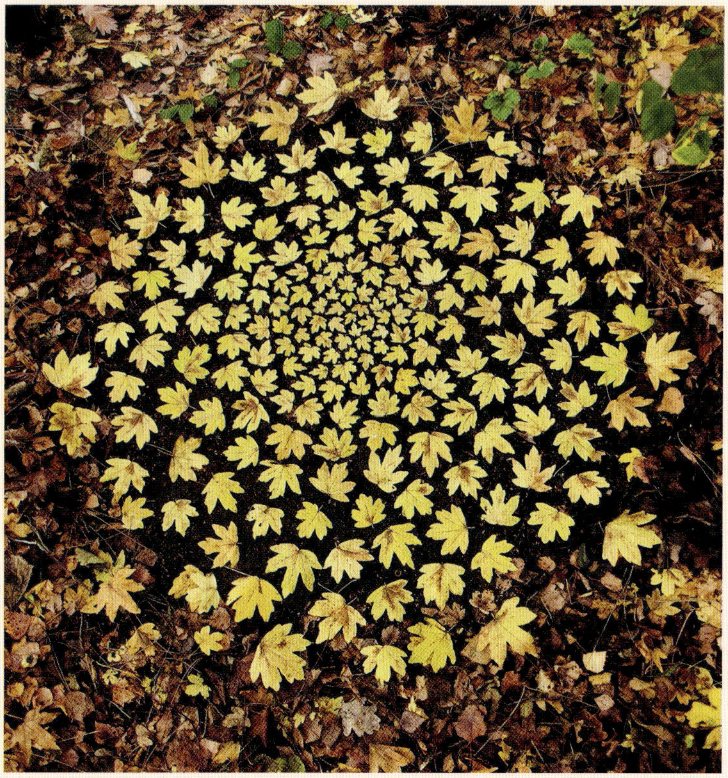

Winter

December

Still
Quiet
Waiting
Empty

Winter begins calm, empty of story. I spend a day with a blackbird working together doing and undoing, under the laurel whose charm has returned, keeping an eye on the compound for a glimpse of the green woodpecker.

***Below:** Work in process. The sharing of my lunch with a blackbird led to this having to be remade, as it grew in confidence and kept hopping across the piece.*

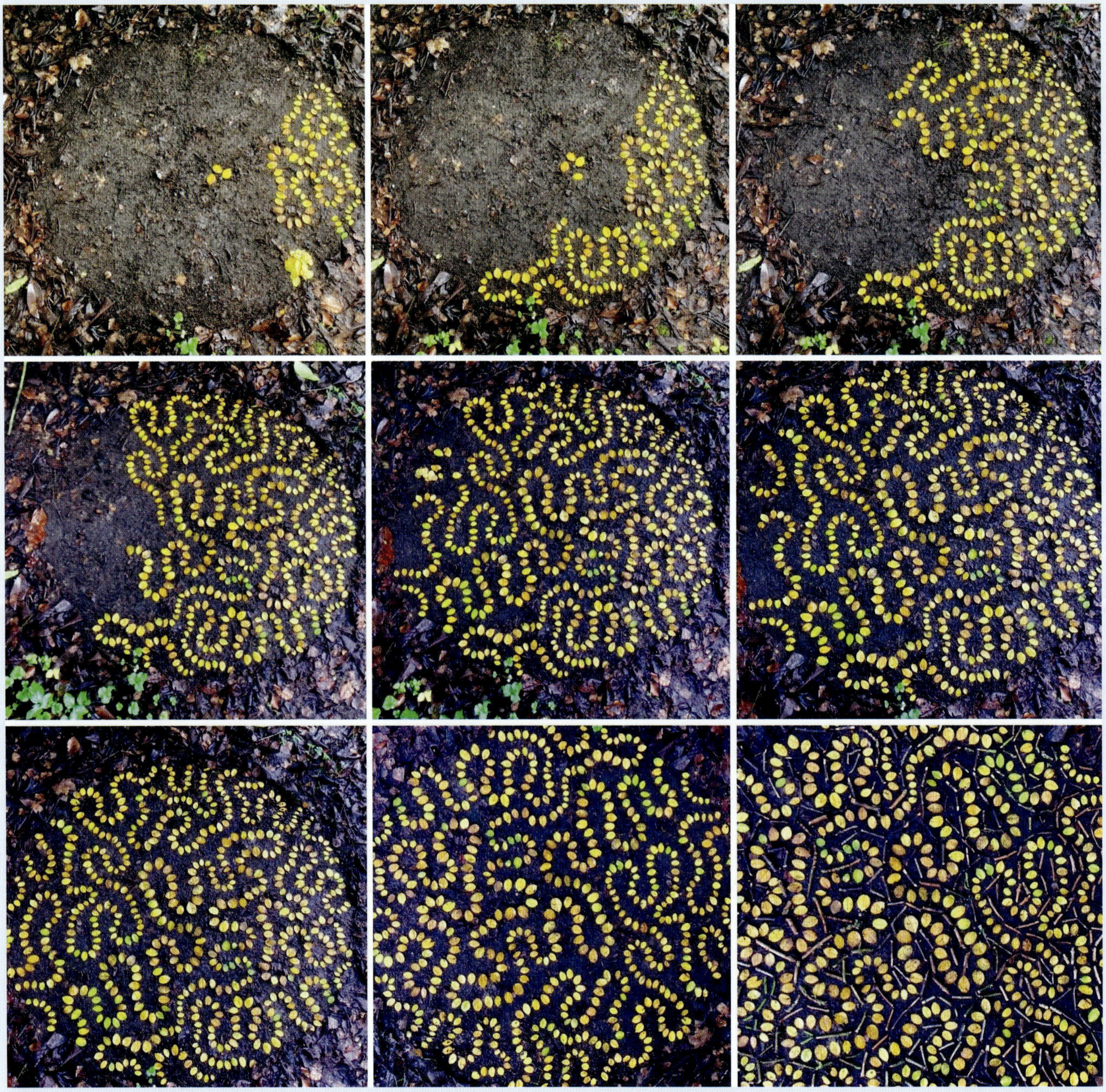

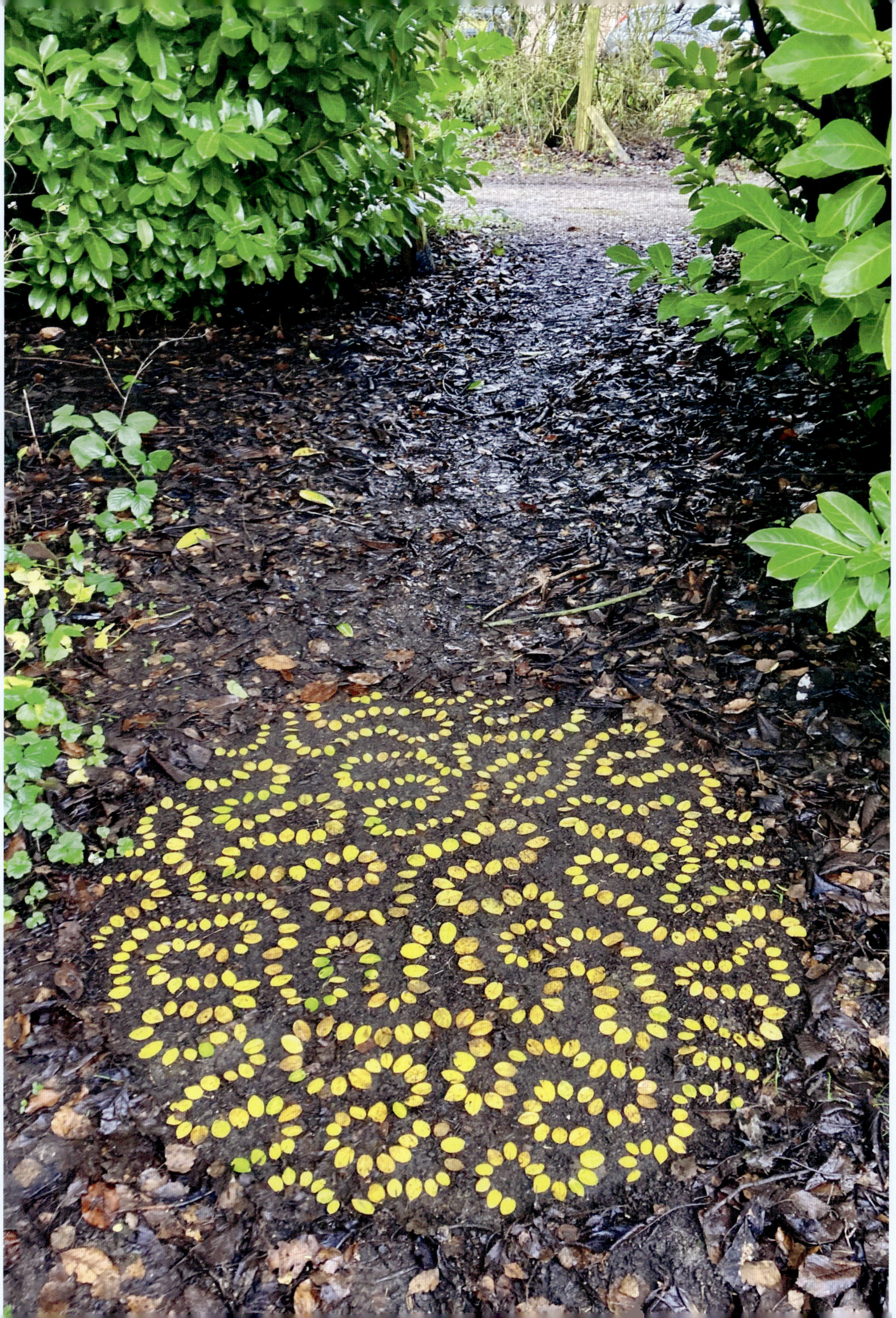

January

Dormant
Resting
Damp
Preparing

New year arrives with no fuss, color is sparse, and the Field seems asleep. I get lost within the trees transforming the floor.

Below: *Winter was a truly magical time for me at Weleda; work flowed freely, and I felt very connected.*

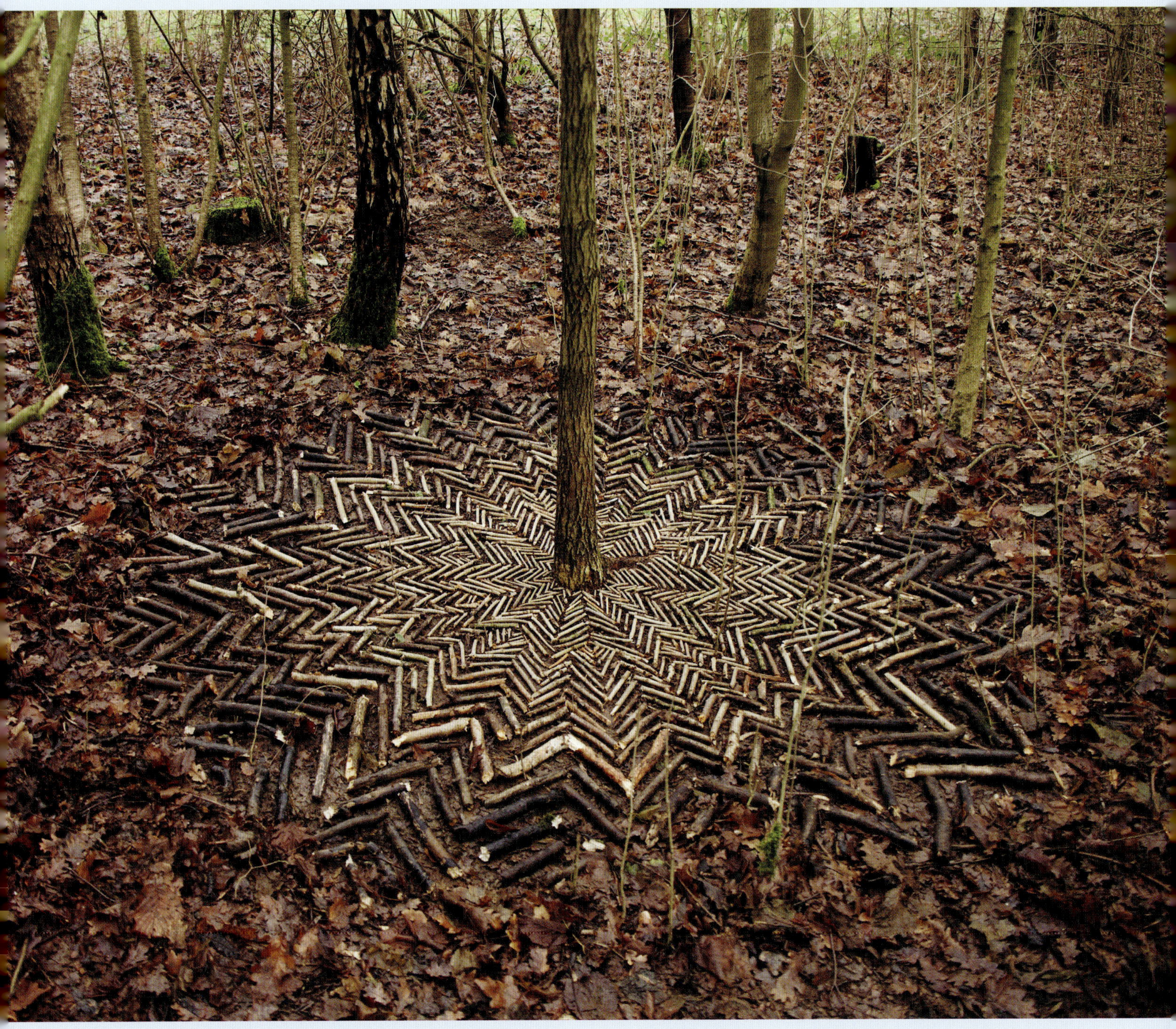

February

Cold
Harsh
Crisp
Purpose

The end of my time and real winter arrives; it's a month of contradictions with harsh and with hope; a day with the ice proves a challenge and reward; a week further on and catkins begin to fall. My last day and last work hold a special place in my heart. A mossy nook I'd walked past many times over the year, always calling and reminding that its time will come. And on that last day it did, drawing me in. My last gift to the Field, for now at least. I hope when I return, the land remembers my touch, accepting and inviting, deemed part of the scene.

Below: *Ice stack. I had an amazing day with the ice on the pond. Creating and experimenting with material and conditions I rarely get to use.*

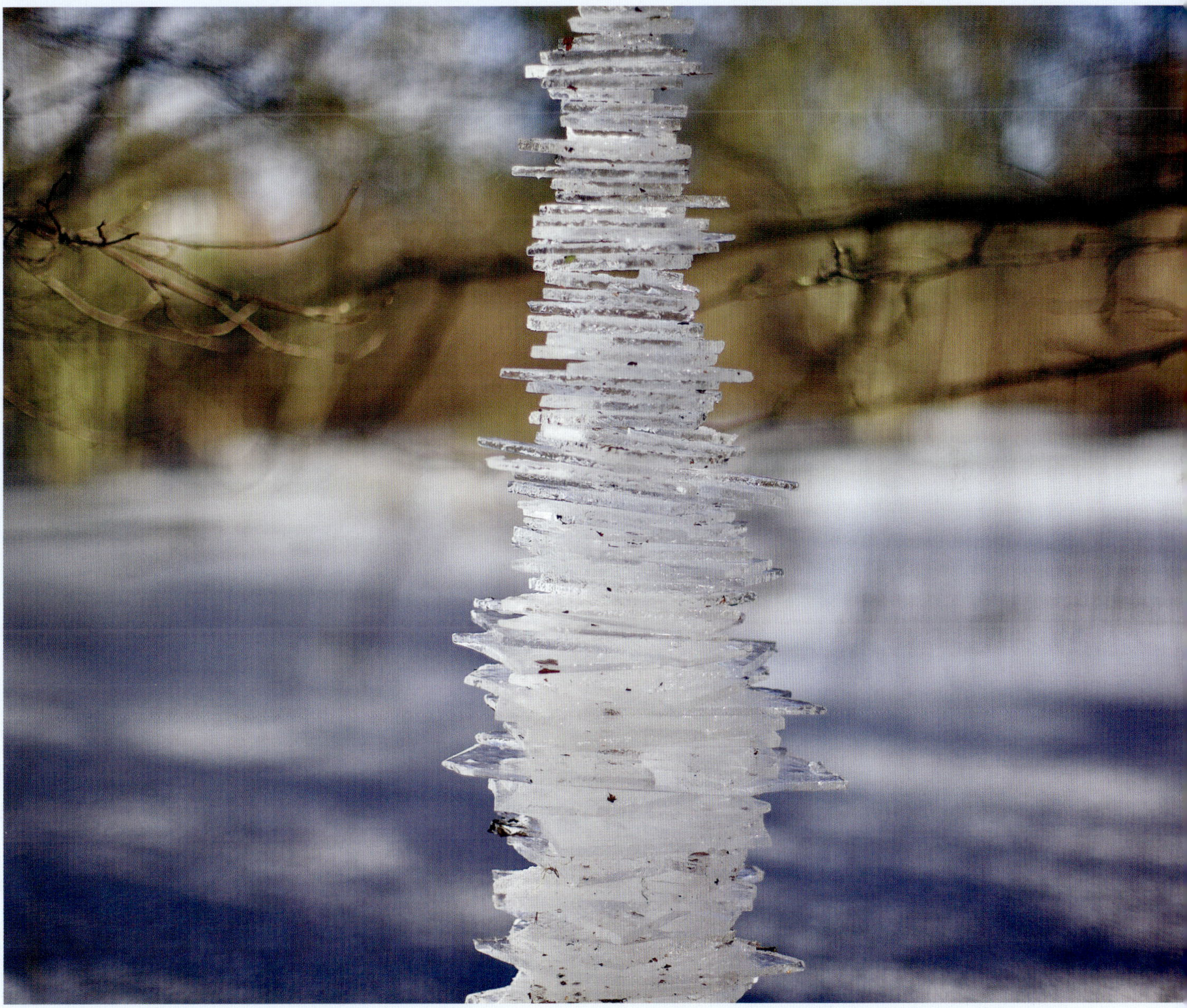

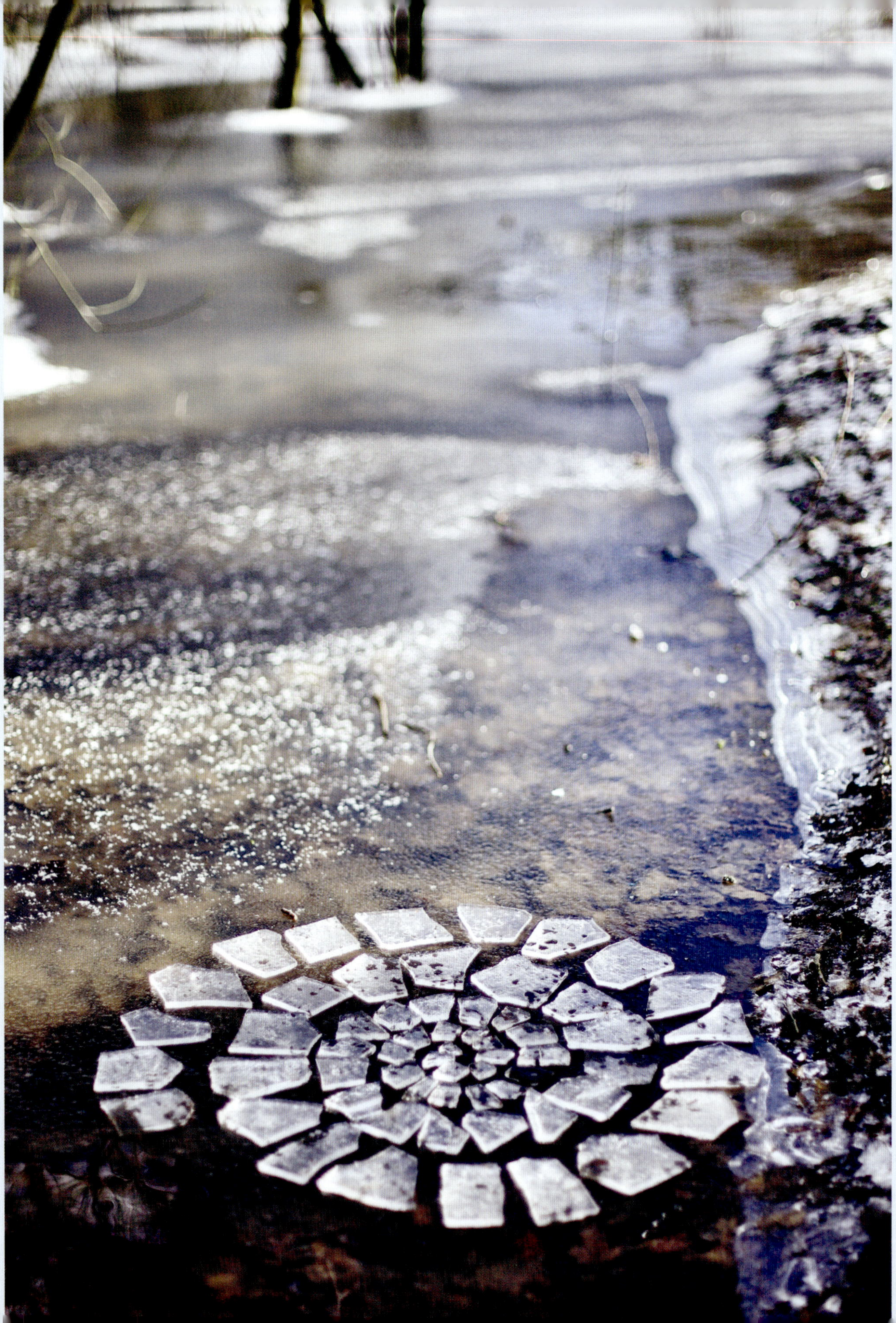

Left: *After the first one sank, I moved locations to try again. Pictured here in its wider surroundings.*

Right: *Ice spiral. The weight of the ice on the frozen surface led to an image seen previously on page 18.*

Below: *Early signs of spring to come. Despite the cold weather, spring and color are already beginning to emerge.*

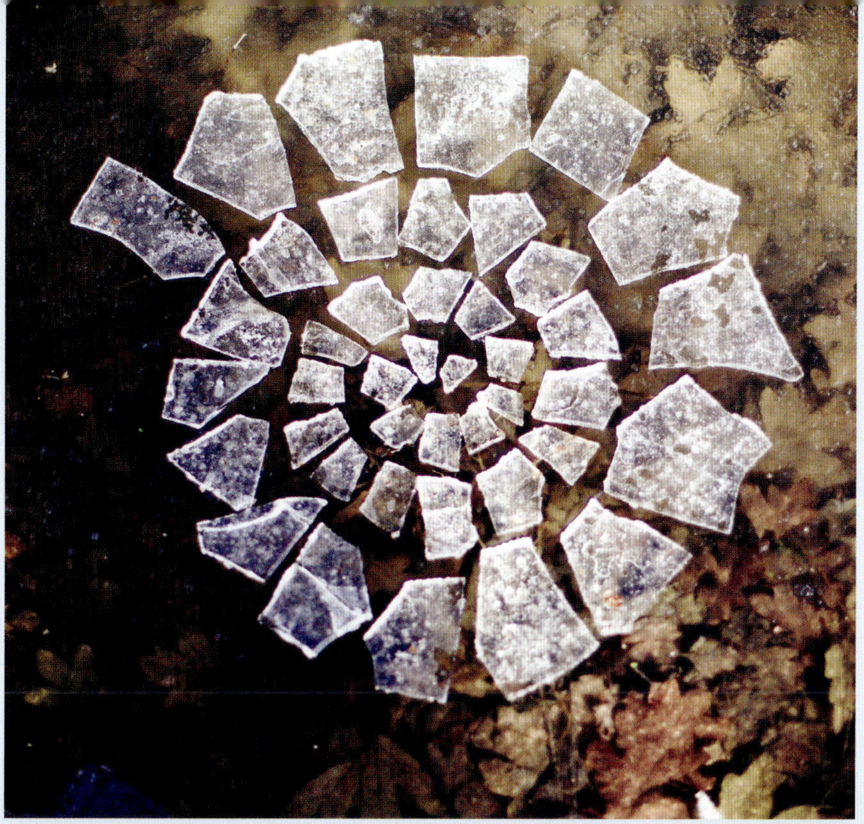

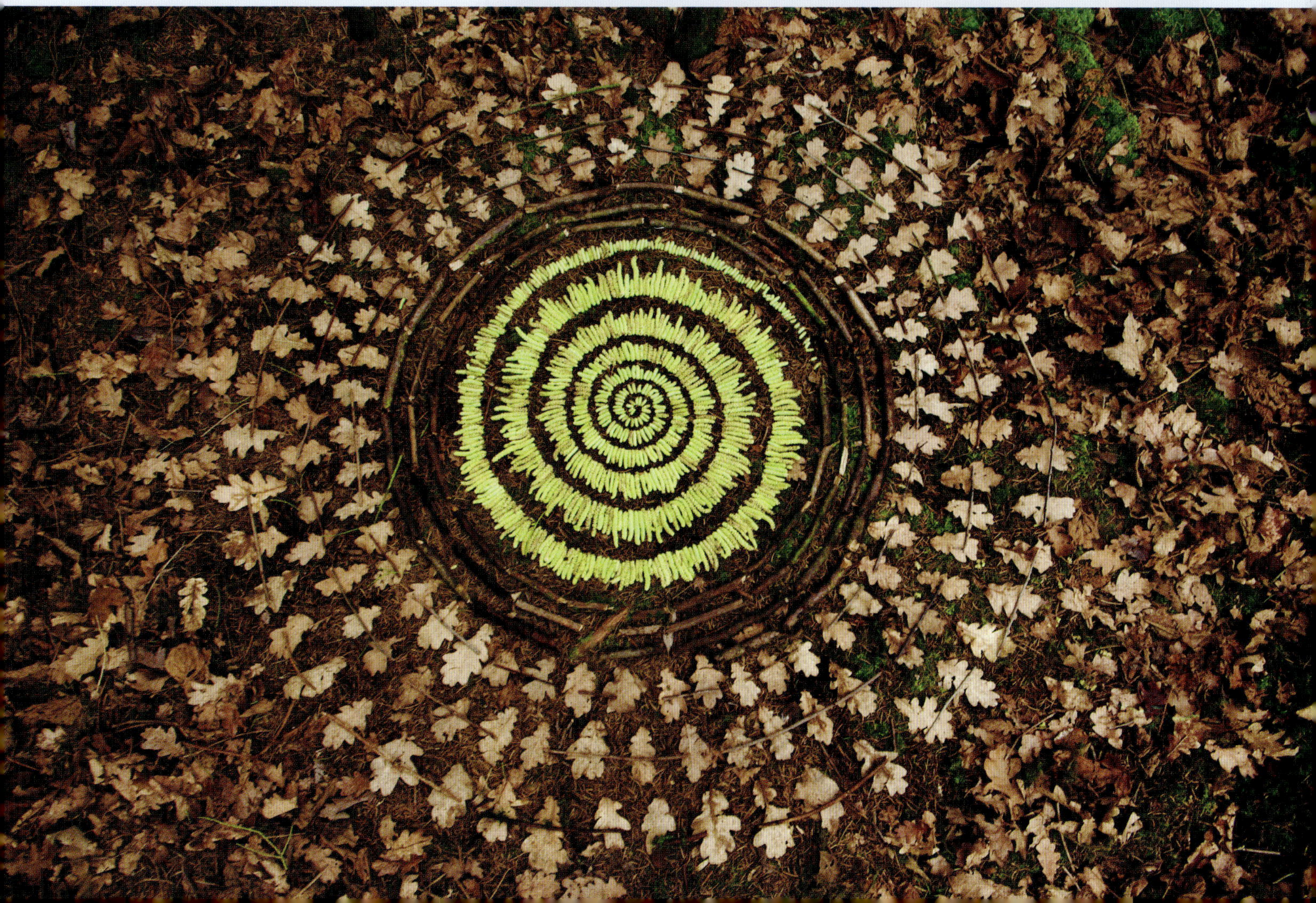

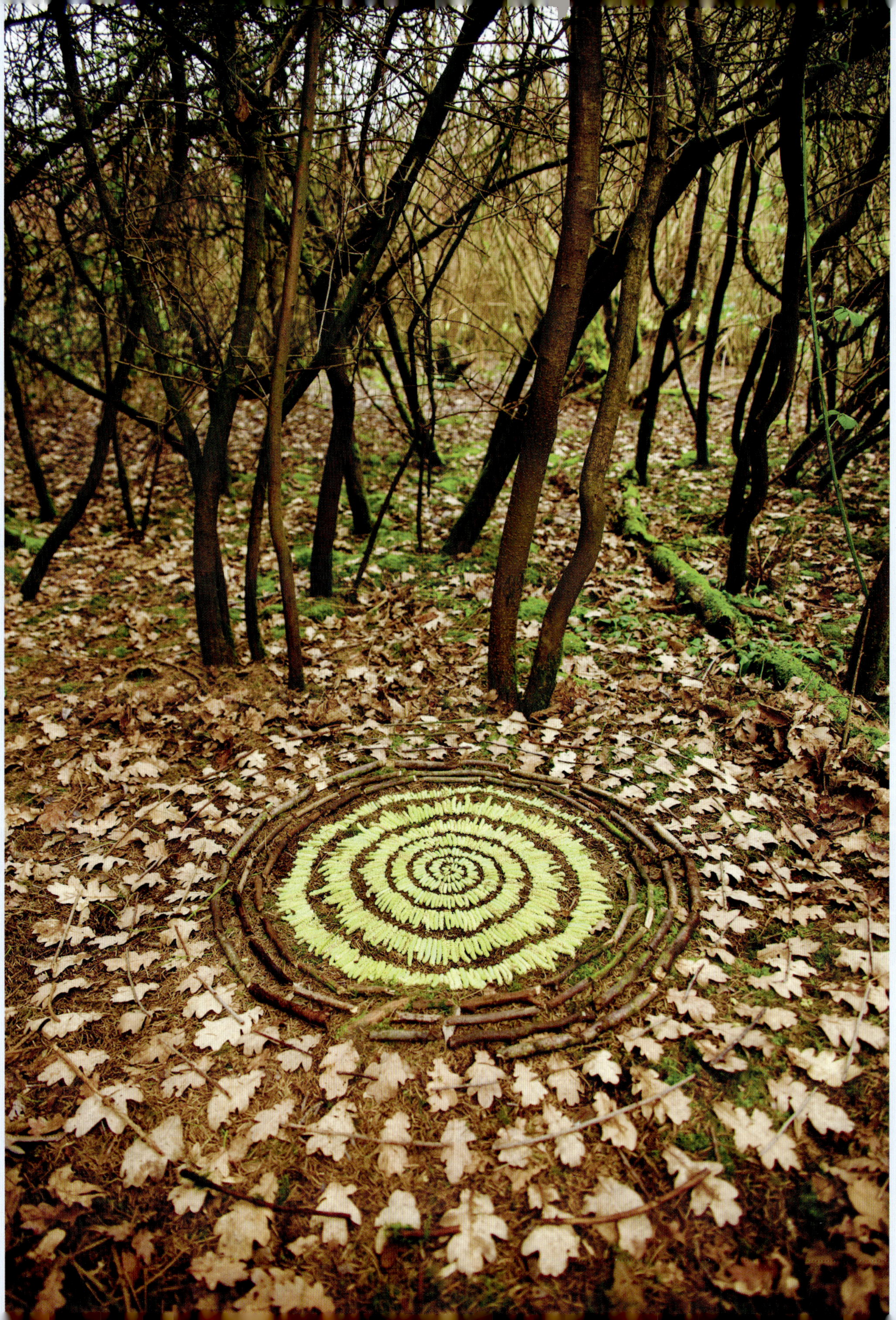

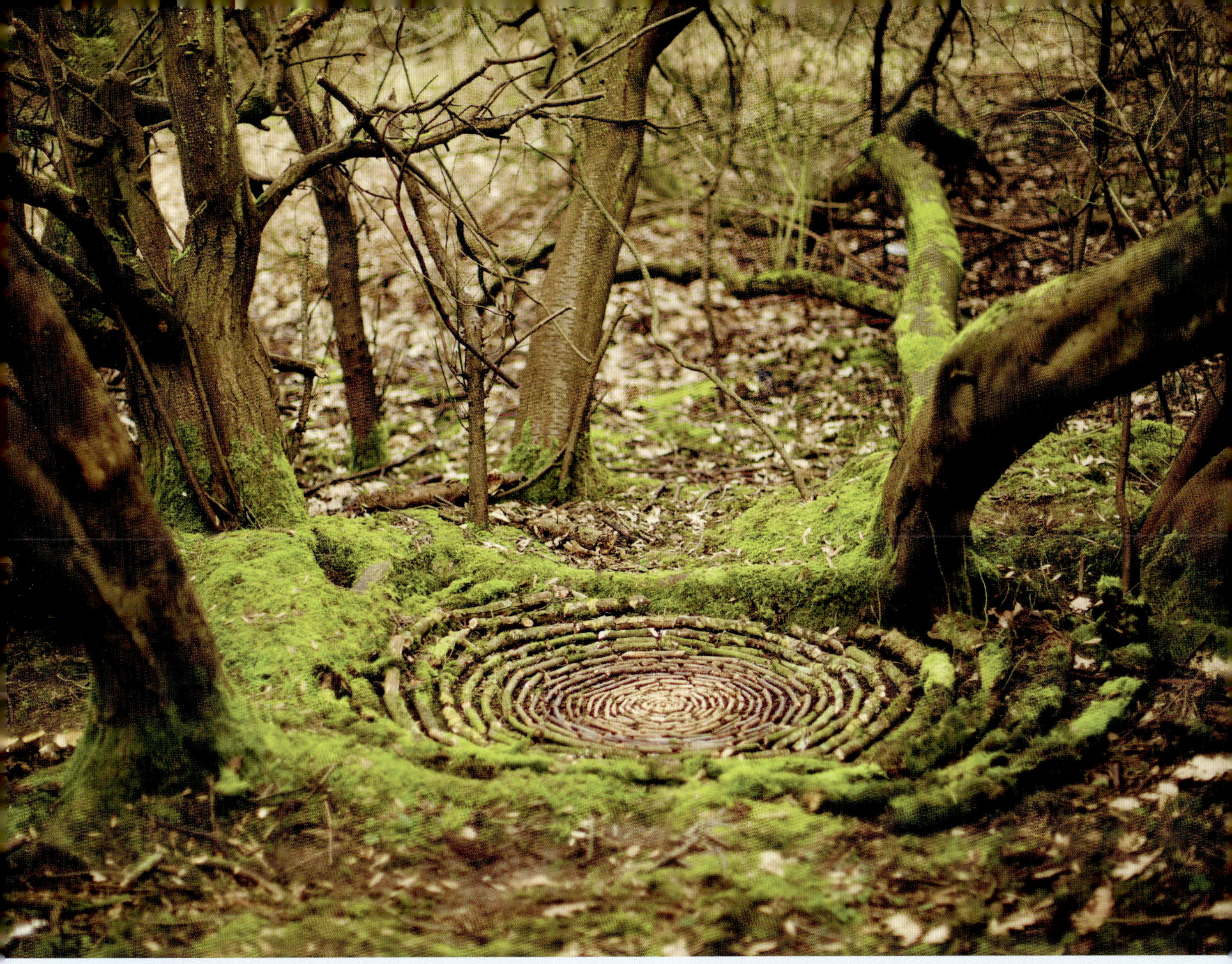

Left: *Weleda is many environments, packed into a relatively small plot of land.*

Above: *My last work at Weleda and possibly my most assured, definitely the most in tune with the land.*

That last work created at Weleda showed me something important, to create work that appears natural, that sits within its space and looks at one with its space. Of all works created, this piece comes the closest. My work is never stronger than when this connection is made, and the work and the boundaries between natural and man-made are blurred.

Weleda was a time to immerse, to play, to find my place, to learn, to understand, to be sympathetic, responsive, open, and accepting. If undertaking my Forest School training was a milestone moment for me, then so was my year at Weleda.

New Works, Reflections, and Memories

Before we start on what I worked on since the year at Weleda, I wanted to just reflect on five works that if I hadn't made, I don't think I'd be here writing this book now. The period since 2015 has been a creative journey that has guided me to this point now, and while I try not to put importance on works or let a previous work influence what I do next, it would be remiss to neglect the fact that circumstances beyond my control have played a key part in my career.

First is this piece from May 2017, created in Anston Stones Wood on a stunning spring day. The water was low, leaving an island of pebbles. The smell of wild garlic was intoxicating, Foxy was with me, and the woods looked lush. It was a triumph of my limited photography skills, with the whole composition being much more important than the rock spiral I'd made. The vivid, fresh greens of the trees, the wild garlic flowers encroaching down the brook banks, the hit of green reflected in the water all combine to lift the work to much more than it was. But also, it looks at home in the picture; it's not invasive. It seems to me a complete photo and probably one of the first I'd managed. Not long after this work, I got the email inviting me to attend my first Llano Earth Art Festival.

***Below:** Stone spiral, Anston Stones Wood, a perfect combination of location, color, smell, and immersing myself into the landscape.*

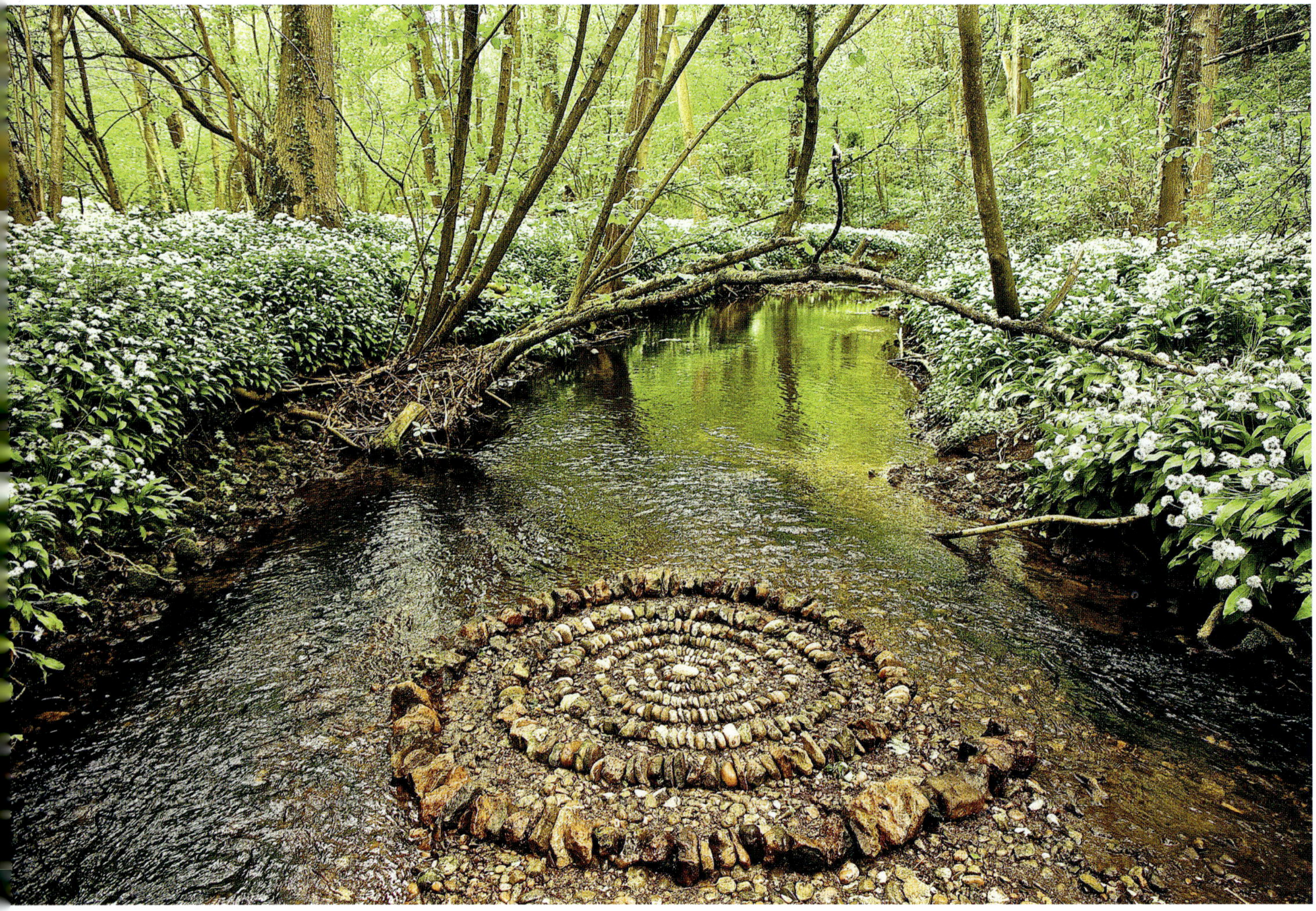

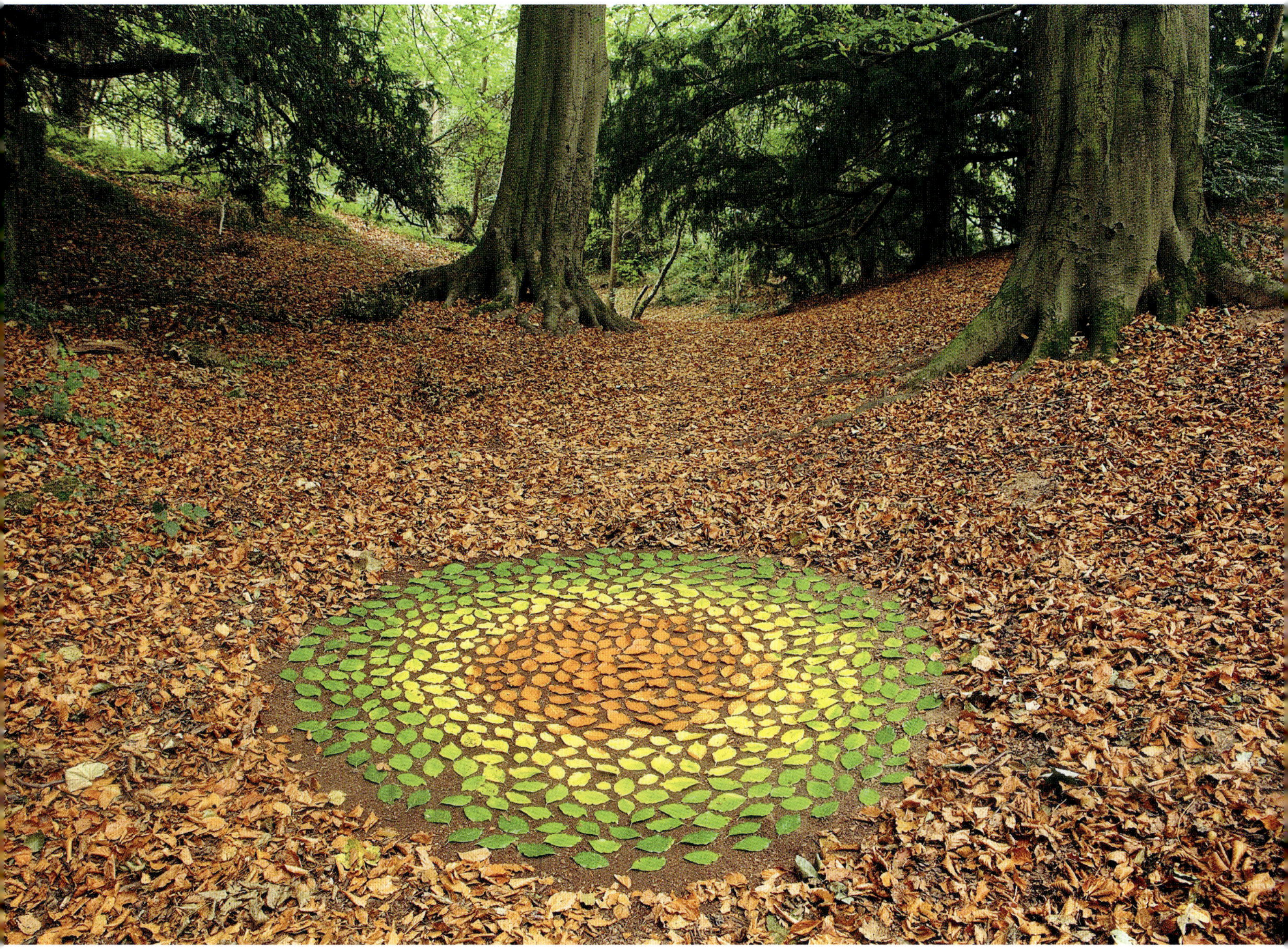

Next, we have this from October 2017. It's a perfect example of how my work is so reactionary to what I find on the day. I'd walked for a long time with not a spark of inspiration, and I was on my way home when I stumbled across a large branch that had recently fallen from a majestic beech tree. All the leaves were still attached to the branch and destined to slowly dry out and decay unnoticed on the fallen branch. From what was turning out to be an uninspiring day, I ended up with this. When working in schools, I often arrive to see this image on a screen in the classroom as an introduction to my work for the children I'll be working with. It's been titled "The Avocado" by children all over the UK. Look closely and you'll find a gap and missing leaf that the breeze has blown out of place. It's only later, when processing images, that I notice these things. I call them "nature's touches"; they make me smile and are a lovely little sign that Mother Nature has already started the process of reclaiming the leaves.

***Above:** Beech leaves, Anston Stones Wood. I had to negotiate many dog walkers and passersby to complete this.*

The next image was created the following month. I'd dropped my car off at a repair shop for some work and decided to walk a new way home over the old colliery pit tops, Foxy and camera with me (just in case). I stopped on the way home when I came across these field maple leaves. The work didn't take too long to make, but again the composition of the final image just works, and the arranged leaves appear very natural within the environment. The little gap where there seems to be a leaf missing on the outer right-hand side of the photo has always stuck out to me. What you can't make out on the photo is a tree root where the leaf should sit. I always try to work around such things, as opposed to find a way to hide them. Unfortunately, in the picture you can't make out the root, so it just appears like a leaf is missing, another of nature's little touches.

Right: *Field maple, Dinnington Community Woodland. I've made many works like this that haven't resulted in this kind of impact.*

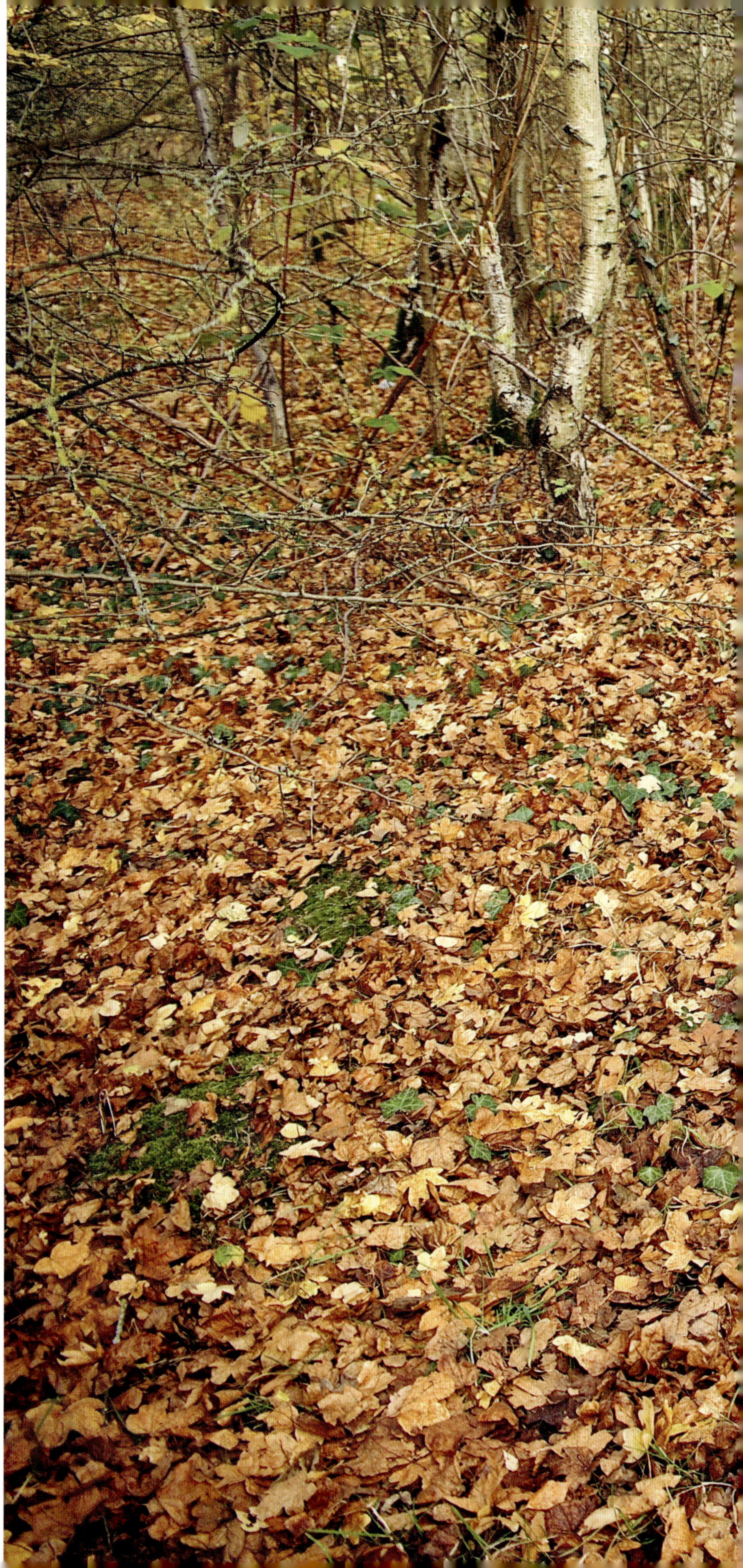

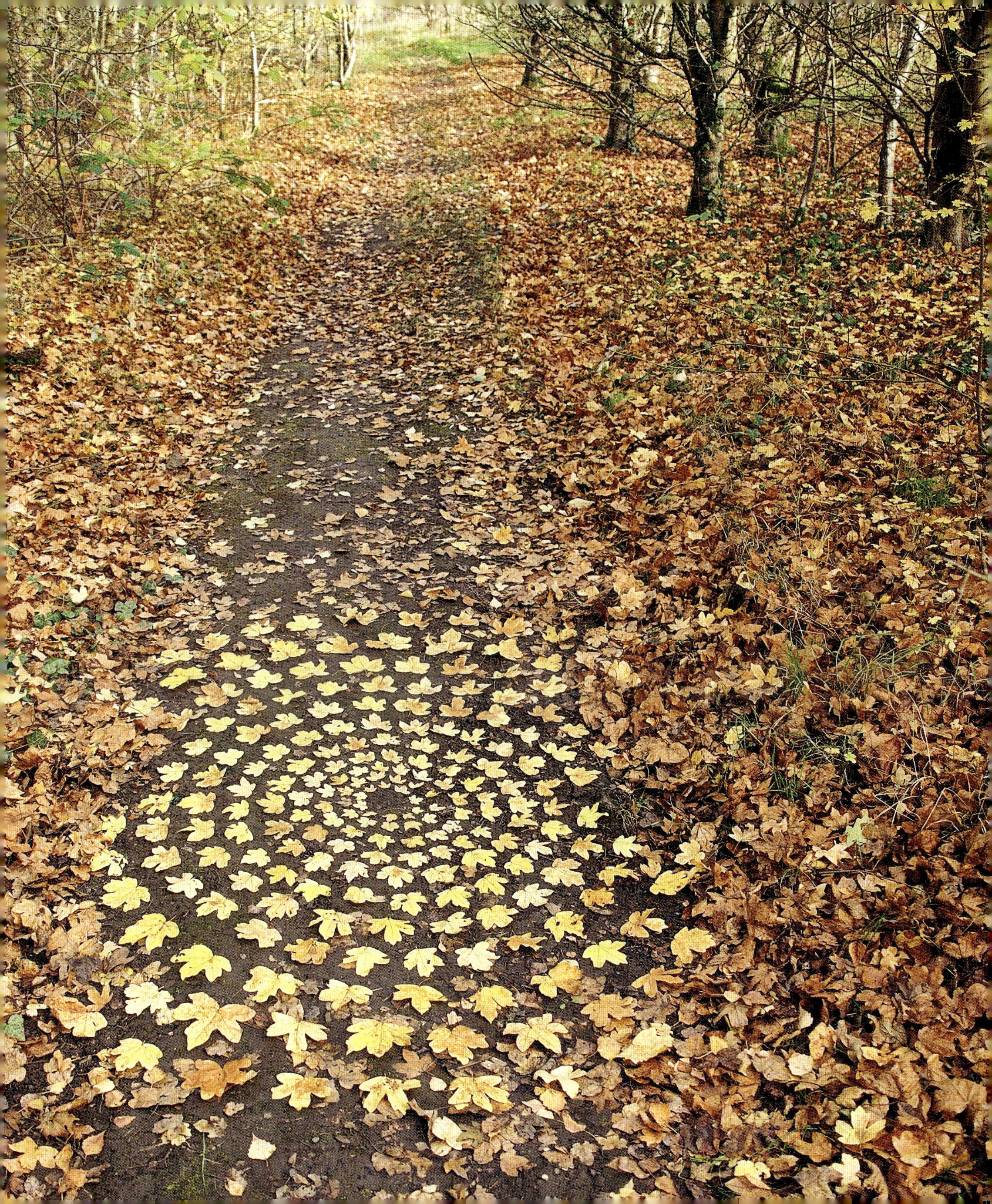

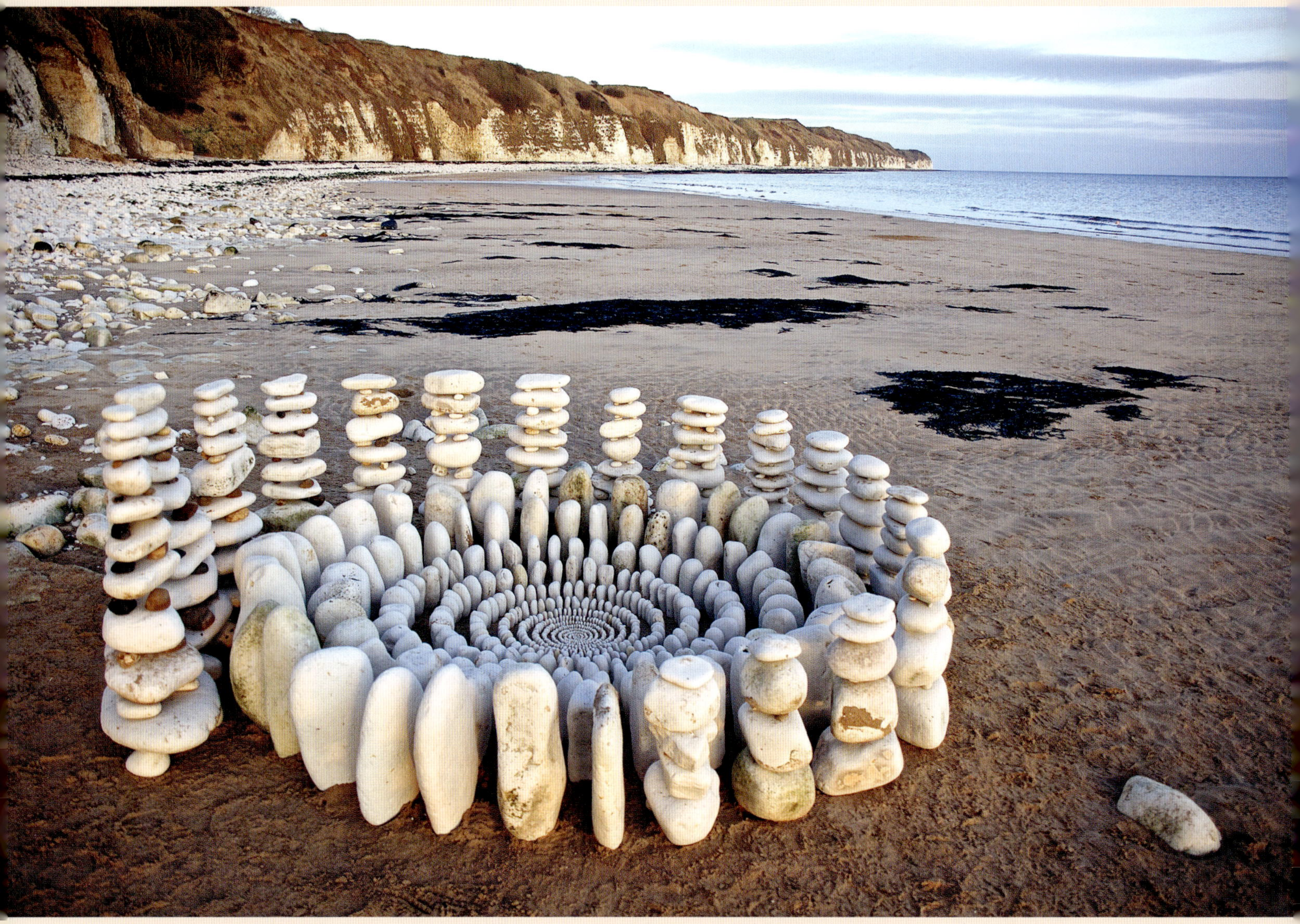

***Above:** Danes Dyke, East Yorkshire; nothing better than winter on an isolated beach.*

Next up, in January 2018, I'd had this thought about taking work more seriously. That if I wasn't just stopping to make things while walking the dog, and I gave myself more time, how would my artwork change? So, I planned shortly to head off to the coast, on my own and with no other agenda than to create. The two works created on those days took the online awareness of my work to another level. This was the first, created at Danes Dyke near Bridlington. It was freezing. I saw one other person walking on the beach all day, and the ocean reclaimed the pebbles and stones with no one seeing the work other than me.

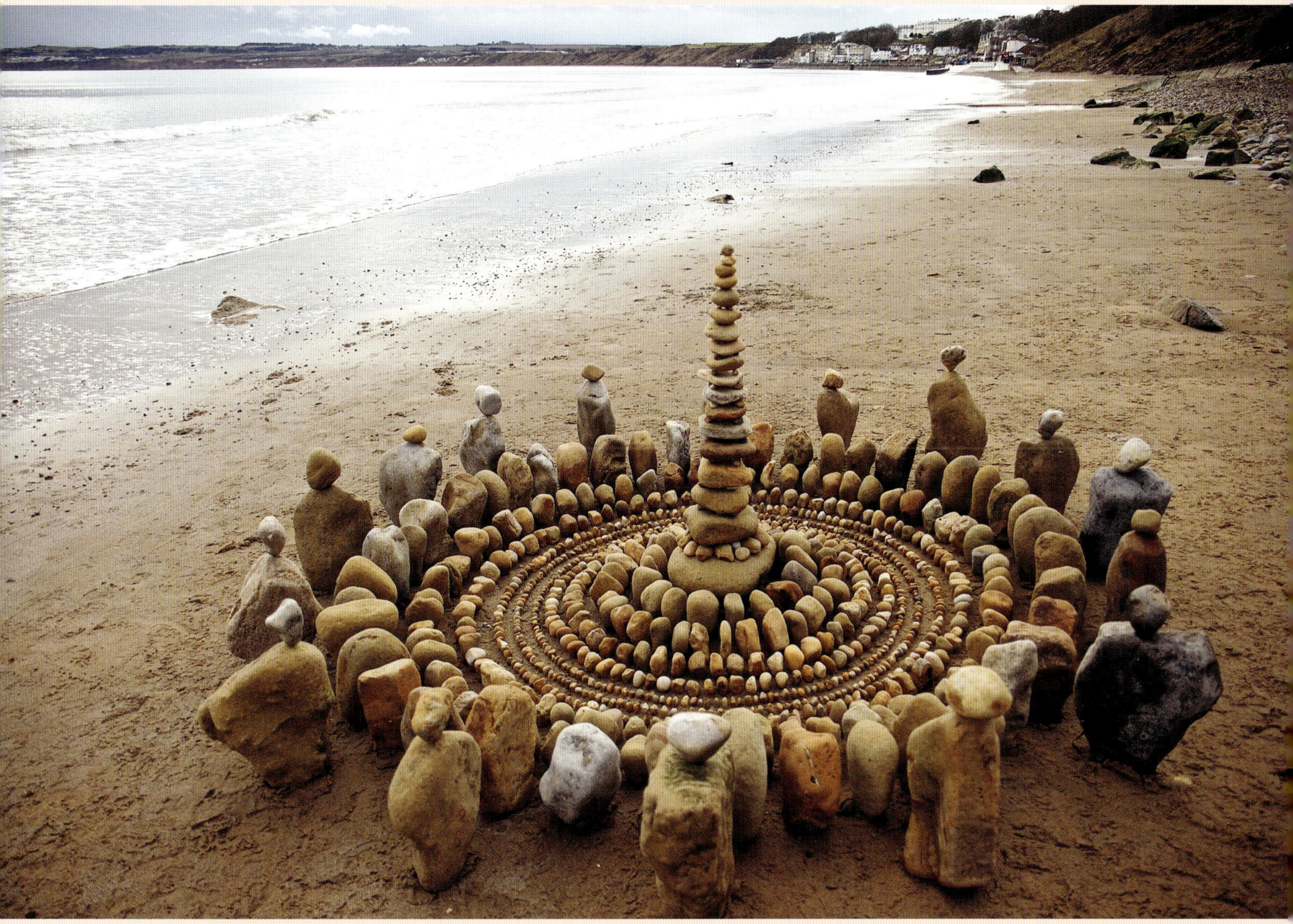

Above: *Filey Beach, North Yorkshire. I was caught out by the tide coming in faster than I expected, so I've always seen this as incomplete work.*

A week later, on another beach (Filey), this was the second of those two works. I posted versions of both works on "Nature Mandalas," a natural-art Facebook page, and they both went viral, unlike any reaction I'd had to any post before. Soon after that, online creative magazine *Colossal* published a feature on my work, soon followed by *Bored Panda* and *Modern Met*. Suddenly things went a little bit crazy; in a matter of minutes I watched Instagram followers go up in their thousands. I couldn't respond quick enough to emails coming in, and for the first time I started to get negative reactions to what I was doing. It was quite stressful for a time, and managing the online world stopped me from getting out as much as I normally would, and as anyone close to me will tell you, that makes me grumpy. Thankfully, events calmed and normality returned.

At my first LEAF in Texas, I remember a very grounding conversation with Michael Grab, who thankfully reminded me of the importance of my daily walks with Foxy, and he was totally right. I'm never more grounded, more in tune, more at ease than when Foxy is with me. There's no pressure to create, no pressure to not waste time; it's just me and the dog, along with the world around me, responding to what each day presents. And that is when the world feels right.

The following pages contain a selection of my more recent works. I'm very excited to share them with you.

I feel like I've been holding on to them for so long. When I started the journey of putting this book together, I made the decision to try to the best of my ability not to change my working practices, so not making work specifically for a book, but making the work I would always have made. Staying as true to what got me here in the first place. I think the collection is an honest representation of me, which is good; it's what I set out to do. Foxy was with me for most, many were fit in between other life tasks, and a good number were opportunistic, seizing an unexpected moment.

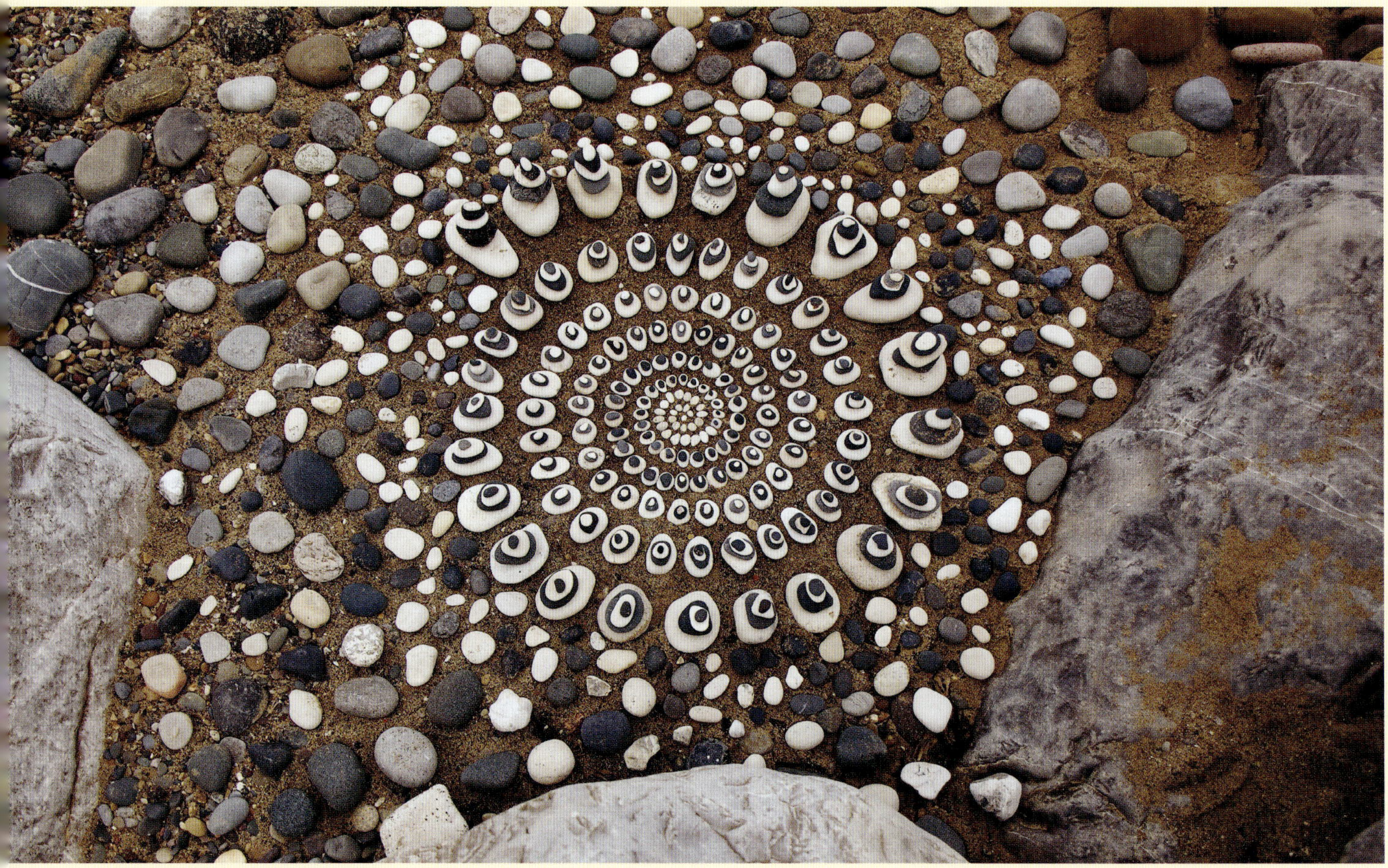

Playing with contrast on Withernsea Beach

I created this during a beach art workshop, and it grew beyond this element to include other colors of stones. As the day went on, more and more people got involved and helped.

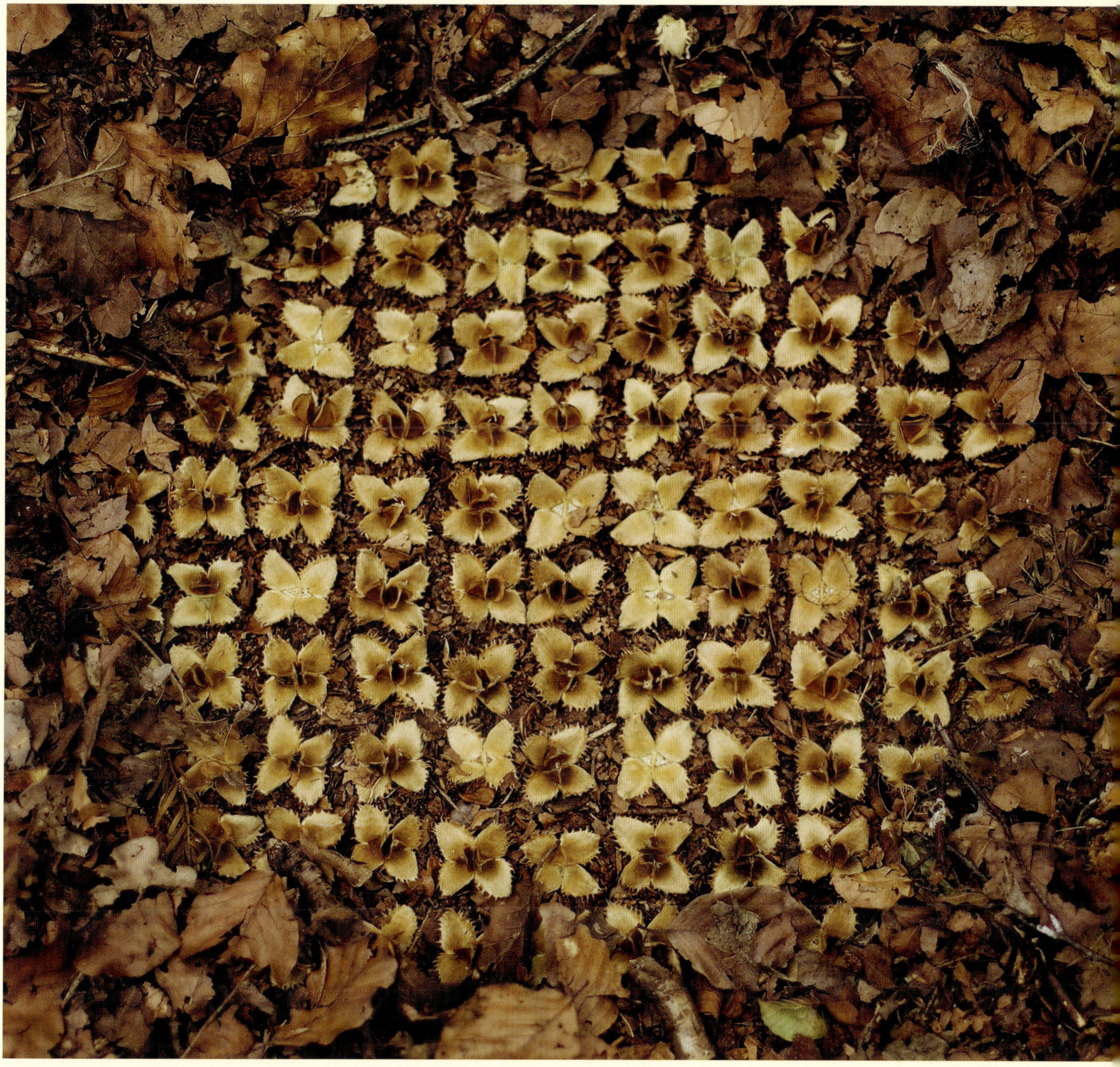

Beech kernels, Thoresby Park, Nottinghamshire

I'd been playing (unsuccessfully) with open beech kernels for a few days before this and had really struggled; the complexity and detail within each shell didn't suit the larger works I'd tried, and it was the realization to keep things simple and small that finally worked.

It was a lesson in working with the object, not trying to manipulate it to my work.

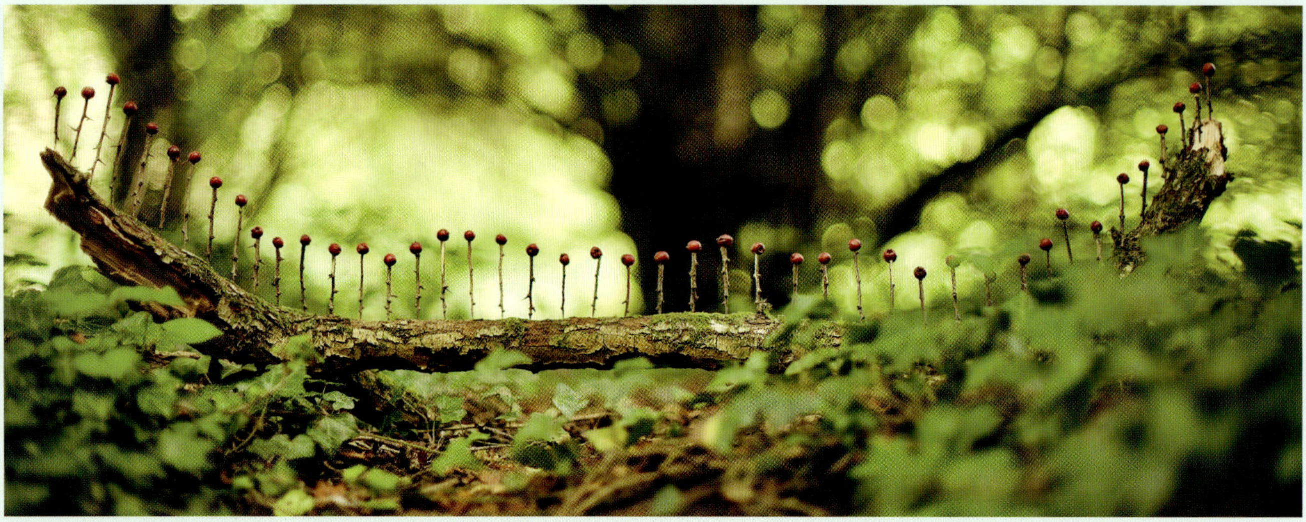

Deadwood and hawthorn

This was the first thorn piece I'd made at ground level, and I think it's definitely an avenue for further exploration.

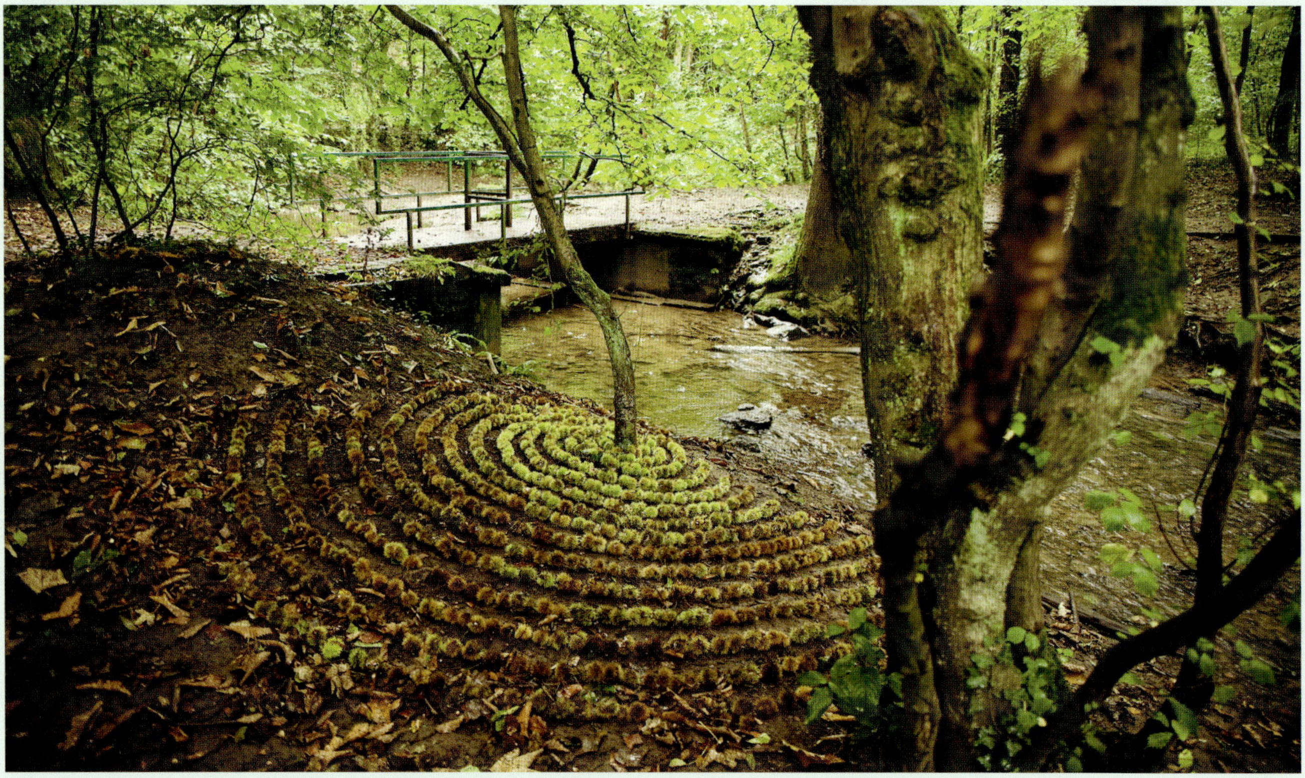

Sweet chestnuts, Anston Stones Wood

The differing age of the fallen chestnuts and variation in color all added to this arrangement sitting very comfortably within its environment.

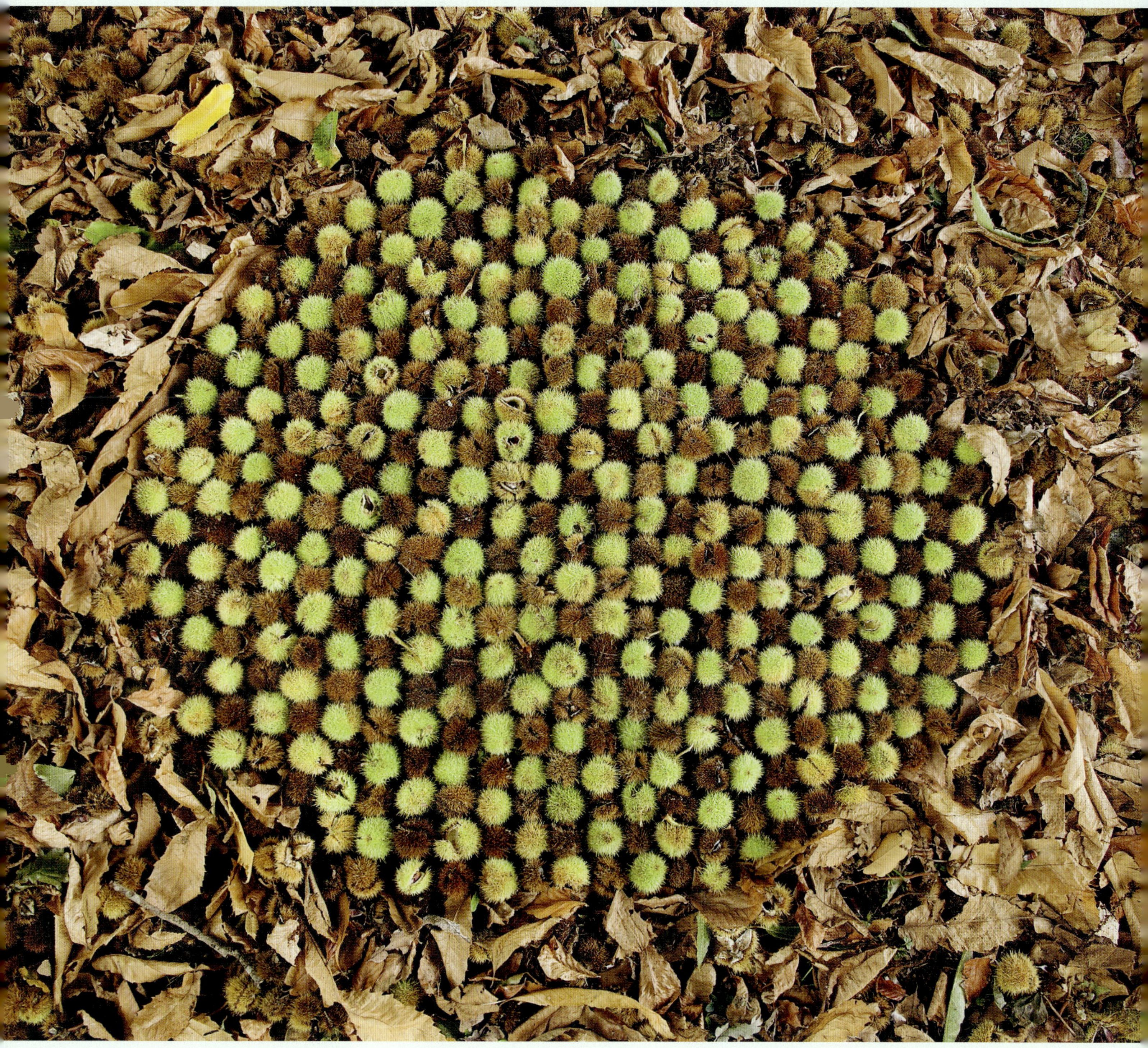

Sweet chestnuts, Elsecar Park

Made during a site visit, the day before a workshop with homeschooled children. Their first task on the day was to find this.

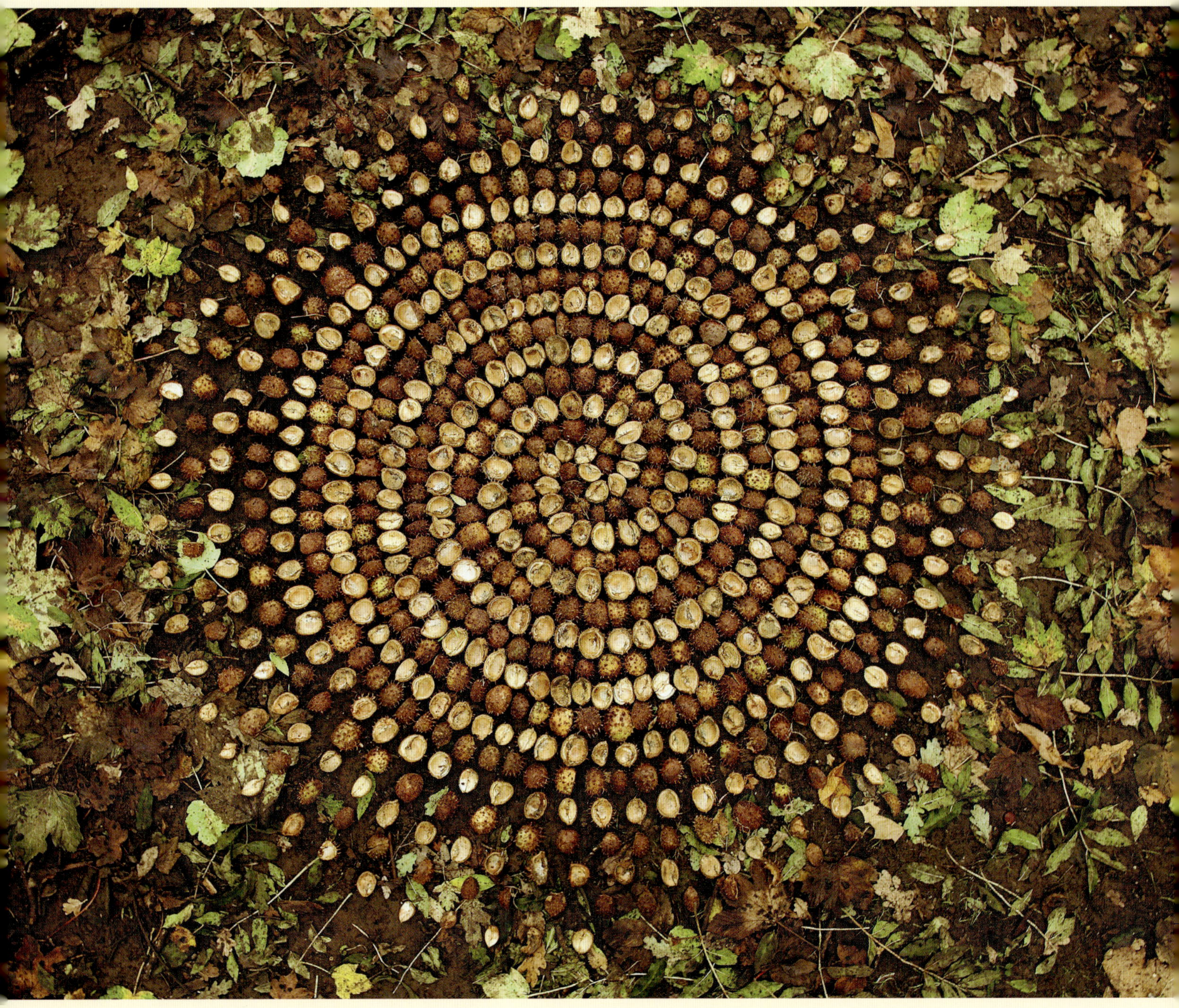

Horse chestnut shells

I collected the shells for an event in Sheffield city center I was working at. I returned them to the woods and made this.

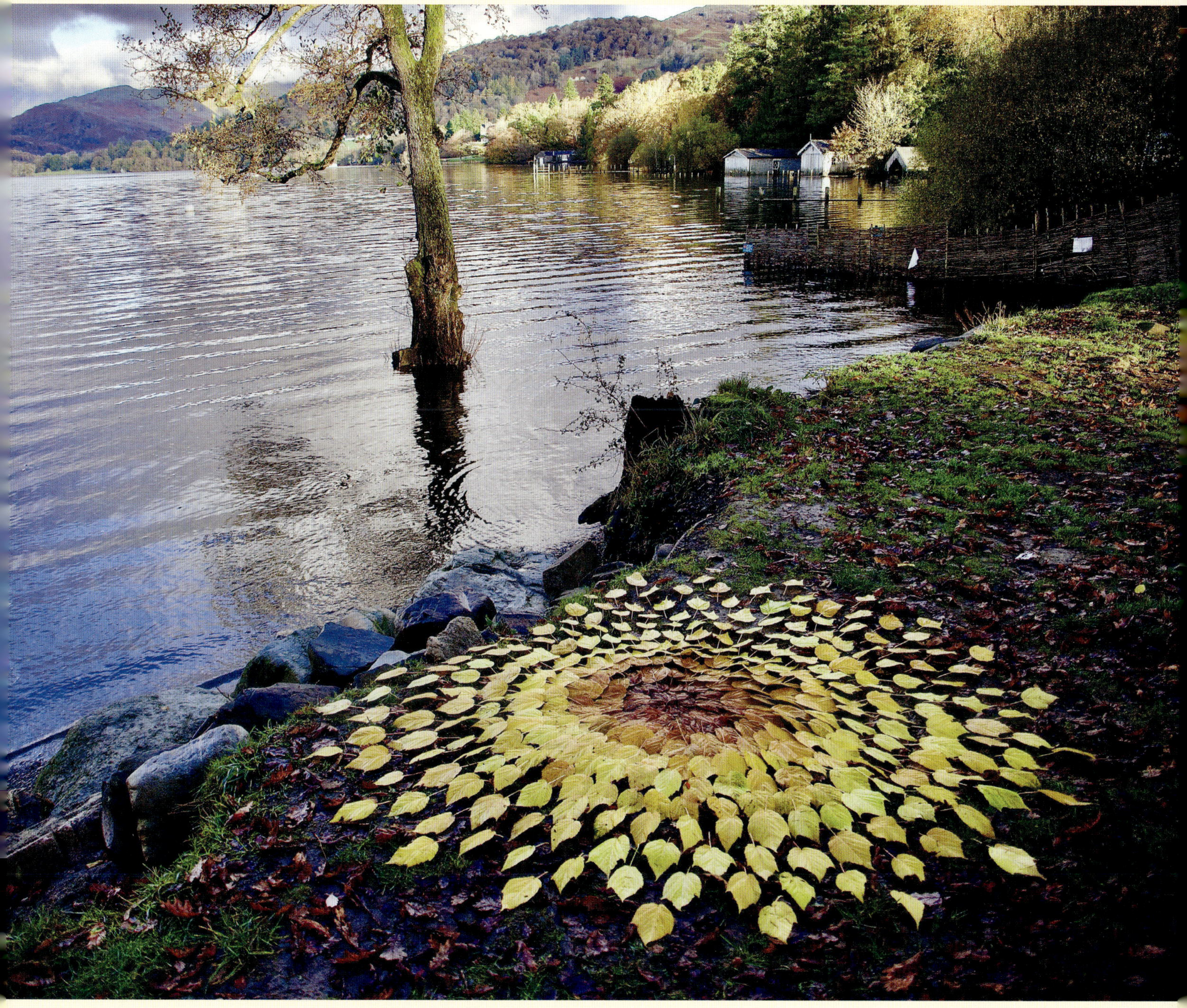

Brockhole on Windermere, Lake District

I was in the Lake District to create a new piece and install an exhibition with Richard Shilling and Julia Brooklyn. The area was recovering from a storm that had brought many trees down. The park itself was derigging from Halloween activities, but I still managed to find stunning backdrops such as this wonderful tree, with the supported outcropping branch. Often, it's stumbling across these compositions that spark the urge to create.

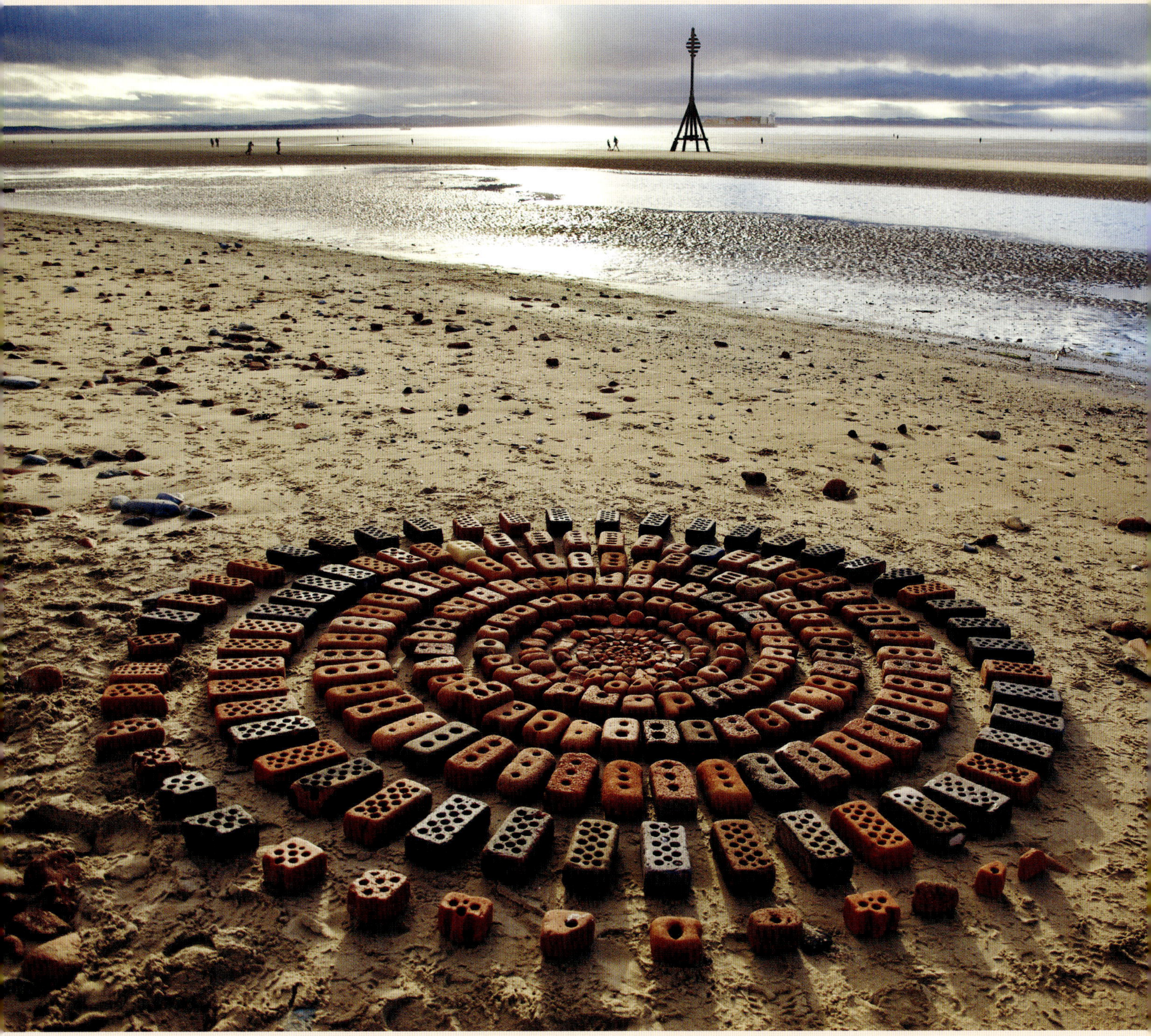

Ocean-worn bricks, Crosby Beach

I love this beach; it's on the opposite side of the UK from where I would normally visit, and so a longer journey to get there, but it's so worth it. Known as Burbo Bank, this section of beach has a long bank of old brickwork and building materials, which are the remains of WWII bombing raids. The rubble was moved to the seafront as part of the ocean defenses. In the distance you can see the standing figures of Antony Gormley.

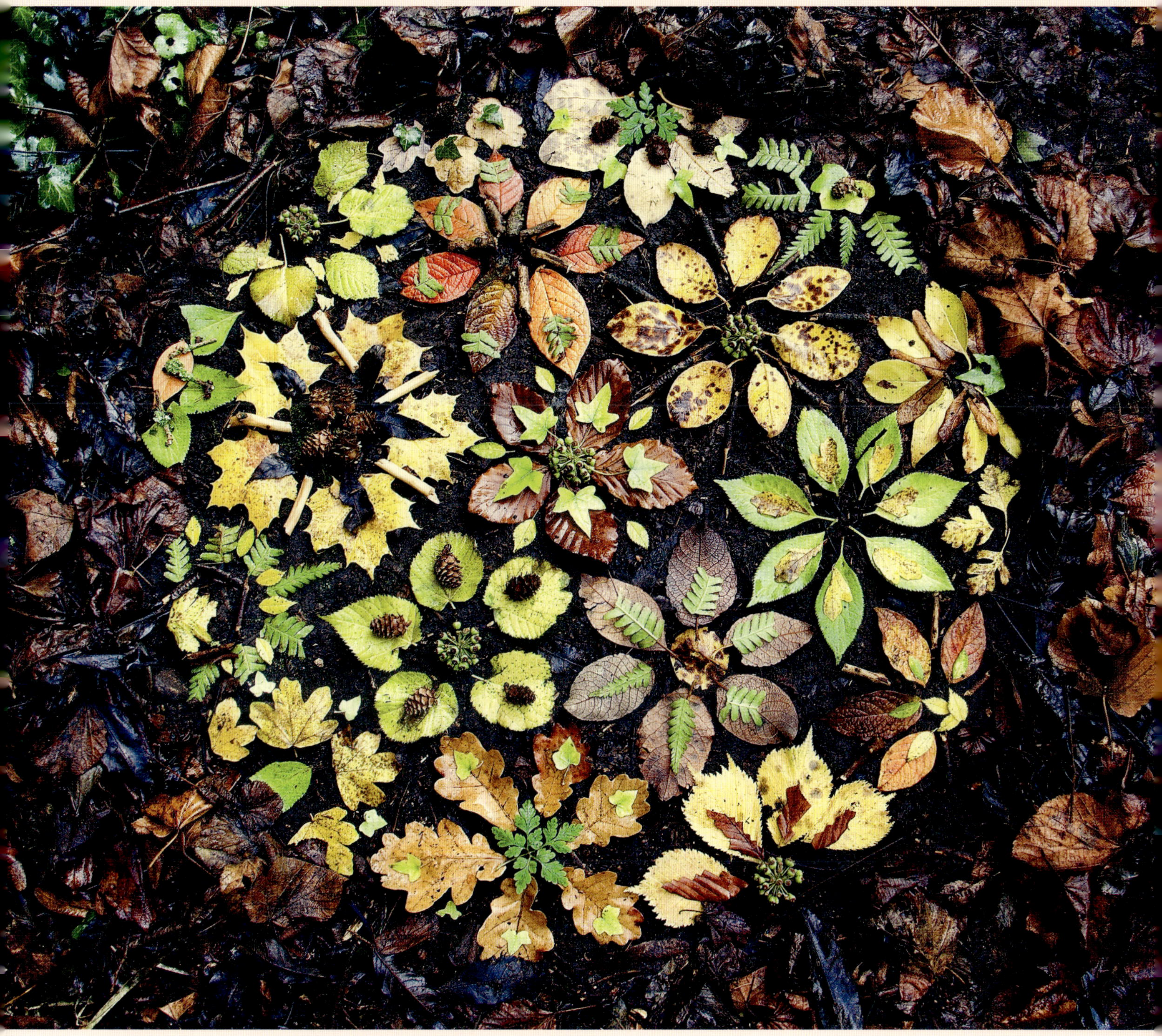

Collected materials, Anston Stones Wood

This was one of those few occasions when I collected materials as I walked; there's no way I would have found all this color in one location in the middle of December. The result gives a false impression of the time of year.

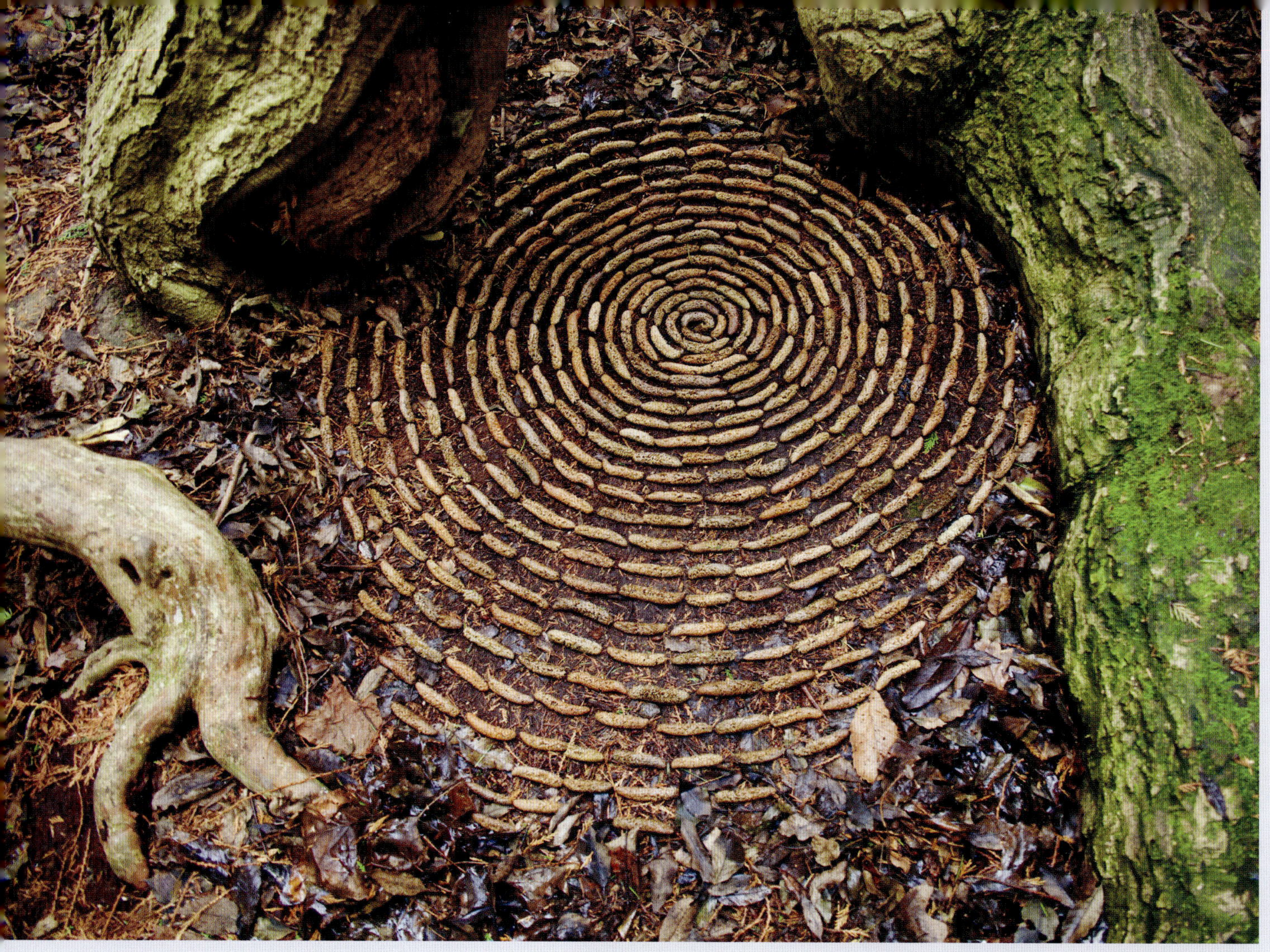

Catkins, Cannon Hall Park and Gardens, Barnsley

I was drawn to this gnarly old tree trunk, without knowing the significance of the tree. What I later learned and what we are looking at here is a grafted ash onto an older ash trunk.

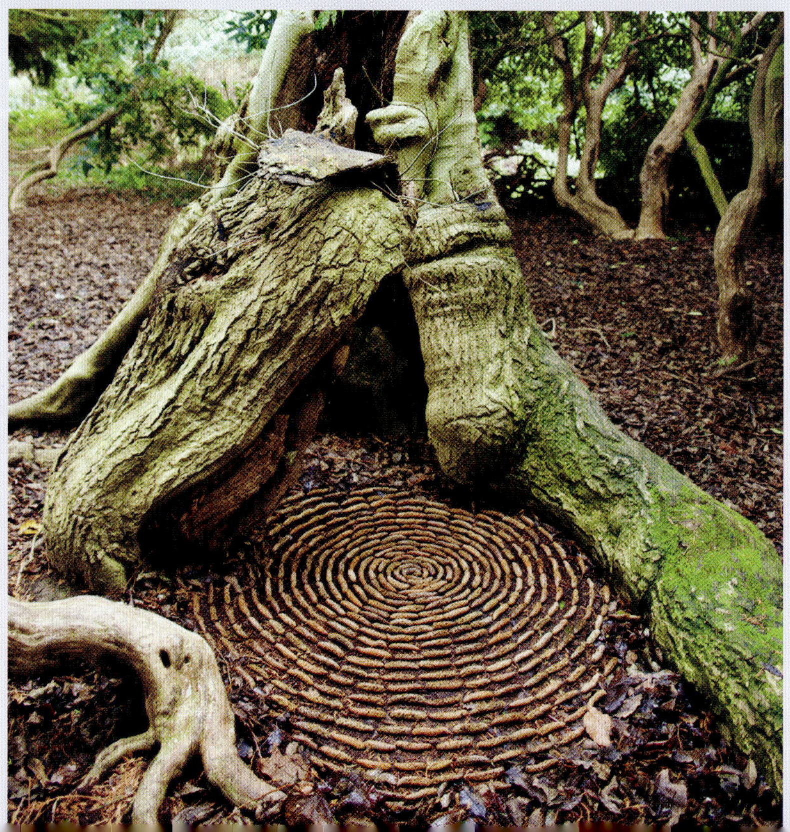

Twigs between branches, Rother Valley Country Park near the Trans Pennine Trail

I've been creating these branch pieces for many years now. It's both a simple concept and very challenging process with endless possibilities for development. There will be many more to come, I expect.

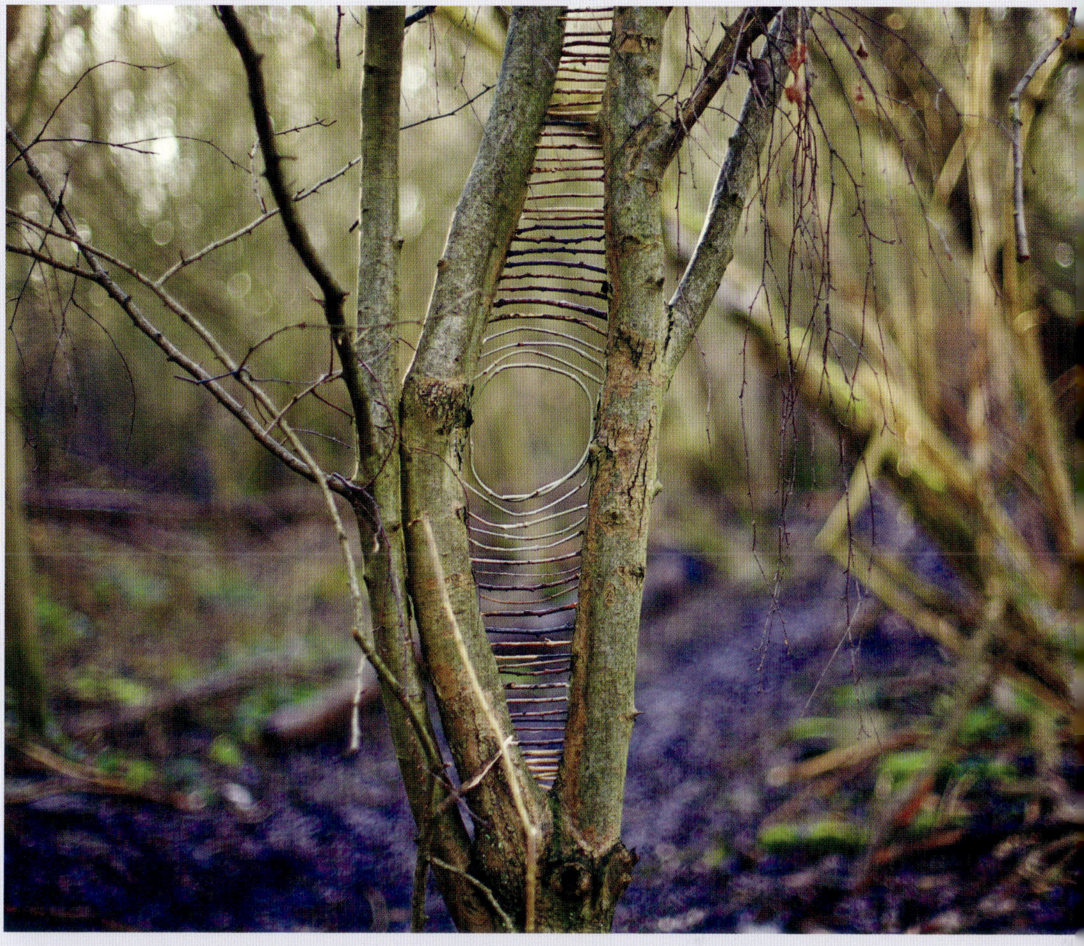

Sweet chestnut mandala, Clumber Park, Nottinghamshire

I had no idea how this piece would turn out, which is often the case. But going with the flow, changing it up when the time feels right, and soon the natural pattern begins to emerge and work evolves to completion.

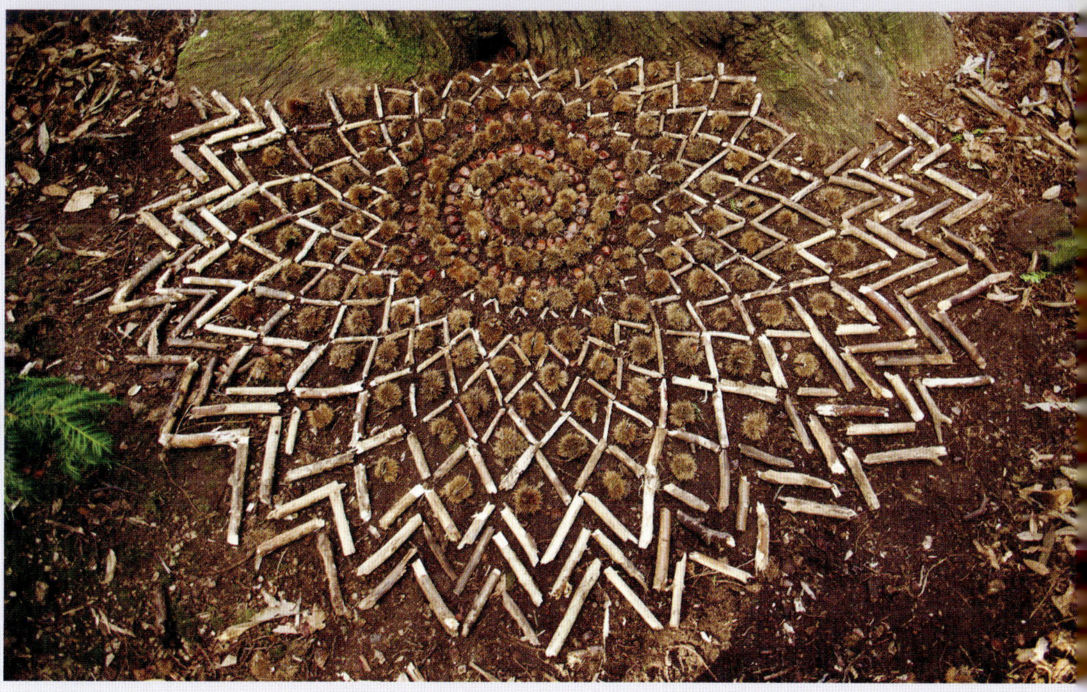

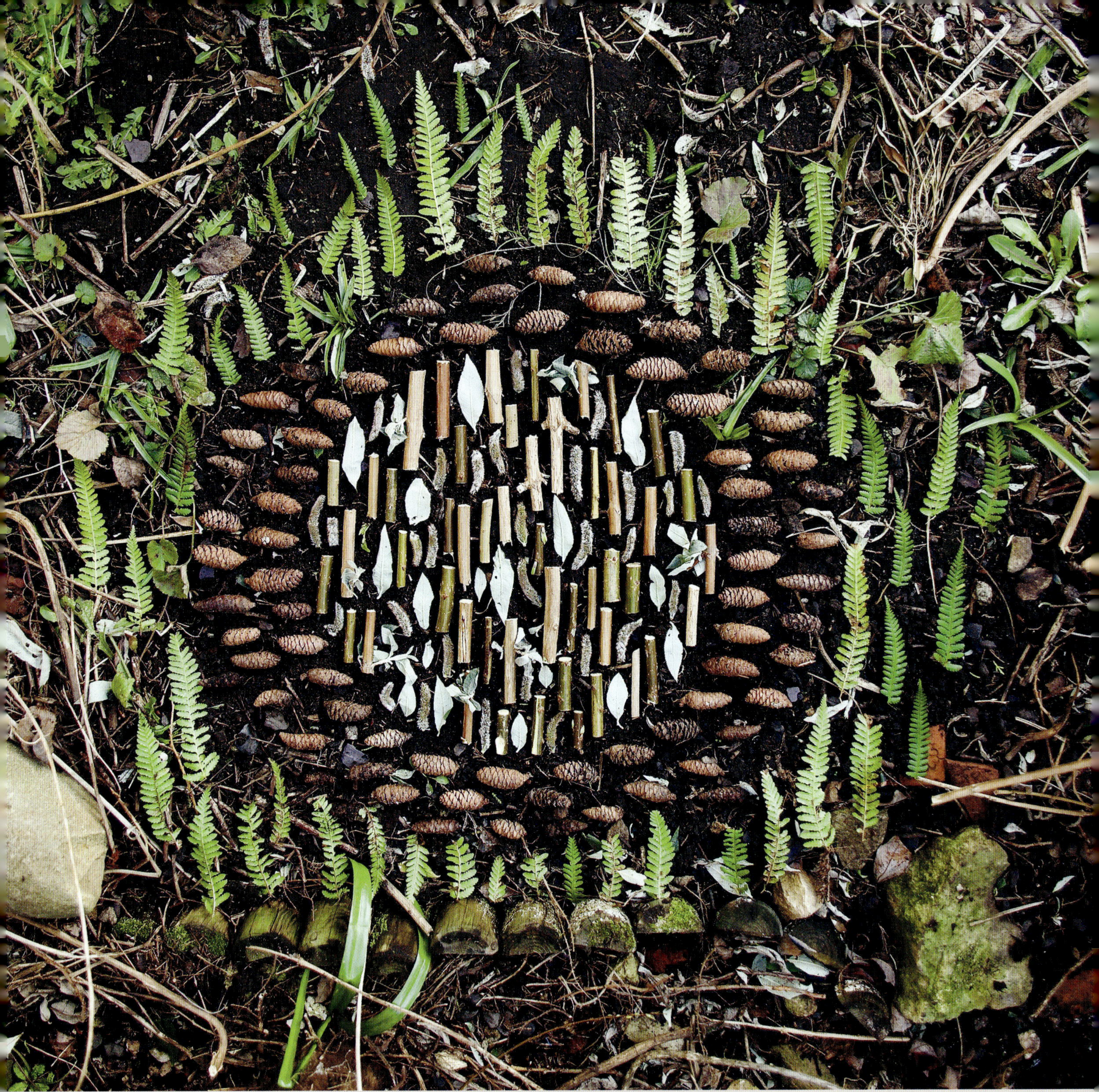

Garden art

The recent pandemic and lockdowns have enabled me to appreciate my garden more. I started making a series of garden artworks, with the intention of sharing and encouraging others to get creative at home. In truth, my garden became a very important space for my own creative well-being too.

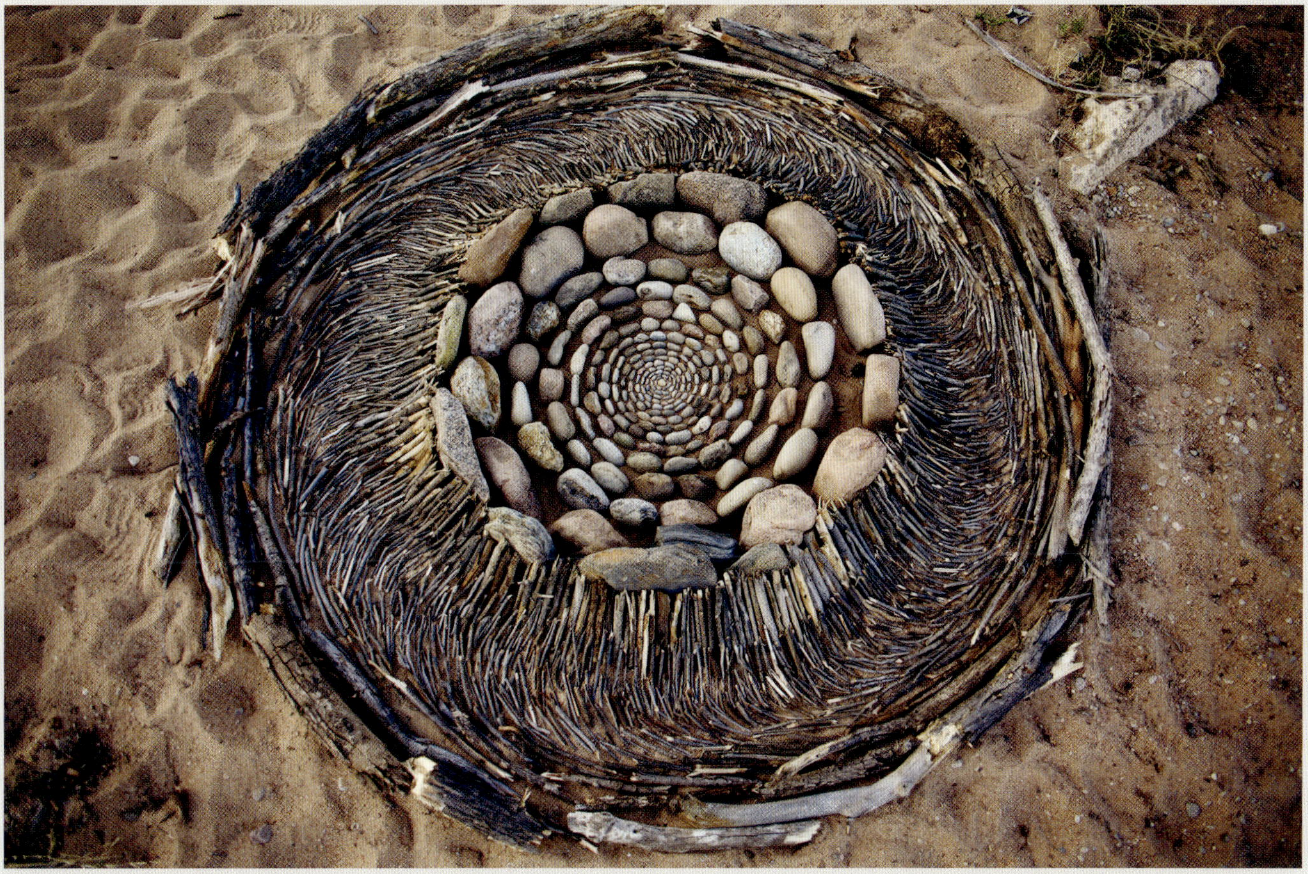

Llano Earth Art Festival, Texas 1

Let's talk Llano! Creating work at LEAF is like nothing I've experienced before. The environment and meandering waterways of the dammed Llano River create dry, ever-changing islands of sand, granite rock, and shrubbery. Poison ivy, barbed cacti, and, if you're lucky, a snake or scorpion provide a constant warning. Artists create alongside each other, helping, sharing, debating. No animosity and no egos. Family, at one with each other, the land, the LEAF team, and the visitors. It's a unique experience, and the family grows each year. Fueling a wider debate about our relationship with nature and the importance of experiential outdoor learning and play.

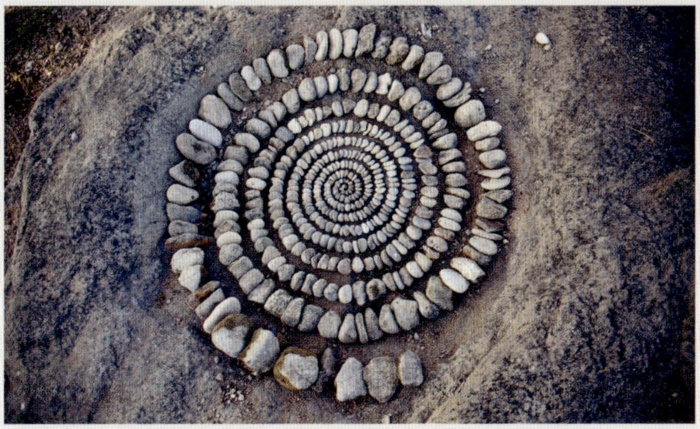

Llano Earth Art Festival, Texas 2

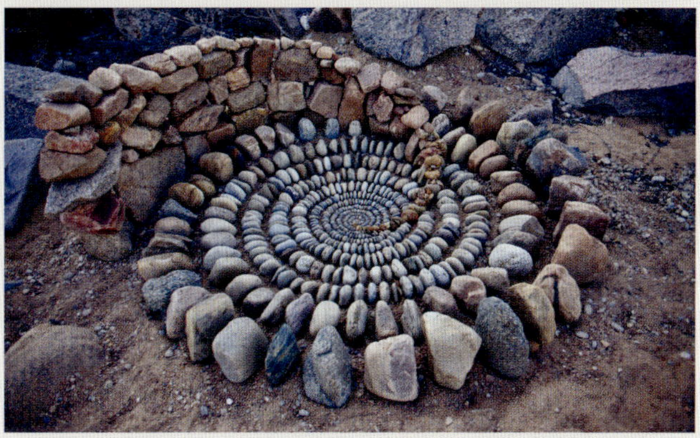

Llano Earth Art Festival, Texas 3

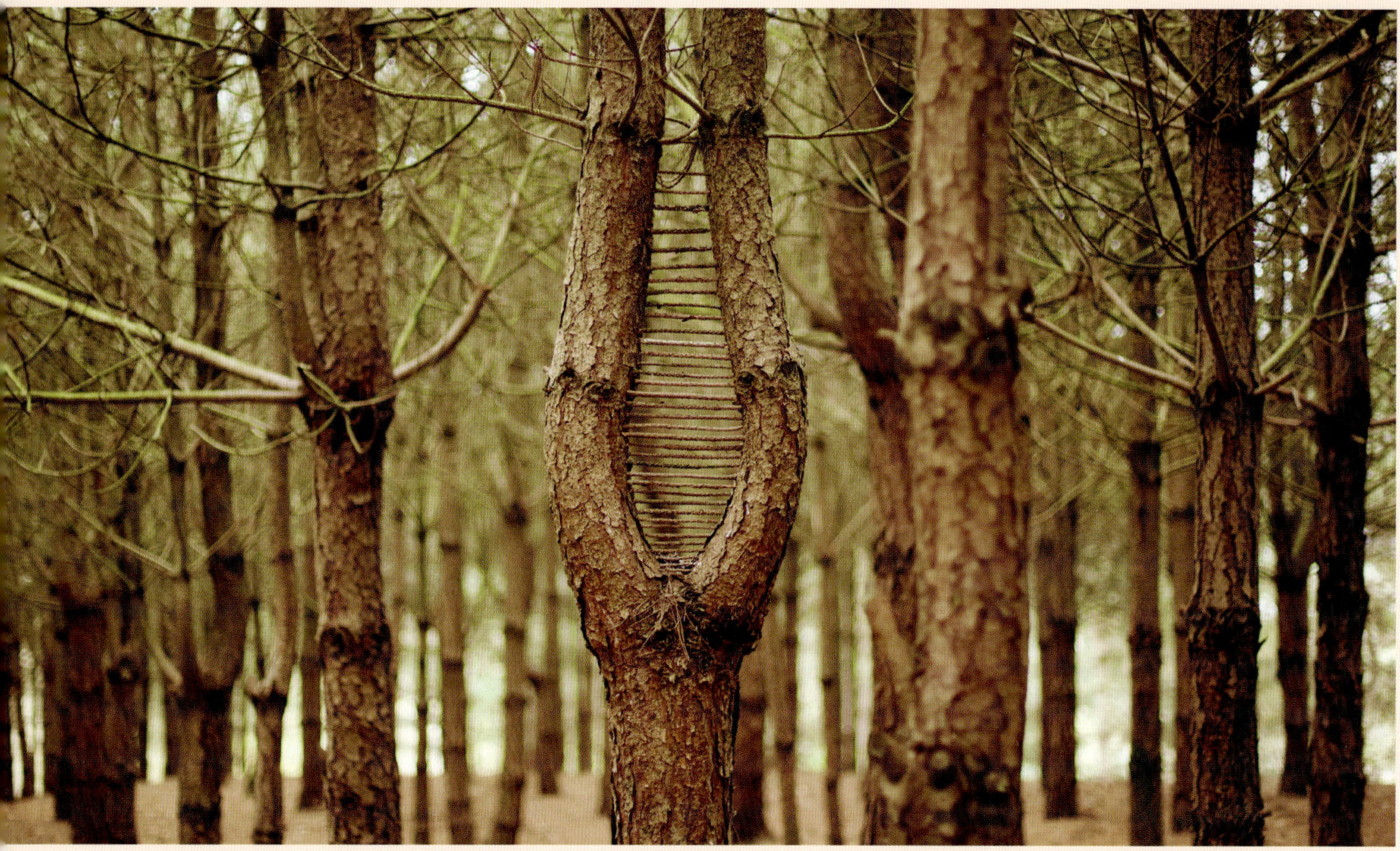

Coniferous woodland, Manton Community Woodland

Where I live, there are several new community woodlands on the grounds of former colliery sites. This was my first visit to this woodland in northern Nottinghamshire.

I was there with Forest Schools trainer and outdoor writer Richard Skrein, with the task of creating a winter mandala for his next book.

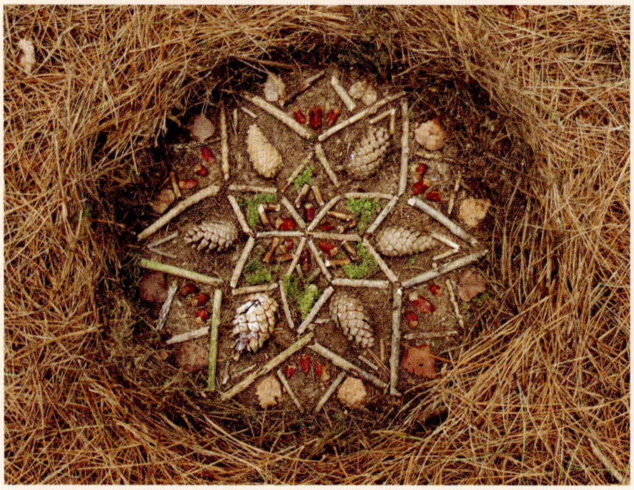

Ten-minute mandala, Manton Community Woodland

I am often asked about how long it takes me to create a piece of work. The answer is, it completely depends: some can take all day, others an hour or two. It all depends on so many variables. I wanted to include this to show people that time shouldn't be a barrier to having a go; it can also be part of the fun. While working on a larger piece, I decided to have a break and set myself a ten-minute challenge.

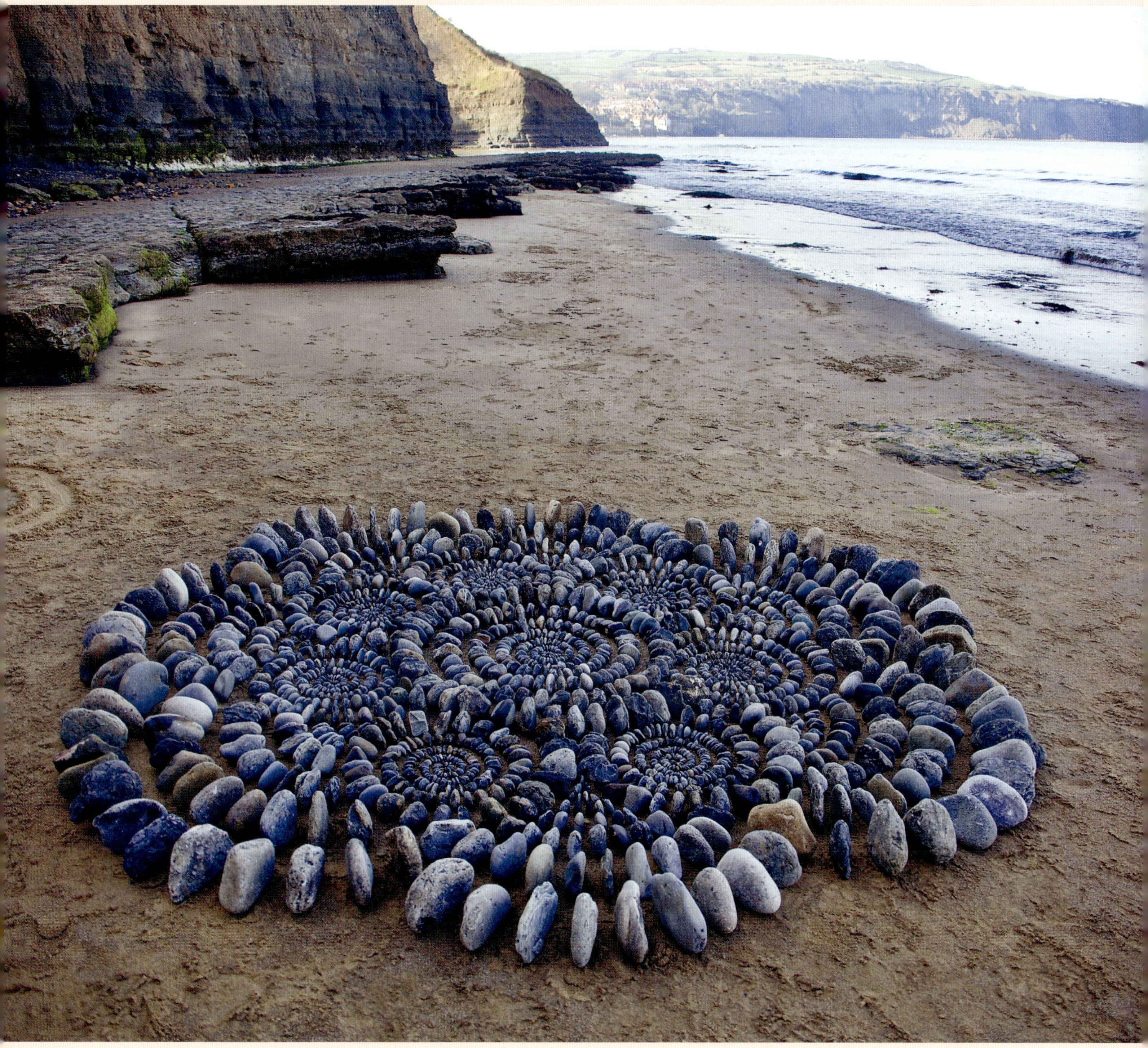

Pebble spirals, Boggle Hole, North Yorkshire

Waiting for the tide to come in and get a shot of the ocean beginning to reclaim the work, I was aware of the tide cutting off my access route off the beach. I didn't mind a paddle to get the shot but wasn't planning on a thigh-deep wade to safety, camera above my head to avoid the waves.

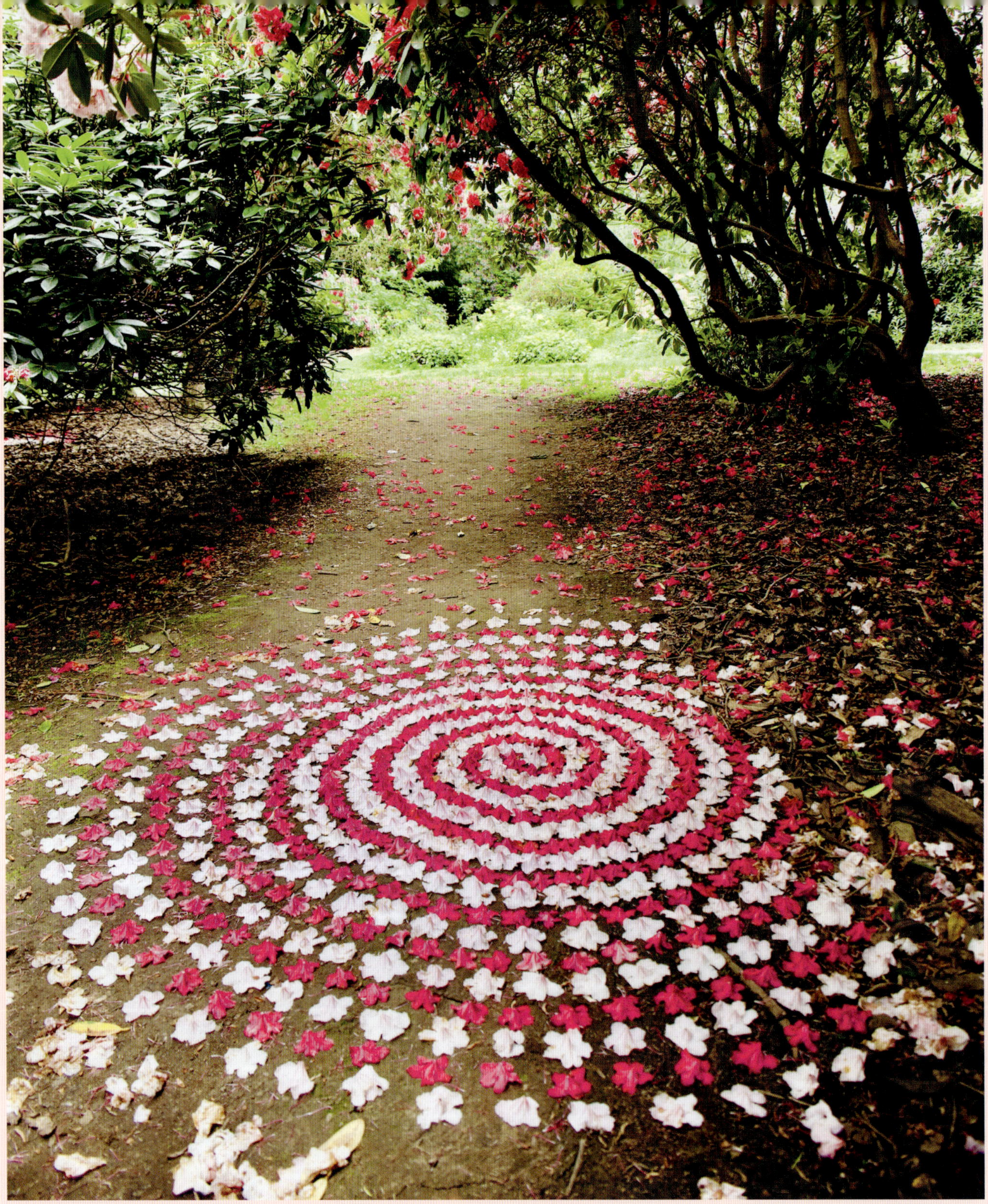

Rhododendron, Cannon Hall, Barnsley

I'd been working here the week before, with Tim Haywood, creating a logo piece for the Lily Foundation, the charity that supports people and families affected by mitochondrial disease. We used the fallen flowers then, and I was so keen to return and work with them again.

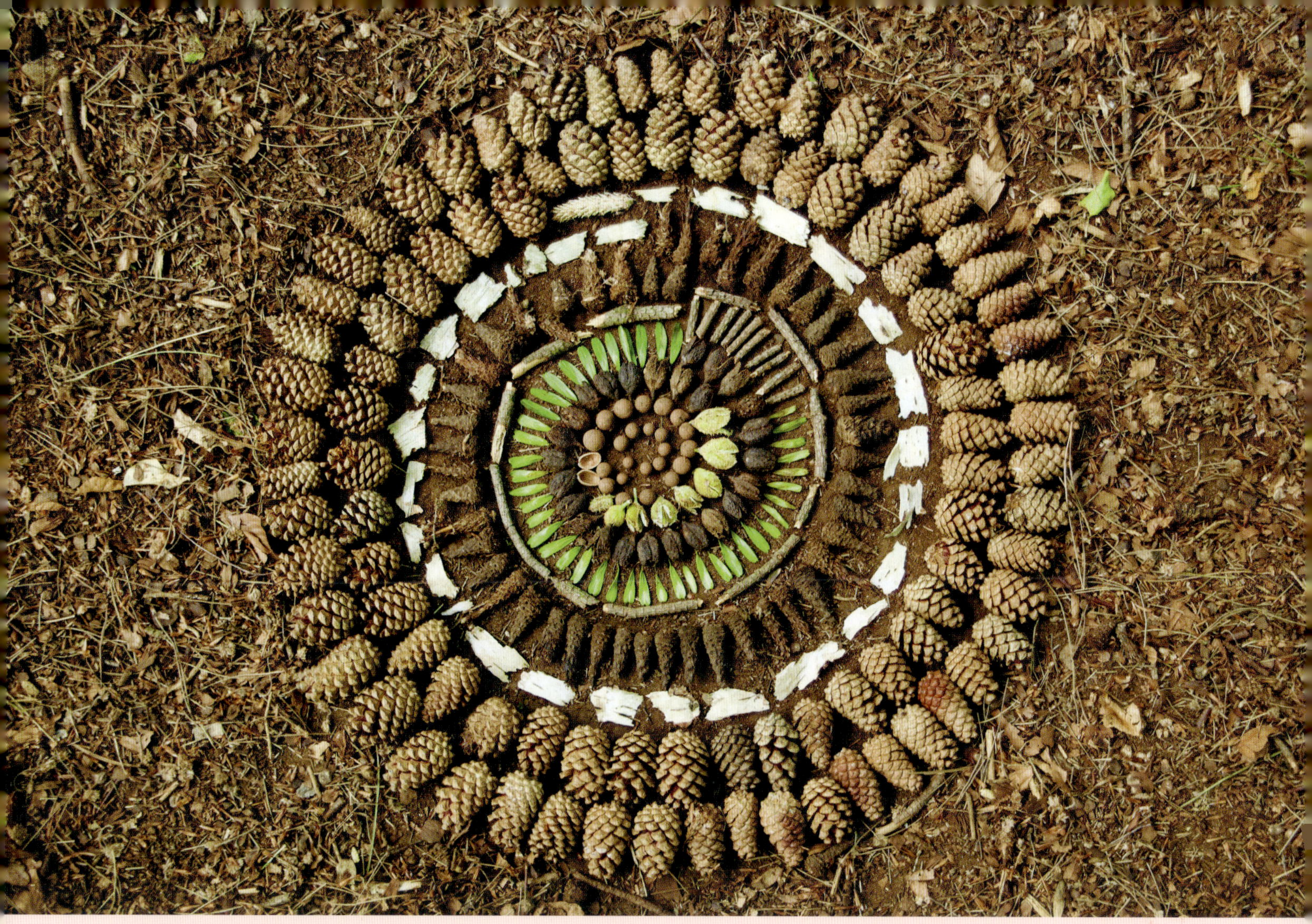

Anston Stones Wood

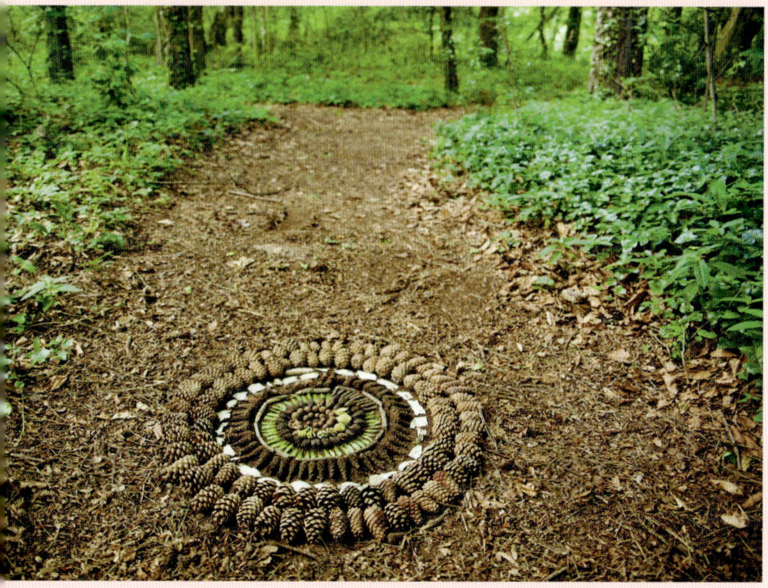

A glorious adventure

It seems so fitting and right that the last new image is from Anston Stones Wood. Concluding this book feels very in tune with walking home with Foxy after spending time in Anston Stones. Leaving the work behind, handed back to nature. Already on the lookout for what tomorrow may bring. Heading home, Foxy with a spring in her step, looking forward to taking her place on the sofa, me to plug camera into computer to see what I have.

I will be back tomorrow to make something new, to be captivated by a new place, but that's for another day. Thank you for taking this journey with me. I hope you take as much pleasure looking through these works as I did creating them.

Jxx

About the Author

James Brunt is an artist and Forest Schools practitioner whose work (play) is enjoyed throughout the world. His natural arrangements and outdoor adventures are followed by a huge online audience, and he is constantly in demand for workshops, creative experiences, and schools sessions—all of which he loves doing.

Thank You

This has been quite a journey and I've a few people to thank for their support along the way. Sam Cleasby, Andy Whitehouse and Odette Brightmore for reading, proofing and generally keeping me on track. The 'Liability' of land artists, for the community. Timm for showing me a different way. Caroline, my partner, for everything really. I wouldn't be me without you. And finally, Foxy the best assistant ever.

Social media accounts

Facebook: James Brunt Artist | **Instagram:** @jamesbruntartist | **Twitter:** @RFJamesUK

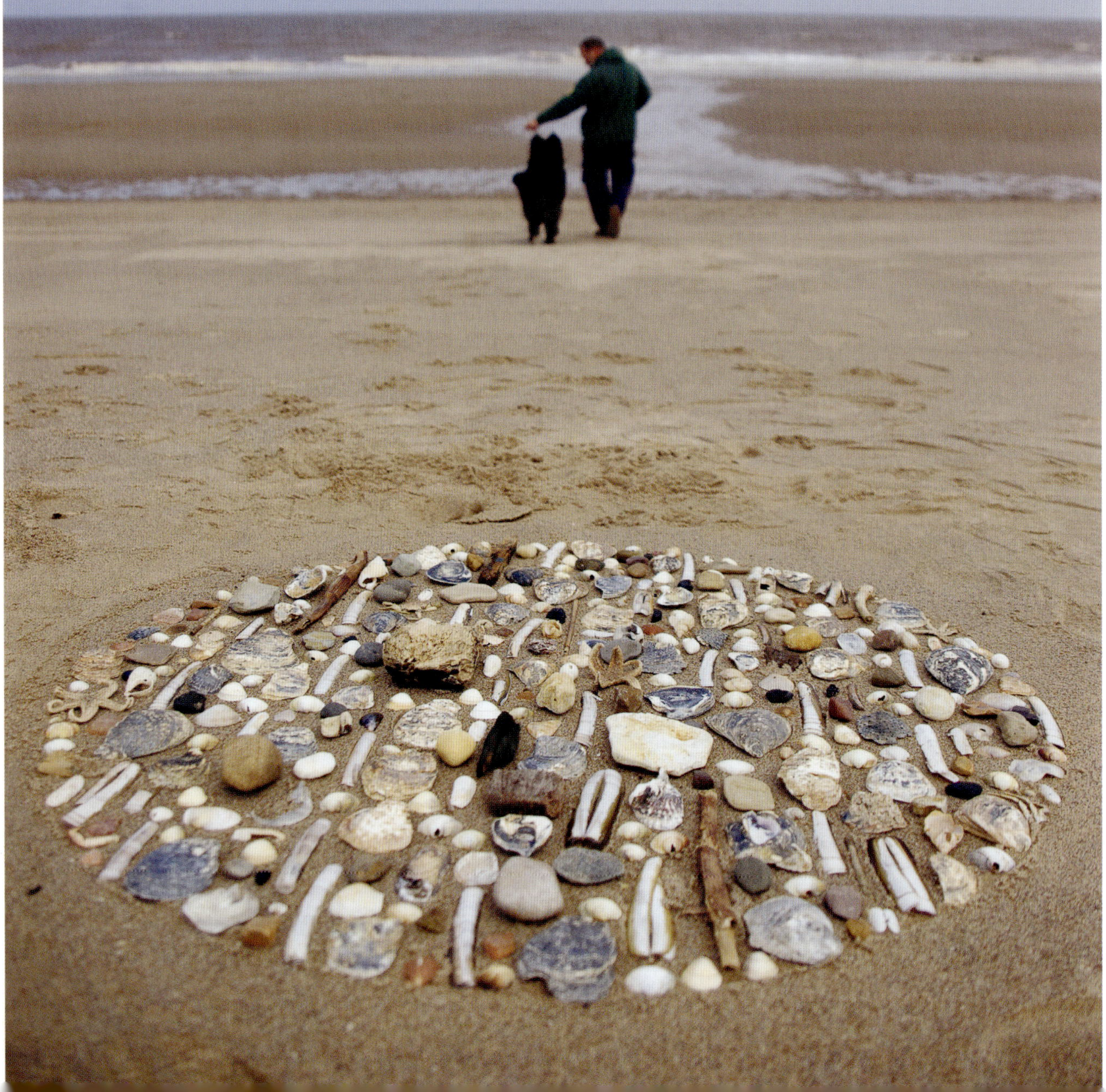